Do Bar Fights Count?

How To Write Your Military Stories

Copyright © 2006 Warrior Tales, LLC.

10-Digit ISBN 1-59113-917-1
13-Digit ISBN 978-1-59113-917-1

All rights reserved. No part of this publication may be reproduced, stored in a retrieval system, or transmitted in any form or by any means, electronic or mechanical, including photocopying, recording or by an information storage and retrieval system—except by a reviewer who may quote brief passages in a review to be printed in a magazine, newspaper or on the Web—without the prior written permission of the author. For information, please contact Warrior Tales, LLC, P.O. Box 1628, Clackamas, OR 97015.

Printed in the United States of America

Warrior Tales is a registered trademark of Warrior Tales, LLC

Permissions acknowledgements appear on page 223.

Cover art by Julie Sartain of www.julesavenuegraphics.com

This publication is designed to provide competent and reliable information regarding the subject matter covered. However, it is sold with the understanding that the author and publisher are not engaged in rendering professional mental health advice. The author and publisher specifically disclaim any liability that is incurred from the use or application of the contents of this book.

The characters and events in this book are based on true events but are not meant to be a comprehensive documentary of the author's life. Any unintended similarity to real persons, living or dead, is coincidental and not intended by the author. Although the author and publisher have made every effort to ensure the accuracy and completeness of information contained in this book, we assume no responsibility for errors, inaccuracies, omissions, or any inconsistency herein. Any slights of people, places, or organizations are unintentional.

Booklocker.com, Inc.

2006

Do Bar Fights Count?

How To Write Your Military Stories

Kimberly A. Cook

*Joyce,
Thank you for your service to the Country and your wonderful friendship!
Kim Cook*

Dedication

This book is dedicated with great love to my two favorite veterans, my parents, James Robert Cook, U.S. Army Air Corps, and Betty June Tuthill Cook, U.S. Marine Corps.

To all of my former students, to all veterans, and to all active duty, Guard, Reserve, Coast Guard and Merchant Marine personnel.

This book is dedicated to all of those we have yet to bring home, and to their families and friends who continue to wait:

Prisoners of War and Missing in Action as of February, 2006

World War II	78,000
Korean War	8,100
Vietnam War	1,800
Cold War Era	120
Gulf War/Operation Desert Storm	1

This book is dedicated to my warrior angels:

Dennis C. Eshleman 1948 - 1969
Scott U. Hall 1954 - 1995
Mikel Mathews 1951 - 1998
Ray Goody 1932 - 2002
Jennifer Lee Alexander Sears 1956 - 2005
Dee Burke Lopez 1919 - 2006

To members of the Oregon Army National Guard and Reserve members who have served and died in Iraq and Afghanistan.

And last, but not least, this book is dedicated to those who serve and die in the shadows, whose stories will never be told, who give so much to keep us free.

Thank you all.

Acknowledgements

I would like to thank everyone I have met in my life for making me the writer I am today. Including the grouchy people. Now that I've covered my ass, I would like to be a bit more specific.

First, a very big thank you to the veterans who volunteered and even paid to take the *Writing War Stories* classes. These men and women taught me more than I ever taught them. A special thank you to the members of the last class, including the three who stayed with me for three years from the first class, Doug Curtis, David Hammond, and Harley Wedel. Also, the second termers who stuck through for three years, Bob Morris, Bob Hill, Phillip Leveque, and the FNGs of the late Ray Goody, Tom LaDuke, Jeff Manthos, Mike DeMaio, Chuck James, Eric Guest, and Don Goodwin who we picked up along the way.

For the rest of the gang who rolled in and out of the class, you were all a joy.

Thank you to Marcia Truman and Rebecca Kenney at the Mt. Hood Community College Community Education Program for supporting my initial proposal and the class.

I could not have even attempted to develop and teach this course if I had not had wonderful teachers my entire life. A special thanks to my first grade teacher Mrs. Rufner who taught me to read, my sixth grade teacher Mr. Hilton who taught me it was okay to be smart, my eighth grade teacher Miss Gotberg who encouraged my creative mind, my ninth grade journalism teacher, Miss Michaelson, who encouraged my writing and was mortified when I told her I wanted to be a stewardess, Mrs. Stephan for taking me on as her aide and letting me try and handle a mimeograph machine, Mr. Gillespie who taught me all writing efforts are valuable and the community college writing instructor who shredded my writing before the noon day sun and accelerated my entry into the Army.

I have been very blessed with writing teachers. My journalism instructor Bob Watkins encouraged me to take a newspaper job before entering public relations. He said I would never regret it and he was correct. Quentin Smith, then editor of *The Gresham Outlook*, who taught me how to start a story. My editor, Steve Beaty, at the *Newport News-Times* who kept me honest and pushed me to try and be creative on deadline.

A special place in my heart goes to the late Dee Lopez, my long suffering novel class instructor who taught me most of what I know about teaching writing. In and out of her class for more than ten years, she put up with me, even helping me edit a romance manuscript requested by Silhouette Publishing as I was being mobilized for Desert Storm. Talk about competing deadlines. A Red Cross veteran of World War II, Dee spent time in Europe helping to entertain and comfort "her boys."

Bill Johnson taught me how to write a screenplay and his book, *A Story Is A Promise*, describes his teaching. He is one of the most brilliant editors I know.

Cynthia Whitcomb, screenwriting instructor, helped put the fun back in writing when this book was driving me to distraction. An accomplished teacher with two books to her credit, including *Writing Your Screenplay*, Cynthia thinks I'm funny, so I know she's a genius.

I think I've earned a degree from all the writing conferences and book readings I have attended and want to thank the writers whose words stick with me to this day; Debbie Macomber, Suzanne Brockmann, Eileen Dryer, Liz Curtis Higgs, Steve Perry, Stephen J. Cannel, Chris Vogler, Sue Grafton, Ron Bass, Ron Howard, Jennifer Crusie, Elizabeth Lyon, Brian Doyle, and Anthony Swafford

I still believe in happy endings and want to thank the romance and mystery writers who kept me laughing and believing when the days got dark; Janet Evanovich, Suzanne Brockmann, Jennifer Cruisie, Jayne Ann Krentz, Rachel Gibson, Debbie Macomber, Merline Lovelace, Karen Monk, Rosamunde Pilcher, Mary Stewart and M.M. Kaye.

I also want to thank the community of authors/friends who have always supported me when life got weird and writing became frustrating - Cindy Hiday, Laurie Gilbert, Irene Radford, Kathie Richards, Carol Timm, Mary Rose Kerg, Pam Girtman, Cindy Trumpower, and Pat Blanco.

Absolute thanks to Maggie Grover, who told me this was my soul work in 1997, and believed in my dream before I did.

A huge thanks and saved money on a therapist goes to the best group of professional writer friends a girl could ever have, members of Oregon Press Women, who had me organize a conference before I was a even a member in 1983. They have survived both me and my social life for 22 years. The blood, sweat, tears, laughter, networking, chocolate, and booze make these the "go to gals" in my life.

My non-fiction critique group who helped me labor through the beginning birth pains of this book and assisted me in dealing with the only case of writer's block I have ever had; Sally Petersen, Jim Petersen, Ann Daughtry, Patti Collins, Janice Stevens, Glennis McNeal and Richard Waitt.

My screenwriting support group members Karen Barreuto, Joe Mondo, Jane Manchee and Marguerite Becker who helped fan the creative flame.

Manuscript readers Bob Morris, Harley Wedel, Betty Cook, David Hammond, Chuck James, Kathie Richards, Cindy Trumpower, Cindy Hiday, Joann LeBrun, Suzanne Sigona, Al Siebert and Rick Rutherford.

My Army buddies who survived me, including my friend, Jan Waters, who still keeps track of me today for entertainment purposes. My Air Force Reserve friends who still keep in touch, Ann Helm, Jody Nyvall, Janice Petroff, Shirley Cameron, Aaron Maness, and Kathy Lux. Plus my fellow Aeromedical Evacuation Operations Officers who truly understand the meaning of herding cats.

A big thank you to the VA Veteran Outreach Counselors who worked and supported me and knew I should be a client; Rich Clark, Mike DeMaio, Deborah Richter, Sandra J. Hardin, and David Collier. A special thank you to Robert and Nancy Fleming for their support and letting me play Cupid.

I would like to thank the Clackamas County Sheriffs' Office (CCSO) for apprehending the serial rapist in my neighborhood, especially Detective Steve Hyson. It really helps a girl's concentration to have that loose end tied up. So to speak.

Another thank you to the CCSO for dealing with my neighbors from hell, and a huge thank you to Portland General Electric for turning off their power so the 24/7 rave parties stopped. It's really the little things in life that count. Like sleep.

A special thank you to my Sheriff's Office friends who supported me, many times without their knowledge; Joann LeBrun, Joyce Nagy, Captain Don Howard, Lieutenant Jack Catto, Phyllis Flowers, Ed Montgomery and Miss Kitty.

Thank you to CCSO Deputy Andrew McVey and Sergeant Damon and Tammy Coates for their cooperation.

A big thanks to my two co-workers who knew what I was up to with this book and still supported me the entire distance, Judy Nastrom and Cindy Trumpower.

Another big thank you to my co-workers who I kept in the dark on purpose to give me room to breathe: Dan Nenow, Laurie Bergstrom, Kathy Streed, Tom Averett, Lane Miller, Carolyn Phelps, Connie Blakemore, Tammy Fuller and Paul Burral.

Thanks to my military veteran co-workers for their service and support: Ron Oberg, Dan Nenow, Randy Shierman, Al Rhodes, Rick Rutherford, Heather McNeil, Jeff Jorgensen, and Bob Cornelius.

My hairdresser, Ronee Tamm, for her wonderful listening ears and artful hair cutting and my excellent manicurist, Mai Nguyen, for keeping my nails in perfect pink shape and discussing the challenges of dating men.

Special thanks to the LeBrun's for loaning me their ranch, snake shovel, tree penal colony, and Cleo, Miss Victoria and Alex kitties to keep me company for the editing retreat on this book.

Special thanks to my handsome and brilliant attorneys, John K. Larson and Walt Karnstein, for putting up with me and covering my six. Thanks to my handsome and talented graphic designer Rob Ottley, of Ottley Design, for his graphic artistry and my logo and trademark.

Thanks to Robert T. Kiyosaki and Sharon L. Lechter for writing the book *Before You Quit Your Job*. Robert is a Marine chopper pilot who served in Vietnam and I think every veteran should read chapter six of his book.

To Toby Keith for his writing, his music and his unwavering support of the troops. To Jon Stewart and Bill Maher for using the freedom of speech I helped defend. In this case the cliché is true; if you don't use it, you lose it.

To my buddy, the great white, Michelle Collins-Hytrek, and her husband, Greg, and son Michael. A friend for all seasons and all reasons thanks for everything from smashed lunches in my school locker on through disco, the wedding of the century, and raising a newborn in their mid-forties. Who could ask for more?

A big group hug to the Warrior Tales Advisory Board who helped me launch this endeavor with humor, snacks and always chocolate: Kathie Richards – Dream Development Director, Betty Cook – Money Maven, Joann LeBrun – Wildside Walker, Ross LeBrun – Grill Master, and Cindy Trumpower – Spiritual Sister.

With great love and thanks to my two favorite veterans, my parents, James and Betty Cook, and my loving and fruit loop family, my sister Karen and brother-in-law Gordon Hubbard (Army veteran who served in Berlin during Vietnam), my oldest amazing niece Sabrina, her husband Nigel, and sons Caleb and Justin Ambler, and my amazing youngest niece, Jennifer Hubbard.

And to my beloved cat, Miss Amber, who never once stepped on the computer keys before she moved on to kitty heaven.

It may take a village to raise a child, but it takes a galaxy to create a writer. Thanks to all my stars!

Table of Contents

Restricted Area = Rules for Significant Others xiii

INTRODUCTION xv

PART I WRITER BASIC TRAINING 1
   Chapter 1 Do Bar Fights Count? 3
   Chapter 2 Throw The Grenade! 13
   Chapter 3 The Mighty MO 20
   Chapter 4 Mission Objective: Conflict 25
   Chapter 5 Eavesdrop For Intelligence 35
   Chapter 6 Ever Sniff A Poncho? 44
   Chapter 7 The Warrior's Sixth Sense 54
   Chapter 8 Build a War Zone 62
   Chapter 9 Forget Forced Marches 67
   Chapter 10 How To Make Foxhole Friends 73
   Chapter 11 Corporal Cupcake Wins A Chew Toy 78
   Chapter 12 The Strategy and Tactics of Publishing 89
   Chapter 13 Certificate of Achievement 95

PART II SPECIFIC VETERAN GROUPS 101
   Chapter 14 POWs/MIAs 103
   Chapter 15 Special Operations, Special Forces, and Military
      Intelligence 112
   Chapter 16 Disabled and Paralyzed Veterans 117
   Chapter 17 Native American Veterans 121
   Chapter 18 Women Veterans 124
   Chapter 19 Minority Veterans 130
   Chapter 20 Gay and Lesbian Veterans 133
   Chapter 21 Biker Veterans 135
   Chapter 22 Incarcerated Veterans 142
   Chapter 23 Corrections Officers 147
   Chapter 24 Law Officers 151

Chapter 25 Emergency Medical Personnel and Firefighters 154
Chapter 26 Australian Veterans 159

PART THREE USING WRITING TO HEAL 163
Chapter 27 Harnessing Anger and Humor..165
Chapter 28 Suicide Sucks and Death is Permanent 172
Chapter 29 Space Shuttle Columbia STS-107..178
Chapter 30 Using Writing To Heal A Soldier's Heart............................180

PART FOUR TRANSITIONS AND SHOVING OFF 191
Chapter 31 Transitions and Parting Shots...193

Appendix A Guidelines for Teachers and Counselors................199

Appendix B Veteran Outreach Centers 209

Appendix C Online Resources 221

Permissions 223

Exercise Nine Shopping List 225

About The Author..227

Restricted Area = Rules for Significant Others

Thank you for buying this book for a veteran. Now I am going to ask you to do something quite hard.

Give the book to the veteran.

Don't ask about it again.

In my class, I did not allow students to show their work to their spouses or significant others for at least six months to a year. Reason? Some very well intentioned loved ones can kill the smallest effort of a veteran writer without meaning to. What seems like nagging or criticism at the wrong time can be worse than a small nuclear device.

I fought for every word and sentence I could coax from some veterans. Other veterans found they could not write. It was too painful to return to some of those dark places.

So, as the Beatles would say, *Let it Be*. (If you don't know who the Beatles are, Google them, okay?)

If your veteran does show you something he or she has written, realize the honor and trust they are putting in your palms. Treat it as a dove of Peace. Find only positive things to say and DO NOT edit spelling, grammar or punctuation. Never! Wait until they have been writing for a year or so and then maybe offer those services. Only if they ask. And use a purple ink pen – no red ink allowed.

An even better idea is to get your own copy of this book. No, I am not out to sell a zillion books. I want you to share in a veteran's writing journey by learning what they are doing and to also take a shot at writing yourself. Every veteran's family members, friends and co-workers have also gone on a journey. Your stories are important too. Write them down and maybe you can compare them along the road. Veteran warriors and domestic warriors. Both journeys count.

Thank you for taking a chance on this book to help a vet learn to write. I will do my best to complete my mission.

INTRODUCTION

I've been listening to military stories all my life. My father was a natural storyteller who served in World War II with the Army Air Corps. My mother joined the Marines to free men to fight during World War II.

Given my gene pool, it seemed natural for me to enter the Army in 1975. However, it turned out to be a shock to my parents. They had been citizen soldiers during World War II, but the post-Vietnam Army I entered was a different breed of beast.

Three years with the Army's Fourth Infantry Division at Fort Carson, Colorado, were followed ten years later with three years in the Air Force Reserve 40th Aeromedical Evacuation Squadron at McChord Air Force Base, Washington. But the one constant through my entire life was always writing.

When I created and started teaching the *Writing War Stories* class 22 years after entering the Army, I did it because I felt veterans had no place to go and learn to write and tell their stories. A veteran myself, I wanted there to be a place for veterans to write their stories and share them with other veterans.

I drew on my experience as a newspaper reporter, fiction and screenplay writer, public affairs officer and photographer. I taught the *Writing War Stories* class at Mt. Hood Community College in Gresham, Oregon, from September 1997 to May 2000. The veteran students taught me more about life, love, forgiveness, pain and my own emotional walls than I could ever have imagined.

First hand I got to experience again the miracle of "buddy love." That unconditional acceptance which binds military members and veterans together based on a common experience. And I had the privilege to tell veterans that they and their service were important. Most Korean and Vietnam War veterans have never heard those words.

This book began the first year of the class, and then I put it down for several years. When I picked it up again, the book and I had changed, so we both started over. The world changed as I worked on the book, from 9/11 to Afghanistan to Iraq. The parallels I see in the veteran students I taught that first night in class who felt their stories "didn't mean nothin" I want to make sure doesn't happen to today's warriors.

As in life, emotion is what holds a reader to writing. Emotion touches our hearts with pain and joy. Without experiencing one, we cannot fully appreciate the other.

Do Bar Fights Count?

Military stories are emotional. Military stories include laughter and tears. War stories occur during peacetime. Some stories are downright funny - the military did invent the word SNAFU (Situation Normal, All Fucked Up).

Growing up I watched the Vietnam War unfold before my eyes on television. When our neighbor's son was in Vietnam, he told his folks several of the soldiers in his platoon didn't get much mail. My mom was my Camp Fire Group leader and we all decided to write to the boys/men in his unit.

I remember getting the two letters from Dennis C. Eshleman from Pennsylvania. The Free Postage stamp drawn on the upper right corner of the envelope. He wrote about Pennsylvania where he lived and how he liked horses. His letters stopped in early 1969. Somehow I knew Dennis was gone.

Twenty years later in 1989, while I was working on the Vietnam Art Show project with the Salem Vet Center, I picked up the book of names on The Vietnam Memorial Wall. I found Dennis's name and I cried. A Private First Class in the Army, he died on January 29, 1969. From that day on I carried his name with me in my flight pouch when I flew with the Air Force Reserve. His sacrifice and my grief knew no time limit.

Some stories explore the dark side of men and women's tortured souls. Men who learned to kill with laser precision and carried out heart chilling deeds our nation asked them to perform. Women have been victims, witnesses and warriors since time immemorial, contributing to the legacy of wars.

My first "official" recording of a war story was interviewing my brother-in-law's Uncle Johnny for a Social Studies project in 1974, my junior year in high school. Uncle Johnny worked as a civilian for the Navy, "to make magnetic minesweepers out of bird boats," in his words. He was a "veteran" of the bombing of Pearl Harbor.

My family went to Hawaii for the first time in March 1974 and we visited the U.S.S. *Arizona*. Later Johnny gave me a box of newspapers of the first thirty days after the bombing of Pearl Harbor that his wife, Maude, had kept. I still have them. A treasure trove of stories on yellowed paper. Yes, I still have the Social Studies report too, complete with pictures. My first written war story.

The act of writing military stories down can help complete the military hero's journey. Classic Greek literature details the age-old warrior path from leaving home before basic training to returning after the battle or service tour for every soldier, sailor, airman, merchant marine, Marine, Guard, or Reservist.

May this book help every veteran understand the importance of their military journey. Please write those events for yourself, your family, the young, the old, and for history. I salute each and every veteran for his or her courage to write. And let's have fun along the way too. Every veteran's story is important.

Move out!

Kimberly A. Cook
February 2006

PART I

WRITER BASIC TRAINING

Chapter 1

Do Bar Fights Count?

Thank you for serving your country. If I am the first person to thank you, I am honored.

This book grew out of the class I taught for three years, *Writing War Stories*. While writing this book, I realize the reason I developed the class and this book grew from two basic emotions—love and anger. Love for the sacrifices my fellow veterans made and anger for how veterans have been treated in this country the past 85+ years.

When I get angry, watch out. I take action. Trying to convince folks I'm just a cupcake with weapons training doesn't seem to work. I'm a warrior woman writer. The universe has been put on notice. For the veteran who wants to learn how to write, this book is for you.

Veterans made personal sacrifices every day in the military, whether in combat, underwater in submarines, risking the challenge of high mountain climbing, watching for blips on radar screens in the Aleutians, or preparing mess hall food in a tent. What you did and do is important. I want the rest of the nation to know what it takes to defend freedom, day in and day out. To do that, I would ask you to write down your military experiences.

This book is my way to thank my fellow veterans for preserving the freedom I love. If thank you is enough and you don't want to write, that's fine. I have accomplished my mission. But, if you do want to write, here is how I taught the class. Let's go over some rules of the road before we get down to writing. You know, that SOP stuff.

Standard Operating Procedures

To answer the chapter title: do bar fights count as part of military service? You bet your ass bar fights count. War time AND peace time service count. Every veteran counts. When the *Writing War Stories* classes started in 1997, I knew it would be important to let veterans know their experiences mattered. Telling their stories made a difference to them. I didn't know then how much I was underestimating the simple act of recognition.

When I first decided to develop the class, I told a former Navy co-worker, Charlie Smith, about the course.

"What's the class called?" he asked.

Do Bar Fights Count?

"Writing War Stories."

He paused. "Do bar fights count?"

"Of course," I stated emphatically.

"I didn't see much action bobbing off the coast of Vietnam on an aircraft carrier," he said. "But there were times when planes didn't quite make it back or smashed into the carrier." Charlie has other war stories, beyond the bar fights, but he hasn't written his stories yet.

Everyone who served in the military has "war" stories. Hugh joined my first *Writing War Stories* class. Hugh went into France on D-Day plus two. He was bombed and strafed. He helped carry the wounded and processed prisoners of war. A stevedore, Hugh insisted he was a non-combatant. By the end of the class, we got him to admit he experienced combat. He also didn't sit off to one side of the class anymore, physically removed from the combat veterans.

Through teaching I discovered my own stories made a difference, both as a woman Army private and later as a reserve Air Force officer. Scholars say we teach what we need to learn. So it was in my case.

It is clear to me every Army, Navy, Marine, Air Force, Reserve, National Guard, Coast Guard, and Merchant Marine service member made a difference. Every man, woman and animal, whether black or white, Native American or Asian, male or female, gay, straight or four-footed matters. Our service guaranteed the freedom we enjoy today and that we must continue to defend.

The legacy of the Korean and Vietnam Wars left many veterans feeling their sacrifices were not important to the citizens of the United States.

In 1975 I only wore my dress green Army uniform in an airport one time. Complete strangers gave me hostile looks. I was carrying a stuffed pink elephant, on my way home from basic and advanced training. How bad a person did they think I was? I always wore my "civvies" when I traveled after that. I learned to be an invisible vet, especially easy for a woman veteran.

Do not doubt the power of putting these stories on paper. Their touch reaches beyond boundaries. I have had veterans send the yearly anthology book we published to their unit historians, and then receive a call from a long lost buddy who read the tale. One veteran was contacted by the children of a soldier who died in Vietnam. They wanted to learn what kind of man their father was through the stories of the last man to see him alive.

Who defines a veteran? I don't use the Veterans Affairs or Department of Defense categories. To my way of thinking, veterans served with the Army, Navy, Air Force, Marines, Coast Guard, Merchant Marine, Active Duty,

Reserve, National Guard, Women's Air Service Pilots, WAVES, WAM, WACs, Army Air Corps, Flying Tigers, Native American scouts, Buffalo Soldiers, and military combat artists and photographers.

Men and women also served with dogs in the canine corps, mules hauling equipment, dolphins for undersea duty, even a few elephants and camels have their stories to be told. The heartbreaking story of the U.S. military dogs abandoned at the end of the Vietnam War haunts their handlers to this day. War seems to be an equal opportunity employer; man, woman, and beast.

Who defines wars? Forget all the categories, in-country, out-of-country, peacetime, humanitarian mission, on-planet and off-planet (military astronauts). If you served in the military or the other services, you are a vet by my definition, with stories to tell. I find peacetime a misnomer—we lost 268 military members in Beirut, Lebanon, 40 in Panama, 19 in Grenada and 8 in Somalia, plus 20 in El Salvador, 1 in Honduras and 1 in Libya, 28 due to terrorism and 148 in the Persian Gulf in 1987--all during peacetime. There are also training accidents, like the 10 Air National Guard crew members of King 56 lost in Oregon, with one survivor, in 1996. In 2000, 17 men and women lost their lives in the terrorist attack on the U.S.S. *Cole* in Yemen.

Then September 11, 2001. We lost innocents, families, children, civilians, veterans, FDNY, NYPD, Port Authority Police, emergency medical workers, a canine police dog, active duty military personnel, Department of Defense workers, and our national innocence. Several days later on September 21, Prisoner of War/Missing In Action Day, I realized we had MIAs buried in the rubble of The Pentagon. This book became even more important for me to finish.

Veterans have always known this country was vulnerable to attack, but none of us could envision such horrific events on 9-11. That day I saw the 1,000 yard stare in co-workers eyes I had only seen before in vet's eyes. I knew we were a nation rocked to our gut. I also knew we had the best men and women in the Armed Forces out kicking butt and taking prisoners—only because prisoners might give information to stop further terrorism.

Veterans have been dealing with tragic loss since before this nation was born. I've had men cry in my class fifty years after a battle. It's okay. These memories do not go away in a year, five years or ten.

Wars claimed 408,306 men and women in World War II, 54,246 in the Korean War, 58,219 in the Vietnam War and 363 during Desert Shield and Desert Storm. We've lost more than 254 Americans in Operation Enduring Freedom and 2,240 in Operation Iraq Freedom, with more than 17,097 wounded in action, as of Jan. 22, 2006. (Figures from www.iava.org)

Combat veterans know who they are and I honor them. Those of us who have not been in combat have still experienced loss and death. The increasing reliance on the Reserves and National Guard ensures everyone has war stories, even during peacetime. At one point in my peacetime Army career, eight soldiers died in training accidents in two months. Stupid accidents, but preparing for war is a dangerous business and people get hurt and killed in training.

Getting Started

When you are ready to begin, write whatever you want about your military experiences. Tell it as truthfully as you remember. It will be the truth, as you experienced and recall it.

Most veterans start writing for their families. So let's consider you are writing a true-life, non-fiction personal history. The combat veterans in my first class thought "memoir" sounded uppity. Or maybe you prefer writing fiction, dressing up your personal experiences. Writing fiction can free a new writer from feeling someone is looking over his or her shoulder. After all, it's not "real." Change the names, physical descriptions, some places and you're home free. Anyone with fiction questions, take a look at Richard Marcinko's books—after his first non-fiction book *Rogue Warrior*, most are labeled fiction.

We've defined "war stories," now let's move onto the writing challenge itself. To begin, let me say "Congratulations." It takes courage to write. My hat is off to those who try the writer's journey.

Whether a few words or a few lines, a paragraph or a book, this is such important work to let others know the toll and the triumphs of military service. If I can help by providing guidelines as you start, I will frolic. It is very little to contribute considering what every one of you has already given.

The Good, the Bad and the Ugly

We need to talk about some special considerations when writing war stories. I told my classes, "I run the Clint Eastwood school of writing; we talk and write about the good, the bad and the ugly." To be truthful, one cannot be politically correct. So, let loose. War and keeping the peace are nasty businesses at best and strong human emotions are involved.

A writer holds his or her readers to a story with emotion. Writers live life twice, once when they experience it, again when they write about it. For some veterans, emotions are the last thing they want to drag up about a war or military experience.

Here is my <u>caveat emptor</u>—buyer beware. Once you open the memory bag and start writing about your experiences, events long forgotten may emerge. Most likely you will experience dreams and perhaps nightmares, symptoms of Post Traumatic Stress. **If at any time these images begin to scare or overwhelm you, please visit a counselor.** I have worked closely with the Veterans Outreach Centers in Portland and Salem, Oregon. I have experienced depression and dreams not only from my own experiences, but from listening to and reading veteran's stories. It happens. Called "vicarious traumatization" or "secondary stress" in counseling circles, I knew the stories would eventually catch up to me after I started teaching the class, but when they did I was still surprised. I was able to deal with the nightmares by reducing my writing classes from two to one.

A World War II combat veteran began having nightmares near the end of the ten-week course. He would write his stories and cry at his computer. "Why is it happening now? It's been more than 50 years since Pearl Harbor. I've never had this problem before," he told me. "Even after I was left in a pile of dead sailors on the ship, until somebody spotted me breathing."

We discussed intrusive memories. "It's happening because you are going back there." He went to see the Vet Center counselors. It helped him to find out he was having a normal reaction to Post Traumatic Stress. Military members don't have time to fully grieve or process events when they happen—survival depends on sucking it up and moving on to the next fight.

In 2000, the crew of the U.S.S. *Cole* had to fight to keep their ship afloat, aid the wounded and locate the dead while still being on alert for another attack. Months or even years will need to pass before these veterans can contemplate revisiting those experiences and sorting them out. Survival takes priority.

That is why I believe Desert Shield and Desert Storm veterans' stories will begin to trickle out now, more than fifteen years after the war. Of course, Gulf War II also kicked in memories for us Desert Storm veterans. Korean and Vietnam War veterans are also finally claiming the importance of their never-told stories.

My wish is for Iraq and Afghanistan veterans to start writing now to help them process their experiences, whether rage or numbness.

Time can be merciful. I encourage veteran writers to use the Veterans Affairs Outreach Centers. Heaven knows you've earned the right. I always gave a Vet Center brochure to each veteran at the beginning of class. A list of Veteran Outreach Centers and a copy of the brochure can be found in

Appendix B. Please use them. If nothing else, to have them tell you it is normal to experience these things.

Some veterans who are dealing with Post Traumatic Stress Disorder (PTSD) have found writing can be a healing way to deal with memories. I encourage PTSD veterans to start or join writing groups at Vet Centers with their counselors; this includes Vet Center counselors treating incarcerated veterans in prisons.

After three years of teaching ten classes, I have experienced and seen the positive healing, forgiveness and pride that comes from writing down these stories and reading them out loud amongst other veterans. It is one way to deal with the pain and joy of the military.

Veterans who are seeking health claims from the Department of Veterans' Affairs many times have only other veterans to rely upon for documentation.

But the power of stories reaches way beyond recounting facts and figures. The connections made through stories can be helpful in a practical way. But perhaps most important, veteran's children and grandchildren need to know these stories to discover the legacy of freedom and the sacrifice required to keep and maintain it.

Which brings us back to the good, the bad and the ugly. Veterans are not perfect. Veterans are not saints. But, veterans are veterans, most doing the best they can. It is hard to explain the experience of being a veteran. The special bond of combat veterans is impossible for the rest of us to understand. But that is exactly why it is so important for combat veterans to write their stories, IF THEY WANT TO. The rest of us need to know, lest we forget.

Book Structure

This book is set up with chapters 1 through 13 the ten-week course on writer basic training. Chapters 14 through 26 illustrate specific veteran groups whose stories are under-represented, in my opinion. Based on personal experiences I've had with these veterans, I encourage them to write their often forgotten stories. Chapters 27 through 30 discuss the effects of trauma and the use of writing to heal. Chapter 31 is my swan song, complete with a personal wish list. Appendix A gives class guidelines for teachers.

I use my personal and family military experiences as examples, because I'm lazy, and there are copyright issues with my former students' work. It also gives the reader a way to get to know me; always important for any reader.

Everyone Is A Writer

Time for the first lesson. My favorite book to read out loud on the first night of class is Brenda Ueland's classic, *If You Want To Write*.

> "Everybody is talented because everybody who is human has something to express. Everybody is original, if he tells the truth, if he speaks from himself. But it must be from his true self and not from the self he thinks he should be. So remember these two things: you are talented and you are original. Be sure of that. I say this because self-trust is one of the very most important things in writing."

Brenda was so right. The night of my first *Writing War Stories* class, I gave the veterans their in-class assignment. When they were finished, I told them they would read their stories out loud.

It was easy to see they would have been more comfortable being sent into a firefight with a spoon. But they obeyed orders, did a great job, and found out they had much in common—rather like getting their heads shaved in basic or women recruits being forced into ugly fitting uniforms.

Brenda Ueland goes on to explain how we have acquired a fear of writing.

> "How does the creative impulse die in us? The English teacher who wrote fiercely on the margin of your theme in blue pencil: "Trite, rewrite," helped to kill it. Critics kill it, your family. Families are great murderers of the creative impulse.... Older brothers sneer at younger brothers and kill it. There is that American pastime known as 'kidding,' - with the result that everyone is ashamed and hang-dog about the slightest enthusiasm or passion or sincere feeling about anything."

Brenda knew about the critics and the creativity killers. I am not the grammar or spelling police. What a beginning writer needs to know is every effort to write is valuable. The effort is half the battle. When I edit or comment on veteran's work, I use purple ink, for several reasons.

My long-suffering novel writing instructor Dee Lopez served in the Red Cross in Europe during World War II. She taught me to receive her constructive writing critiques using purple ink. Purple is a nice color. Besides being connected to the Purple Heart and royalty, I think it held me in good stead with my students too. Red or blue ink jars and reminds one of school. So, think purple when you self-edit your work. Be kind with your beginning efforts.

From the first class, I noticed all of the veterans started writing at a high level. I believe the greatest reason is they write from the heart. They also know I will not pounce on their efforts and shred them before the morning sun. A bond of trust is created between the beginning writer and instructor. This must be true if you join a writing class, develop your own critique group, or write on your own. The forestry management writing method of slash and burn is NOT the way to teach beginning writers. Brenda says so.

> all people who try to write .. become anxious, timid, contracted, become perfectionists, so terribly afraid that they may put something down that is not as good as Shakespeare.
> And so no wonder you don't write and put it off month after month, decade after decade. For when you write, if it is to be any good at all, you must feel free, - free and not anxious. The only good teachers for you are those friends who love you, who think you are interesting, or very important, or wonderfully funny; whose attitude is:
> "Tell me more. Tell me all you can. I want to understand more about everything you feel and know and all the changes inside and out of you. Let more come out."

Welcome to Writer Basic Training

Writer Basic Training is not an easy job.

Writing about personal experiences is like performing heart surgery on one's self, but the rewards can be great. You will start out as a new recruit and end up a trained writing machine. Or as my Vietnam guys would say, you're an FNG now, but stick with it and you too can be an old guy writer. For those of you not familiar with the FNG term, let me explain it does not stand for "Fun New Girl" as one woman informed me while I was on a biker trip to participate in Rolling Thunder. "Fuckin New Guy" is a Vietnam acronym.

Before I go too far down the road of instruction, a note to my fellow women veterans. I've had a couple women veteran writers in my class. They are a joy, especially when we fell into the most divisive topic—swearing. More about swearing in chapter five, women veterans in chapter 18.

There are more than 1.2 million women veterans in the United States. Their stories must be recorded for history and accuracy, to quote my favorite historian, Sharon Nesbit, from the Troutdale Historical Society in Oregon. "Historians kill for these kinds of personal accounts," she emphasized to my first class. **"If you don't write these stories down, somebody who wasn't there will and they will get it wrong."**

I never thought it unique to go into the Army at eighteen. My mother had served as a Marine during World War II and my dad was in the Army Air Corps. Perhaps their greatest gift to me as a child, besides all the TAB paperback books I could order at school, was the confidence I could do anything I wanted to do.

This may have been a shock to some of the men I ran into in the post-Vietnam Army in 1975, but I didn't even see my being a woman as an obstacle, so I assumed there were none. I almost pity the Fourth Infantry Division when I look back. But, they did survive me. That is part of my story as a woman veteran. What is yours?

Writing Goals

If you want to write only one paragraph—great! A twelve-page story? Terrific. A book? You go to it. It's all done one word at a time.

There are steps and tricks to writing, but no secret handshakes to learn. Really. There is also no one "right" way to write. This book describes what worked in my classes, so it might work for you.

Learning to write stories is like building a house—first you need excavation, then a good foundation, you build the walls and fill in the details like wall paint, fixtures and picking out carpet. (Spelling and grammar are paint and carpet, by the way. Don't even think about them. We are going to work on the foundation—the stories.)

Perhaps this book was given to you as a gift and you don't want to write your military stories. That's okay. Use this book as a doorstop or pass it along to another vet. Every writer decides to write or not. Your choice. Unlike in Basic Training, you can say no to writing.

If you do want to write, come along with us through Writer's Basic Training. Forward, H'arch!

Assignment One

Write down three paragraphs about the best or worst advice you ever received from someone in the military. Do it right now. If you have trouble starting, write me a letter.

Dear Kim, The best advice ...

Finished? Good job! Now, read it out loud. It helps if you have a veteran writing buddy or group, but you can do it alone. (Editing tip—reading out loud is the one sure way to find out if a story doesn't work, sounds wrong or a sentence is too long—you can't breathe!) Excellent. How did it sound? We have just taken the hardest step. Now we're ready to start the writer's journey. One boot step at a time.

Assignment Two
List five scenes or events you want to write about from your military days.
1.
2.
3.
4.
5.

Now pick one of these events, the one that interests you the most. Write three paragraphs about it. Take your time. When you have finished this assignment, move on to Chapter Two. Great job. Isn't this more fun than passing a Physical Training test?

Resources:
If You Want To Write, by Brenda Ueland
Rogue Warrior, by Richard Marcinko with John Weisman

Chapter 2

Throw The Grenade!

Working as a journalism intern at *The Gresham Outlook* newspaper, an article lead (first sentence) was giving me a terrible time. Nothing fit. Seems I had lucked out with "natural" leads on my first two stories. This one I'd have to wrestle. I wanted it to be perfect. I cared a lot about this story.

The editor, Quintin Smith, gave me advice that has never failed about beginnings. "You are trying to create a word picture," he said. "Describe what is happening." I'm sure he saw the four-foot fluorescent light switch on over my head.

Here is the lead, which came out on the front page:

> Sharon Hamnett is spending her days waiting for the telephone to ring and glued to the TV.
>
> She is worrying about her son, Greg Matthews. He is an airborne military policeman in Grenada.
>
> "The phone rang at 10:45 p.m. Tuesday and it was Greg," said Hamnett. "I told him the news was scaring me and he said, 'That's why I'm calling mom.' He shipped out for Grenada an hour later."

Quentin told me "good job," when I finished the story. I went to the parking lot and did handsprings, Quentin was not known for giving flowery praise. I felt like I'd won the Pulitzer.

A speech given by Eileen Dreyer, a romance and mystery writer, reinforces how to begin any story. "I had started out my opening chapter with the usual woman riding on horseback over the rolling hills kind of scene," she said. Her critique group didn't let her get away with it. The opening line became, "It had been a long time since she had undressed a man."

Gets your attention, doesn't it? That is exactly what it means to "start in the middle" of the action. When I wrote an article for *ARMY* magazine in 1992, the opening had to be an attention grabber. "I stared hard into the large brown eyes of the 1,200-pound retired Army combat veteran and saw my military career crash and burn." The editor liked the opening and the story about a girl and her ass, er, mule.

Do Bar Fights Count?

This doesn't mean you can't start your story out with when you left home, before you went to basic training. It means, tell us about a scene from the middle, not when you woke up in bed the last morning, but when you said goodbye at the door or the train station, something like that.

Consider the exciting hand grenade as an example. *The Soldier's BCT Handbook*, May 1969 edition, Department of the Army, Chapter Three, Aim to Kill, describes the little beast.

> The hand grenade is a weapon with many uses. However, it is dangerous and you must learn to handle it carefully as well as effectively. All hand grenades have two common characteristics: short range and small effective casualty radius. There are two types of fuze action: delay and impact detonating. Hand grenades are composed of three main parts:

Hold me back. This is how educational writing can make even a hand grenade seem dull. Now try this for a beginning.

> Drill Sergeant Tucker watched the Army recruit fumble the live grenade into the pit. "Throw the grenade!" he yelled, diving for cover.

Gets your attention? Starts in the middle of the action? When starting your story, remember the grenade.

But first, don't drive yourself nuts worrying about the opening sentence. JUST WRITE. It is more important to get started. You can change the sentence later. The best opening line will come while you drive down the freeway or change the oil. The writing muse is weird. There probably won't be a pen or paper around either, so make a dash for a writing implement and get it down. Be ready when inspiration sneaks up on you.

This is when you truly begin to understand what it's like to be a writer. Writers are people, who appear normal, sitting quietly, then suddenly jump up, grab a napkin, and use the soy sauce to write the first sentence of their book on it. Welcome to my world. I always carry paper, pen, and my pocket PC. It's much less messy than soy sauce and packs easier.

So remember, try to create a word picture with your beginning. What's happening? I use several opening lines from books to let my students know how other authors have started out. I usually don't tell them the author and I ask them to guess what time period the story is set. See how these examples work for you. It is not a requirement to have the time and place in the start of a story, but a writer must always catch a reader's attention.

1. "The cold passed reluctantly from the earth, and the retiring fogs revealed an army stretched out on the hills, resting. As the landscape changed from brown to green the army awakened, and began to tremble with eagerness at the noise of rumors. It cast its eyes upon the roads, which were growing from long troughs of liquid mud to proper thoroughfares."

2. "Boylar was on fire."

3. "A Liberty boat full of sleepy hung-over sailors came clanging alongside the U.S.S. *Northhampton*, and a stocky captain in dress whites jumped out to the accommodation ladder."

4. "A trip by troop transport in convoy is a remarkable experience."

5. "My first memory of West Point is lunch—eating lunch in an enormous, drafty room with four thousand men."

6. "It was a bad time. Billy Boy Watkins was dead, and so was Frenchie Tucker. Billy Boy had died of fright, scared to death on the field of battle, and Frenchie Tucker had been shot through the nose."

7. "By ten-forty-five it was all over. The town was occupied, the defenders defeated, and the war finished. The invader had prepared for this campaign as carefully as he had for larger ones."

8. "We were flying fast and low, so low that the pilot of our helicopter had to pull up to fly over the convoy of American trucks streaming through Iraq."

9. "The choppers appeared just after the sun."

10. "When Radar O'Reilly, just out of high school, left Ottumwa, Iowa, and enlisted in the United States Army it was with the express purpose of making a career in the Signal Corps."

11. "We are at rest five miles behind the front. Yesterday we were relieved, and now our bellies are full of beef and haricot beans. We are satisfied and at peace."

12. "The sky was black and ominous, and the cloud cover threatened a heavy early-evening rain. Staff Sergeant Deverton Cochrane's assessment was just as dismal."

13. "We are T-minus thirty seconds and counting..."

Nathan West was strapped tightly into his launch seat. He listened to the steady, feminine voice of the mission commander through his helmet's comlink. It didn't matter that Nathan had heard her run through the checklist over a dozen times in the past; each and every time her voice made his adrenaline pump.

14. "In the late summer of that year we lived in a house in a village that looked across the river and the plain to the mountains. In the bed of the river there were pebbles and boulders, dry and white in the sun, and the water is clear and swiftly moving and blue in the channels. Troops went by the house and down the road and the dust they raised powdered the leaves of the trees."

15. "Where today are the Pequot? Where are the Narragansett, the Mohican, the Pokanoket, and many other once powerful tribes of our people? They have vanished before the avarice and the oppression of the White Man, as snow before a summer sun."

16. "Only a day or two before, three boiler tenders and a machinist's mate had reported aboard for duty, turned their service records over to the quarter-deck watch and disappeared into the bowels of the ship, never to be heard from again."

17. "The Marines, hard men and realists, had never heard of the Chosin Reservoir, but they did not believe the war was over. Not yet. Nor did they truly trust MacArthur."

18. "I go to the basement and open my ruck. The basement is in Iowa, after a long, harsh winter, and deep in the ruck where I reach for my cammies, I still feel the cold of February. We were supposed to turn in our desert cammies, but I kept mine."

19. "The sun rose over the mountains to the east, flooding the valley with light. While it remained dark, we could still tease ourselves into thinking that the job we had to do today was some way off. But the sun, creeping up over the Hindu Kush, reminded us of the immediacy of our fate."

20. "I stood on the hardstand, staring up at the big gray-and-white airplane. The wings and four turboprop engines of the EP-3E ARIES II reconnaissance aircraft were outlined sharply in the portable floodlights the maintenance people had used in the night to prepare for today's mission."

21. "It was a Friday night, and Gate 14 at Norfolk International was not crowded. American Airlines Flight 405 was a scheduled hop from Norfolk, Virginia, to Miami, with continuing service to San Juan, Puerto Rico."

Book Title Answers:
1. *The Red Badge of Courage* by Stephen Crane
2. *Courage Under Fire* by Patrick Sheane Duncan
3. *War and Remembrance* by Herman Wouk
4. *Here is Your War* by Ernie Pyle
5. *In The Men's House* by Captain Carol Barkalow with Andrea Raab
6. *Going After Cacciato* by Tim O'Brien

7. *The Moon is Down* by John Steinbeck
8. *She Went To War* by Rhonda Cornum as told to Peter Copeland
9. *M*A*S*H* by Richard Hooker
10. *A Soldier's Heart* by Kathleen Korbel
11. *All Quiet On The Western Front* by Erich Maria Remarque
12. *LRRPs In Cambodia; MIA Rescue* by Kregg P.J. Jorgenson
13. *Space: Above and Beyond* by Peter Telep, based on an original script by Glen Morgan and James Wong
14. *A Farewell to Arms* by Ernest Hemingway
15. *Bury My Heart At Wounded Knee* by Dee Brown
16. *The Ship With A Flat Tire* by Todd Hunt
17. *The Marines of Autumn; A Novel of the Korean War*, by James Brady
18. *Jarhead; A Marine's Chronicle of the Gulf War and Other Battles*, by Anthony Swafford
19. *This Man's Army; A Soldier's Story from the Front Lines of the War on Terrorism*, by Andrew Exum
20. *Born to Fly; The Untold Story of the Downed American Reconnaissance Plane*, by Shane Osborn with Malcolm McConnell
21. *Warrior Soul; The Memoir of a Navy SEAL* by Chuck Pfarrer

By reading these different beginnings, you may discover something I learned while working at the VA Medical Center in Portland, Oregon. I also saw it dawn on the faces of veterans. Technology changes; the military and war does not. When veterans from four different wars listened to each other in class, they realized the "generation gaps" between Vietnam and World War II or Korea and the Gulf War didn't exist.

The military is the military and war is war. Whether one serves in combat, supports those who do, or fights to maintain the peace.

I hope you've enjoyed this exercise and perhaps there are a few books you want to add to your reading list. News flash, writers also READ. A LOT.

Here are more tips, or shortcuts, to use to help strengthen your first attempts at writing.

- Focus on one person for the reader to identify with in the beginning. You can add other characters later. Whose story are you writing? Yours? Then show the story through your eyes.
- This will also help you decide what is called "point of view;" first person, "I," or third person, "he" or "she." Basically, who tells the story? Beginning writers can be self-conscious about using "I" when

they start, but they quickly begin to fill in with their nickname or by using last names only, common in the military.
- There should be some kind of conflict in the beginning. The reader should know this is not a "normal" day for the character. One of those Murphy's Laws of Combat Operations kind of days when everything goes wrong.
- Put in a few details so the reader knows the time and place they are venturing into. "Sarge grunted at the approaching wave of choppers. Night came too quickly in the Nam bush." Let the reader know if they are entering the frozen tundra of Korea, the blistering heat of the Kuwait desert, or the dangerous ground of the basic-training firing range. Is it 1952 or 2001?
- **Give the reader a picture frame for the word picture.**

Assignment Three
Take the opening paragraphs you wrote in chapter one and look them over.

- Have you created a word picture?
- Does the reader know who is telling the story?
- Have you set time and place?
- Did you start in the middle of the action?

Don't rewrite what you have written too much. Beginning writers can edit two sentences into a complete breakdown of the original thought. Make a few changes, and then move on to the next exercise.

Assignment Four
Now continue from your opening paragraphs and write two double-spaced typed or hand-written pages of your story. Yes, two pages. One. Two. You can do this. You're a veteran. You've eaten C-rats or MREs. Either write the two pages or "drop and give me twenty."

If you hated PT as I did, two typed pages are easy compared to twenty push-ups. For those of you who chose the push-ups instead, make them one-handed push-ups. That ought to make you think twice.

After you finish, pat yourself on the back. It's my way of telling you "Good job!"

When you have finished your two pages, move on to Chapter Three. We will discuss the Mighty MO. Yes, sixteen-inch guns are involved.

Resources:
Refer back to list of book titles. Then READ some of them!

Chapter 3

The Mighty MO

During World War II, my dad was assigned to the Americal Division. He volunteered for The Alamo Scouts. Dad stood behind another recruit, sweltering in the hot, humid South Pacific weather. He heard the sergeant question the man.

"Can you swim ten miles?"

"Hell, no," replied the young soldier, aghast.

"Okay, thanks for coming," the sergeant said. "You can go."

When the sergeant asked dad the same question he replied, "I don't know, but if someone was shooting at me, I'd sure as hell try."

The sergeant smiled at him. "That's the attitude we're looking for," he said. "We don't expect anyone to swim ten miles, but we expect them to try."

Motivation. Every story depends on your character's motivation in any given situation. Writers need to know what motivates their characters.

A character is the centerpiece of a story, whether the writing is non-fiction or fiction. The writer must know the characters to help the reader care about them and continue to read. This is especially challenging when you're writing about yourself.

Everything storytellers write tells something about their lives. We can only write from our own experiences over our lifetime, with our personal filters, prejudices, imagination and selective memories. That's how it works. No two writers will ever tell the same story. Many in my classes find this to be true when comparing notes with other veterans in their units. The same firefight is different when seen through the eyes of two soldiers fighting six feet apart.

Remember when you joined or were drafted? What was your motivation? I thought surviving basic training was a good goal. "Bolo" (failing) was not in my vocabulary. The word "recycle" did not mean separating bottles and cans when I went through basic training. If you got "recycled," you had to repeat basic training. Motivation varies.

To get to know yourself and your character better, complete assignment five. As a writer, you may be surprised how well you really do know yourself, hence your character. This assignment is an exercise to help jog your memory and to get in touch with your motivations in that military galaxy far away.

Assignment Five

Write one typed or hand written page about your main character's background and motivations. Use this list to build a picture of your character in a specific place and time. Make sure to answer the questions based on the age and time period of the character's life you're writing about. Writing about yourself? Answer these questions using your background.

Name:
Age:
What clothes did you wear?
What clothes did you like?
Favorite foods?
State of your health?
Hobbies?
Favorite sports?
What kind of work did you do?
Family?
What did your house look like?
Who were your friends?
Education?
How much traveling had you done? Where?
What were your ambitions?
What did you want most in life?
What did you fear most?
What did you read?
What music did you like?
What were your religious beliefs?
What were your sexual beliefs?
What were your bad habits?
Why did you join the service?

Answering these questions will build a strong picture of the character, either you or someone else. Sometimes it is a good idea to do this exercise not only at the age you're writing about, but also from the writer's current age.

In response to this exercise, veterans have recalled favorite T-shirts or clothes they used to wear, music groups and forgotten foods. I remembered a flashy dark blue Mickey Mouse Fantasia long-sleeved blouse I wore to basic training. It got locked away with the rest of my civvies for the duration of

Army basic. I'm not sure whatever happened to that blouse, but I hadn't thought about it for years, until I did this exercise myself.

Do the exercise now. Take your time.

Welcome back. Did you recall anything long forgotten? This is the start of opening your personal memory bank to help write stories.

I picture my brain as a series of file cabinets; some drawers are easier to open than others. Some file drawers require a quick hit or grease, but eventually they open and the strangest memories pour out. If you have letters, newspapers, or photos from your military service, they can act as a crowbar for prying open stuck file drawers in your brain.

Think about emotions that motivate us to take action. Love and friendship are two powerful motivators. Strong emotion motivates. Examples of motivators romance author Susan Wiggs references are:

- love and hate
- discovery
- self-sacrifice
- vengeance
- grief and loss
- rivalry
- persecution
- betrayal
- the quest
- ambition
- survival
- rebellion
- and catastrophe.

Wiggs adds thirteen more examples of story spicers: deception, material well-being, authority, making amends, conspiracy, rescue, mistaken identity, unnatural affection, criminal action, suspicion, suicide, searching, honor and dishonor.

I adore Shakespeare. He used all of these motivators and sometimes most of them in one play. *Romeo and Juliet* display the first list. *Hamlet* and *Macbeth* use most of the second thirteen. I'm not asking you to write a play, just a few pages. But if you get a chance, go see a Shakespeare play or movie. *Henry V* is a marvel with Kenneth Branagh. One of my favorite haunts is the Oregon Shakespearean Festival in Ashland, Oregon. Whenever I need my creative cup refilled, I head there to watch war and love stories acted out on stage. Perhaps a fishing trip is in order for others. Did you fish in the military?

Think about the different things you did in the military. In my case, I asked myself what motivated me to get a tattoo? Why did my best friend think I was drunk when she first met me, when I was stone sober? Why did I light the floor wax with a match, intending to melt it to buff floors and proceed to fricassee my hand instead? How come I liked standing under a hovering Chinook helicopter to hook external sling-loads? Why did I get every goat-rope aerovac mission while I was in the Air Force Reserve? In how many locations did my mascot Air Bunny Bear have his picture taken? These are the important questions I ask myself. What were my motivations?

Motivation also includes why the troops around you acted the way they did.

- Why did the Nam door gunner wear a Willamette National Forest decal on his helmet?
- Who got the best care packages from home?
- What made an English boy and his brother kill a Japanese soldier?
- Who never got any mail and why?
- Who made an art of preparing the best cup of hot cocoa with C-4?
- Why did the "Fucking Monkey" pick Bob's head to fall in love with?
- What brand of liquor was your preferred choice?
- What do "Tootsie Rolls" mean to Marines who fought at the Chosin Reservoir in Korea?
- Why does a sailor know about Bennie Boys in the Philippines?
- Why did some troops go AWOL?
- Why did Santa Claus get busted by the MPs in Saigon?
- How did someone expect women to wear flightsuits made for men?
- Why did we paint rocks?
-

Questions like those help you figure out a character's motivation. Except for the rock thing. Why the military paints a perfectly good rock is beyond my comprehension.

Writing down real stories creates a motivation of its own for veterans. "Stories do save lives," says author Tim O'Brien, "not bodies, but lives. One of the chief reasons that you write about war is you end up preserving the lives of real people." **Writing down stories honors and remembers our brothers and sisters in arms.**

Do Bar Fights Count?

How's that for motivation to write your stories? You honor those with whom you served by writing down these stories.

By the way, dad was in the Alamo Scouts for a month. While training to invade the coast of Japan in rubber boats to map landing sites for the inland assault, the atomic bombs were dropped on Hiroshima and Nagasaki. The Alamo Scouts disbanded. Dad returned to the Americal Division and sailed into Yokohama Harbor, right past Mighty MO, the U.S.S. *Missouri*, another Mighty Motivator, now a museum in Pearl Harbor, Hawaii. On her final voyage to her resting place, the Mighty MO stopped at Astoria, Oregon for a week. Dad and Mom went down and got to tour the regal lady, 53 years after he sailed past her in Japan. I like to think she stopped by to say hi to dad.

Who were the Alamo Scouts you wonder? The Alamo Scouts were formed as an ad hoc unit in November 1943 and disbanded in November 1945.

"The Alamo Scouts are considered to be the Army's first Long-Range Reconnaissance Patrol and Long-Range Surveillance Unit. In 1988 the Alamo Scouts were awarded the Special Forces Tab by the John F. Kennedy Special Warfare Center & School at Fort Bragg, recognizing them as the forerunner of the modern Special Forces,"

according to authors Lance Zedric and Michael Dilley in their book, *Elite Warriors: 300 Years of America's Best Fighting Troops*. How do I know about the Alamo Scouts? Somebody wrote it down!

Assignment Six
Pick up that pen or mouse right now mister, or missy, and give me two pages. It'll be fun. Trust me. I'm from the government.

Resources:
The Power of the Reimagined Life by Tim O'Brien
Elite Warriors: 300 Years of America's Best Fighting Troops by Lance Zedric and Michael Dilley

www.alamoscouts.org
www.ussmissouri.org

Chapter 4

Mission Objective: Conflict

Conflict keeps a reader interested in a story, waiting to see what happens next. Many people might think there is enough conflict in any war or military story. But conflict goes beyond bombs blowing up and machine gun fire. True conflict is how those bombs and machine gun bullets **affect** the characters we are reading about, how it **changes** them.

"It's not *Nam* that I care about, really. Bullets and bombs and military maneuvers mean nothing to me. They never did. *The Things They Carried* is not *about* war; the war is a backdrop. The obsession is in the stories that are set in the war, of friendships, of guys in love, of ghost stories. War is a great setting for issues of the heart, because the stakes are so high. There's a built-in stress to the stories. It's life and death, even in love stories." Tim O'Brien, *The Power of the Reimagined Life.*

Conflict can be seen as a raised eyebrow, or a lone tear. Dwight Swain, professor emeritus of the University of Oklahoma's Professional Writing Program, plus former newspaper man and foreign correspondent, lists eight general sources of conflict:

> Character against character
> Character against himself
> Character against nature
> Character against the clock
> Character against circumstances
> Character against society
> Character against change
> Character against God and the supernatural

"Nobody goes to the theater, or switches on the tube, to view a movie entitled The Village of the Happy Nice People," says Richard Walter, screenwriting teacher at the UCLA School of Film. I attended his screenwriting weekend course to learn more about story structure. I also learned more about earthquakes and human behavior that weekend. After the four a.m. jolt Sunday, everyone got up and went to the bathroom. I figured Los Angeles had no water pressure at that point, illustrating the conflict of woman against society.

Another famous Los Angeles teacher, Syd Field, teaches the three-act structure of screenwriting this way.

>   Act I - Get your hero in a tree.
>   Act II - Throw rocks at him while he is in the tree.
>   Act III - Get him out of the tree.

The writer must realize what the conflicts are in a story. The writer can then think about the overall structure. How does the conflict escalate?

One of the best visual examples I've seen describe conflict comes from my screenwriting teacher, Bill Johnson. Silhouette Publishing had just rejected my military romance novel because it was "too military." I was pissed. I signed up for Bill's class and proceeded to write the most military cathartic screenplay I could think of, titled *Reserve Wars*. Bill's challenge was to get me focused on structure, not an easy thing to do with a mad woman warrior.

He used the movie, *The Hunt for Red October*, where each step of the story raises an additional conflict. The story premise is Freedom defeats Oppression. (Covered in his book *A Story Is A Promise*) Bill believes the story question of the movie is, "Will Ramius make it to America and gain his freedom?" He diagramed the plot of the movie as stair steps cut into the side of a mountain, each step another challenge which raises the stakes for Ramius's quest for freedom.

While most beginning writers can think about structure, I encourage them to keep these thoughts in the back of their minds and continue to write. True conflicts often are not evident to the writer of a story or book until they are well into the process.

Another way to think about how a story might progress or be structured is offered by Chris Vogler in his book, *The Writer's Journey - Mythic Structure for Storytellers and Screenwriters*. Chris, an Air Force veteran, explored the work done by Joseph Campbell in myths and legends and put it in a modern form. His use of the Hero's Journey is an amazing study guide in class. First I go over the steps of the journey as described by Chris. Next, we study his breakdown of the movie *Star Wars* as a hero's journey.

I then have veterans put their own military experience into the slots of the hero's journey. This can have a profound impact. Most veterans never thought of their military service as connected to those of the Greeks so long ago. For

Korean and Vietnam veterans, the phrase "Hero's Journey" had never entered their consciousness.

Does Greek mythology influence the United States military? You bet. When I joined the Women's Army Corps, our insignia was the Pallas Athene. She was the goddess of war with power and wisdom, her mission to maintain law and order. She was known for her resolute courage, ship building skills and love of animals.

The Navy has a class of submarines called the tridents. The trident is a "three-pronged spear forming a characteristic attribute of the sea god Poseidon, or Neptune," says *Webster's College Dictionary.*

The trident is also part of the Navy Sea, Air, and Land (SEAL) team members' hard-won insignia, worn by the best among the best. SEALS and submarines have combined for some legendary stories of their own. Maybe even of mythological proportions.

A myth is not necessarily a lie. The dictionary defines a myth as "a traditional or legendary story, especially one that involves gods and heroes and explains a cultural practice or natural object or phenomenon." Read descriptions of the actions of Medal of Honor recipients and see if the deeds of those men and one woman are myths or legendary stories.

We are more familiar with the stories of Atlas holding up the heavens, Pandora opening the box, and Midas's touch turning things to gold. The story of Achilles has special relevance to veterans. Achilles was among the greatest of all Greek warriors, known for his courage and fierce fighting. A great fighter, he was vulnerable at the base of his ankle. An arrow eventually killed him in battle, striking his heel. An excellent book by Jonathan Shay discusses the challenge of modern warriors to deal with the trauma of war. The title? *Achilles in Vietnam: Combat Trauma and the Undoing of Character.*

One of my favorite myths is the story about Cupid and Psyche. While trying to cast a spell of revenge for his mother on the beautiful Psyche, Cupid drops his arrow and stabs himself, falling madly in love with her instead. Being careful with your weapons is always a good idea, even for Cupid.

The Stages of the Hero's Journey from *The Writer's Journey* by Chris Vogel, reprinted with his permission.

1. **Ordinary World**
Most stories take the hero out of the ordinary, mundane world and into a Special World, new and alien. To show a fish out of his customary element, you first have to show him in that **Ordinary World** to create a

vivid contrast with the strange new world he is about to enter.

2. Call To Adventure
The hero is presented with a problem, challenge or adventure to undertake. The **Call To Adventure** establishes the stakes of the game, and makes clear the hero's goal.

3. Refusal Of The Call
This one is about fear. Often at this point the hero balks at the threshold of adventure, **Refusing the Call** or expressing reluctance. The hero has not yet fully committed to the journey and may still be thinking of turning back.

4. Meeting with the Mentor
By this time many stories will have introduced a Merlin-like character who is the hero's **Mentor**. The relationship between hero and Mentor is one of the most common themes in mythology, and one of the richest in symbolic value. However the Mentor can only go so far with the hero. Eventually the hero must face the unknown alone.

5. Crossing the First Threshold
Now the hero finally commits to the adventure and fully enters the **Special World** of the story for the first time by **Crossing the First Threshold**. He agrees to face the consequences of dealing with the problem or challenge posed in the **Call to Adventure**.

6. Tests, Allies and Enemies
Once across the **First Threshold**, the hero naturally encounters new challenges and **Tests**, makes **Allies** and **Enemies**, and begins to learn the rules of the **Special World**. Character development occurs as we watch the hero and his companions react under stress.

7. Approach To The Inmost Cave
The hero comes at last to the edge of a dangerous place, where the object of the quest is hidden. Often it's the headquarters of the hero's greatest enemy. When the hero enters that fearful place he will cross the second major threshold.

8. Supreme Ordeal
Here the fortunes of the hero hit bottom in a direct confrontation with his greatest fear. He faces the possibility of death and is brought to the brink in a battle with a hostile force. The **Supreme Ordeal** is the 'black moment.'

9. Reward
Having seized death, beaten the dragon, hero and audience have cause to celebrate. The hero now takes possession of the treasure, the **Reward**. Sometimes the sword is knowledge and experience that leads to greater understanding and a reconciliation with hostile forces.

10. The Road Back
Crossing into Act Three now as the hero begins to deal with the consequences of confronting the dark forces of the **Supreme Ordeal**. This stage marks the decision to return to the **Ordinary World**. The hero realizes that the **Special World** must eventually be left behind, and there are still dangers, temptations, and tests ahead.

11. Resurrection
The hero who has been to the realm of the dead must be reborn and cleansed in one last ordeal of death and **Resurrection** before returning to the **Ordinary World** of the living. The hero is transformed by these moments of death-and-rebirth, and is able to return to ordinary life reborn as a new being with new insights.

12. Return with the Elixir
The hero returns to the **Ordinary World**, but the journey is meaningless unless she/he brings back some **Elixir**, treasure, or lesson from the **Special World**. The **Elixir** is a magic potion with the power to heal or it might simply be knowledge and experience that could be useful to the community someday.

The stages can be deleted, added to, and drastically shuffled without losing any of their power.

The Hero's Journey is infinitely flexible, capable of endless variation without sacrificing any of its magic, and it will outlive us all concludes Vogel.

I decided to try my luck at this exercise and fit my Air Force Reserve experiences into the structure.

The Hero's Journey   Kim joins the Air Force Reserve

Ordinary World
   1. Working as a Public Affairs Officer for the Portland VA Medical Center, life seems a little boring.

Call to Adventure
   2. Nurses at the Medical Center think I would be a great addition to their Aerovac Squadron. They need a medical logistics officer and I am a former Army supply sergeant. They promise me I can be on flight status and "shop the world."

Reaction to the Call
   3. Not sure I want to go back into the military. They put on a full court press, including working with the unit on a joint hospital and military patient disaster exercise, getting to fly with the Squadron.

Meeting with the Mentor
   4. Meet Scott and John, my two trainers, and proceed to learn what it takes to be a Medical Services Corps officer, including Squadron politics and passing the altitude chamber.

Crossing the Threshold
   5. Two weeks before my scheduled solo mission, I am thrown onto a training flight as Aeromedical Evacuation Operations Officer (AEOO) to pick up Air Force Reserve brass to ferry them to our Squadron for an inspection.

Tests, Allies & Enemies
   6. I bond with my fellow AEOOs and begin to learn the ropes. surviving challenging training missions and live patient evac flights out of Alaska begin to give me a sense of knowledge and confidence.

Approach to the Inmost Cave
   7.   While on a special two-month assignment to The Pentagon to develop a health promotion marketing plan, Iraq invades Kuwait. I prepare to mobilize my unit for war.

Supreme Ordeal - Greatest Fear
   8.   The first of five waves of reservists are activated at my Squadron. I work non-stop to provide them with air and land chemical warfare kits, weapons with ammo, atropine syringes, narcotics, cold and warm weather gear. I ship out all of my fellow AEOOs, except one, and say goodbye to my close friends on the medical crews.

Reward
   9.   Mobilized to St. Louis, the war ends and I return to the Squadron. It is three more months before all my fellow AEOOs and medical crew personnel are home. I am grateful everyone returns home safe from our unit.

The Road Back
   10.   The Squadron struggles to put ourselves back together with the help of counselors and chaplains. Split in so many pieces around the world, the unit is fractured. More volunteers are asked for in the coming months and eventually Somalia raises its head. Tired of working full time and in the reserves, I find I am not 100 percent committed to the Squadron. I resign my commission. Two years later my friend Scott, my trainer and fellow AEOO, commits suicide.

Resurrection
   11.   I develop and teach the Writing War Stories class for three years I join biker veterans and realize I have become an invisible veteran. I begin to write the book about the class for other veterans who want to write their stories. Mikel Mathews, my next door neighbor who invited me on the biker trip, succumbs to lung cancer and leaves his family behind, the legacy of his 1st Aviation Brigade days in Vietnam. Ray Goody, a Chosin Few Korean War Marine veteran, former student, dies from cancer. His completed book of war stories is one of my greatest treasures.

Return with the Elixir
   12. The process of writing the book gets me in touch with the love I have for my fellow veterans, but more surprising, the anger I feel for how they have been treated. I join the American Legion, Post 1, and ship the book out to readers and query an agent interested in it years ago. Unfortunately, Sept. 11, 2001 and the Iraq war make my need to honor and thank veterans, active duty, Reserve, Guard, and Coast Guard members an even higher priority. I finish the book and send it out to my fellow veterans.

Now it's your turn to try out this structure format.

Assignment Seven
   Using the following outline, fill in your military experiences as they relate to the Hero's Journey.

The Hero's Journey

Ordinary World   1.

Call to Adventure   2.

Reaction to the Call   3.

Meeting with the Mentor   4.

Crossing the Threshold   5.

Tests, Allies & Enemies   6.

Approach to the Inmost Cave   7.

Supreme Ordeal - Greatest Fear   8.

Reward   9.

The Road Back   10.

Resurrection   11.

Return with the Elixir   12.

This structure can be used for one story, one chapter, or an entire book. I encourage veterans to read this material and think about it, but don't dwell or analyze too long. Many veterans worry too much about what structure their stories will take or how they would put a book together.

FIRST, the book must be written, words on paper. Part of the fun of the creative process is how a structure will appear from the stories. Some writers use a chronological approach, beginning to end. Others take only the stories that mean the most to them and create a thread for a book. Still others have many short stories, any way is fine, but the words must be written down first.

Assignment Eight

This next assignment is subversive, sneaky, and fun. I want you to eavesdrop on conversations around you. Shopping malls, public transit, lines at the movie theater, and grocery stores are great places to hear what people are saying. This exercise will train your ear to recognize real dialogue. People do not talk in perfect English. They use slang, cuss words and regional dialects. Incomplete sentences.

It all adds spice to your writing and helps define your characters. When a soldier huddles in the rain on guard duty in Vietnam, the grunt from Texas is not going to sound the same as the kid from Brooklyn.

Next, write down three sentences of dialogue you overhear. Think about how the words fit together and what actual information was conveyed.

One of our favorite replies to this class assignment came from Eric. He overheard two World War II veteran swimming buddies in the college pool locker room.

Do Bar Fights Count?

"Hey, you know that salt peter stuff they gave us during the War?"
"Yeah," replied his swimming bud.
"It's starting to work."

You never know what you might hear out there. In the next chapter we will discuss dialogue. And perhaps a little OPSEC/COMSEC (Operations Security/Communications Security) thrown in too. Are you listening????

Resources:
The Writer's Journey, Mythic Structure For Storytellers & Screenwriters by Christopher Vogler
The Writer's Journey, 2nd Edition, Mythic Structure For Writers by Christopher Vogler
www.thewritersjourney.com

Chapter 5

Eavesdrop For Intelligence

"I can't find the shampoo," I said to Jan.

"Maybe the British PX doesn't carry it," she said. "Did you buy it in a German store?"

"Can't remember. Found it the first month we were here. It's in a brown bottle with Evergreen something on the label."

"That pointy small bottle?"

"Yeah."

"I don't see it. Why don't you get something else?"

"The smell helps me forget the freezing water from the five-gallon can."

"Don't you need a conditioner? We've got to be back with the Jeep in 30 minutes."

"I can't freeze my head like you for a second rinse," I whispered.

"Cookie?"

"Uh huh?"

"Why are we whispering?"

"I think people are staring at us because we have accents."

"Right. We're American women Army soldiers carrying M-16 rifles, in full-combat gear, mud up to our knees, shopping for shampoo. Trust me. They're not listening to our accents."

The year was 1978. We were in Germany for Reforger (Return Forces to Germany) shopping in a British Post Exchange.

How much information are you able to find out from the dialogue? Could you tell who was speaking? How much did you learn about our personal traits and environment?

When people speak they convey information, some intended, some not. Dialogue is a key element for writing. Listening to how people really talk makes a better writer. People do not string English composition sentences together in real life.

With that in mind, how did the eavesdropping assignment from Chapter Four go? Did you learn people don't talk in exact sentences, answer questions, or even listen to each other? Did you realize people talk about the most intimate details of their private lives in public places? On cell phones?

Do Bar Fights Count?

Dialogue makes stories come alive. Working as a journalist, I learned to listen for keeper quotes; sentences or phrases that are unique and different, and express a lot about a person in a few words.

One interview resulted in this quote from a Norwegian sailor who delivered large sailboats around the world for 15 years:

"I don't know if I like the ocean so much. I like the land less. The world is getting pretty complicated," said Kjell Dale of Seattle, Washington.

Those three sentences tell the reader a lot about Dale. Even two and-a-half hours into the interview, relaxed with rations of Puerto Rican rum, I knew those quotes were keepers.

One of the challenging aspects of being a writer is having a constant tape recorder running in your brain. I tell folks writers are never "off work." Suppose I am minding my own business at a coffee shop on Saturday and hear someone say, "You bought the wrong brand of handcuffs. Get the ones with the silver key."

Now, I don't know about you, but my imagination starts racing. What handcuffs? For what? Is this a sex pervert or a deputy sheriff? How can you get the wrong brand of handcuffs? Isn't there a recommended brand? Why do these people need handcuffs? How does one know so much about handcuffs? Do I need to switch coffee shops? All from two small lines of dialogue.

So, even on weekends the recorder in my writer's brain is listening for good dialogue and story ideas. One day that handcuff line will end up in something I write. (It just did.) My writer's mind is awake to clues all the time. Train your ears and brain to do the same. Dialogue is important to create a world for your reader to explore, identify and enjoy. Dialogue provides the clues and details which re-create the writer's world.

Many authors tell beginning writers to take a screenwriting course to improve their dialogue writing. They make an excellent point. I took a screenwriting course to practice dialogue and for revenge, after the rejection of one of my fiction manuscripts. It helped me meet both goals. Here is an excerpt from a scriptwriting article by Lawrence Ditillio, June 1996, *Writer's Digest* magazine.

> ... opt for a line that will do what a line of good dialogue must do: reveal a facet of Jack's character.
>
> Jack moves to the body and gestures to a police officer who lifts the sheet to show him the victim. We know immediately it's a horrid sight, either by showing it directly or showing the reactions of other people on the scene to the sight. Either way, we know what we want from

Jack. He doesn't react; he has seen such sights too many times. He turns from the body and says to a nearby officer: 'Order me a sandwich. Roast beef, rare.' Then he begins his examination.

The sandwich the police officer ordered casually tells the reader quite a bit about this particular detective. The next time you go to a movie, close your eyes and listen. Hear how much can be expressed with dialogue. Screenplay dialogue is somewhat different from real life, but still a good training ground for a writer.

My screenplay course helped me focus on every word of dialogue. Coming from a journalism background also helped me. I believe a fiction book is like Jessica Rabbit from the movie, *Who Framed Roger Rabbit*. A novel is voluptuous and filled with curves and padding, scenery, dialogue, the five senses and even internal thoughts of a character.

A newspaper article is like an anorexic woman. Skin and bones. Just the facts. The information comes across and only the important quotes appear as dialogue.

A screenplay is the woman's skeleton. Words and limited lines of action are all there is to tell the story. Fibula, tibia, that stuff. Screenplay writing is an excellent way to practice dialogue and story structure.

Think about the dialogue in the stories you're writing. What slang terms did one buddy use that were distinctive to him? How about the others? The infantry grunt from the Bronx in New York sounds and talks different than the platoon mate from Dallas, Texas. These details are critical when writing dialogue.

I remember one Army basic training conversation that helped me understand regional accents.

"You want to go to a potty?" my platoon mate Sue asked.

"What?"

"A potty. Delta three is having one on the third floor."

"But, we have potties here."

"We're not having potties."

"We're not?"

Sue stopped and looked at me, understanding finally getting through. "Not a potty. A paw-tie."

"Oh! A party." Her Boston accent got me every time. "I couldn't figure out why I needed to go to the third floor for a toilet. We've got at least eight toilets here," I said, shaking my head.

"It's like p-aark the c-aar in the gar-aage," she laughed back.

But be careful when using dialects or accents. A reader needs to be able to easily read your work. Sprinkle enough accented dialogue to give a hint, not make a story impossible to read because it is all in Louisiana Cajun. A few words will do.

This rule especially applies when dealing with "English" speakers from our allied forces. I spent three months camping through Europe in 1983 with mostly Australians and New Zealanders. One night in Switzerland, I spent an entire hour unable to understand a thing anyone was saying. It started off with "Fair dinkum" and went downhill from there. Not only does slang catch you up, but there are different meanings for words.

When I explained I slept in an Army cot in Germany in 1978, raucous laughter burst out.

"What did I say?"

"You couldn't have slept in a cot! Baby's sleep in a cot!'

"No, babies sleep in cribs."

"A crib is a flat!"

"A flat is a tire."

And so the slang wars continued until we made a list of them in the Day Book, alias trip diary. Cap'n Joe, our nickname for an Australian Navy veteran on the trip, made an additional list of the Auz Navy versus my Army terms.

American beer is piss in Australian. Tea is a brew. Seconds are slops. Smokes are durries. Doing laundry is do dobeying. Laundry detergent is dobey dust. Candy is mackers. Car hood is bonnet and car trunk is the boot. And people wonder why we have trouble communicating since we all speak "English." And of course I couldn't forget the famous chunder chart in the back of the book; who puked and when. Remember our allies and how they talked. It will liven up your writing a great deal.

Swearing

I find it amazing that of all the bloodshed, gore, sex, racial slurs and down right crazy funny situations my students wrote about, the most challenging topic we discussed was swearing.

Having veterans from four wars in my class at any given time allowed for a major cross-section of experiences and potential generation gaps. One spirited discussion centered on the difference in swearing between World War II and Vietnam veterans.

The World War II vet was concerned about the amount of swearing used by a Vietnam veteran. We discussed the Vietnam veteran was writing the truth, what words were actually used during his tour of duty. The word "fuck" was such an integral part of the Vietnam experience; it had to be used. When the class learned there is a lizard in Vietnam who says the word, we figured it was indigenous to the culture and countryside.

The World War II veteran's main concern was what his family would think if they read his story. My solution? **Each writer decides exactly what does and does not go into his or her writing.** Another way to get around it is to put a disclaimer at the front of the book or a sentence stating the language may offend some, but the veteran has written the truth to the best of his or her recollection.

"I don't expect Ward said 'oh, cupcake,' when he was blown off the bridge of his Navy destroyer," I told the student. "But you put what works for you."

Another Vietnam vet explained how he has handled the situation. "My kids get a big kick out of reading my stories," Dave said. "They've never heard the old man swear, then they read how I sounded in Nam. They think it's funny."

The situation of who the swearing might offend in class came up at the same time. Some of the students didn't want to swear in front of us women veterans. But, we women vets, we're a hardy lot. "We used to swear just as much as these guys," said Mary. "We can probably out swear them."

It all works out fine. One cannot be politically correct or muzzled when writing the truth about the military. So, swear words? Use 'em if you've got 'em.

Operations and Communications Security alias OPSEC/COMSEC

A special area of consideration for military writers is security. Some members of military intelligence signed pledges they would not discuss their classified work for at least 30 years. The mission of the Navajo Code Talkers of World War II was not declassified until 1968. Submariners cannot talk about their work, but an excellent book, *Blind Man's Bluff* by Sherry Sontag and Christopher Drew, gives a window to their world.

Writers are responsible for what they reveal when it comes to OPSEC/COMSEC. Veterans know little details add up if someone is watching or listening. I bring this up as a reminder of national security. I remember a friend at the Pentagon telling me the news media always knew when something big was coming down the pike during Desert Storm by watching Domino's Pizza. When a lot of folks were working very late, they would order pizza delivered. It's not terrorist pepperoni, but observant writers. Read books written by former intelligence veterans and see how they have dealt with this issue.

Back to learning about dialogue. There are basic mechanics about writing dialogue. Each time a different person talks, they get their own, individual, paragraph. This way the reader can easily follow who is speaking and every line doesn't have to end with "he said, she said." Check a recent popular fiction book. Flip the pages and see how much "white space" (open space without writing) is on the pages with dialogue. Words seem to float in space from the air dialogue lets into a story. Compare it to any textbook and see the difference.

Not only does the white space rest the reader's eye, but quick, short sentences increase pace and tension. Varying the length of sentences creates a rhythm. With varied sentence lengths, words become puzzle pieces to assemble a story. The more action or stress, the fewer words and the shorter the dialogue.

Think: Ready? Aim! Fire! If all a puzzle's pieces were shaped the same, boring. The same goes for sentence length.

At this point, don't concentrate so hard on sentence length that you forget to write. Write first. Try dialogue. Then afterwards go back over it. In the final editing process, see how long or short your sentences are, whether they vary in length. Are all your characters listening to each other and answering all their questions? It isn't realistic in daily conversations. It may happen in a military mission briefing, but not day to day in the military.

What's the best way to check or edit your dialogue? Read it out loud. For that matter, reading everything you write out loud is a great way to "hear" how the words sound. They may ring true or sound stilted. Some writers read into a cassette tape or CD recorder and listen to it in the car. They can hear their work without concentrating on reading it. Focusing on driving is a good idea though.

Abbreviations

A special note here about abbreviations. The military seems to breed alphabet soup. This came home to me one day while at my part-time job after the Army.

"I need to talk to you," said one of the stockbrokers at the discount brokerage firm, rushing into my area. "I need to talk to this guy and they keep telling me he's TDY. Where is TDY? I told them I don't care where he is; I need to talk to him about the sell order on his stock. Why won't they let me talk to him?"

"TDY means temporary duty," I replied. "It means he is not on the base, maybe not even in the country. He might even be on a classified mission, so they can't even tell you where he is."

"Oh." Her shoulders slumped. "Why didn't they just say so?"

"The military uses its own language. They forget civilians don't know the code."

Given my military, medical and federal government background, I also have to watch out for conflicting abbreviations. When I first started working for the county, my boss had to cover a meeting.

"I'm going to the EMT," she said.

"EMT?"

"Yes."

"Why are you meeting with Emergency Medical Technicians for cable television business?"

"It's the executive management team."

"Oh." Watch out for those dueling abbreviations at all times.

Given their military background, a frequent question from veterans is how much to explain. I remember a particular bloop gun discussion. The Army guys knew the bloop gun was an M-79 grenade launcher. The Air Force, Navy and Marine veterans didn't have a clue.

Military lingo, abbreviations and acronyms can be service-specific. Air Force and Navy carrier veterans will know that FOD is flying object debris. Any Army veteran will know a grunt is an 11B, infantryman. In the Army my job code was my MOS, but the Air Force called it my AFSC. A good rule is to spell out the acronym the first time it is written, like in journalism, then use the abbreviation later.

I told my students to write their story with the words they would use when talking to a fellow squad member, sailor, flight jockey, or Marine. They should not explain each abbreviation in parentheses, as it will drive the reader mad. When stories may be read by a variety of people, the author should consider creating a glossary of terms for the back of the book.

If the primary reason for writing your military stories is for your family to read, a glossary will be required. Considering which era of military service you served in, the time frame will also have to be explained. The military didn't always have night-vision goggles, laptop computers and global-positioning-satellites. These details can be looked at on final editing, but keep them in mind as you write.

Do Bar Fights Count?

Your goal is to make sure the reader can clearly understand your stories. Help the reader be able to see and feel the military world. Bring in the details that make up the military environment.

In the next chapter we will discuss using the five senses in writing. I mean sight, hearing, taste, smell, and touch. To prepare for chapter six, here is the homework assignment. You will need a trusted assistant and I do mean trusted.

Assignment Nine

Your assistant will conduct this assignment. You, the writer, will need a pen or pencil and writing paper. Your assistant will give you five items to awaken your senses. In a short period of time, 30 to 60 seconds each, you will examine the items.

Your assistant's responsibility is to gather the list of items needed before the exercise, choosing from the list in the back of the book, depending on availability. Note to assistants: DO NOT use icky stuff. The writer trusts the assistant. Be nice.

Note to writers: Don't peek at my shopping list in the back of the book. It defeats the purpose of the homework. Thanks. (Kids and grand kids love being the assistants when veterans try this exercise at home.)

The assignment will explore the senses in the following order:

The writer keeps his or her eyes closed. The assistant will take the actions listed below. After each sense is tested for 30 to 60 seconds, the writer opens their eyes and writes down immediate impressions, before moving onto the next item.

When finished, the writer reads aloud their impressions and the assistant shows them the actual item.

> Smell - Wave the item under the writer's nose, two to three times, slowly.
> Touch - Place the item in the writer's outstretched hand and let them feel it.
> Taste - Place it in the writer's hand and let them unwrap it and put it in their mouth.
> Hearing - Play an audio piece for a short amount of time.
> Vision - Display the item for 30 seconds.

Homework assignment complete? Good. Think about what you learned. Move onto the next chapter to find out why all the senses must be used in writing. Ever sniff a poncho?

Resources:
Listen……. What words do you hear?

Black Hawk Down; The Shooting Script by Ken Nolan
Dialogue by Lewis Turco
"The Art of Listening" by Brenda Ueland at
http://traubman.igc.org/listenof.htm

Chapter 6

Ever Sniff A Poncho?

"Needs more color, more smells." Dave once again was a victim of the classic critique.

"But, I can't get them," he said one evening. "How can I get the smells?"

"Ever sniff a poncho?" I asked. The class laughed but got my point. "In an Army surplus store the other day, I walked by a row of ponchos. That smell brought back such memories. How do you describe the acrid, plastic and musty smell of a plastic poncho? Give it a try."

Another veteran, Tony, a forensic psychologist, told us smell was the oldest sense we humans have. It is even located in a different part of the brain from our other senses. I took his word for it.

Senses are the spices which make a writing piece come alive with flavor and subtle detail. The small things really do make a difference.

My advice to Dave? Visit a surplus store and if really brave, how about a Vietnamese grocery? But be prepared for a potentially powerful experience of recall. Smell is the Cro-Magnon sense of the five.

Think about the importance of smell in your life; Douglas fir trees during the holidays, the odor of car oil from your first oil change, fresh baked bread from anywhere and the favorite perfume or cologne worn by a loved one. It is a powerful reminder.

Smells

Some military smells which bring back strong memories include:
- Smoke
- Sweat
- Phosphorous
- Brasso
- Starch
- Web Gear
- Gunpowder
- Floor Wax
- Blood
- Mess Hall SOS

- Latrine, Head, Comfort pallet, Slit Trench
- GP Medium Tent canvas
- Camouflage netting
- Sweaty feet
- M-16 cleaning oil
- Shaving cream
- Sewage
- Mosquito Repellent

What is on your list? I encourage veterans to sprinkle two to three senses on each typewritten page. Now, I know you are going to start counting. STOP. This is a guideline to get you to think about the senses while writing. It is a suggestion, not a rule.

Sound

Military sounds help add a sense of realism to any story. Do you remember?
- Whump, whump of an incoming chopper's blades
- The metal clank of the deuce and a half's chains rattling on the tailgate
- The bosun's whistle onboard the ship
- The pitch of your drill sergeant's voice at 5 a.m.
- Rain dripping on a wet tent
- Sucking sound of mud by boots being lifted out of the muck
- Ripping Velcro from flightsuit cuffs and oxygen line wraps
- The tent zipper
- Radio static
- Jet engines
- Marching
- Reveille
- Hatch closing
- Pick up game of football
- Locking and loading
- Tank treads growling across the desert
- Windstorms
- Jeep horns
- 40s, 50s, 60s, 70s, 80s, 90s, 00s music
- Shifting gears of a five-ton truck

Do Bar Fights Count?

- Rush of wind across the deck
- Sliding torpedoes into the tubes
- Closing clam shell doors on a C141B
- Clank of web gear
- Click of bullets being put into a magazine

And those are just a few. Perhaps you didn't realize how many sounds were a part of your military experience. Add in the animals, nature and war, and sound is everywhere. Even losing hearing from the concussion of a blast—because then the sound is gone and silence reigns during chaos.

How long do sounds affect us? My friend Kathie's son programmed reveille as her cell phone ring. She calls it her vet finder. "Whenever it goes off, I can always tell the vets. Their heads pop up when they hear reveille."

Touch

We use our fingers to feel where we are in the world, whether stroking a child's hair when we say goodbye or assembling a weapon in the dark. What textures do you remember?

- Sleeping bag
- Ship mess trays
- Toilet paper
- Smooth weapons
- Starched, grimy, clean or dirty fatigues
- Dress cap
- Ribbons
- Duffle bag
- Wool socks
- Fireproof longjohns
- Scuba gear
- Helmet
- Canvas aircraft seats
- Entrenching tool
- Sleeping on rocks
- Cot
- Field jacket
- Pea Coat
- Gas mask seal

- Red lensed flashlight
- M-60 machine gun
- Bullet bandoliers
- A 16-inch round
- Trigger
- Wooden bench
- Pouring rain
- Dirt and rocks
- Frozen ground
- Scorching sand

Were they smooth or rough? Did it cut or hurt? How did your skin feel when it was bruised, scraped, calloused, whiskered? What does a week's worth of sweat and dirt feel like on the skin? Can you grow vegetables in your ears? Hot Jeep hoods and wet zodiacs. What does being in the military feel like?

Taste
One very important sense is taste. How do meals ready to eat taste on your tongue? Are flavors spicy, rancid, pasty or sweet? What does dirt and/or sand actually taste like? What can you write about a surprising taste you encountered?
- First taste of SOS
- First German beer
- Drinking fresh milk on the docks after getting off the ship after World War II (dad's memory)
- Favorite meal when you got home
- Coke, Pepsi, Mt. Dew or Dr. Pepper?
- Candy bars
- Coffee with a pinch of salt
- Dry mouth
- Chewing sand
- Turkish apple tea
- Powdered milk
- Local delicacies
- Kimchi
- Salt tablets

- Pie
- Crab for Thanksgiving
- Anything out of those green Mermite hot food containers
- The best mess hall food
- Leftovers on KP duty
- Blood
- Sweat
- Tears
- Chocolate
- Rope
- M&Ms
- Scuba mouthpiece
- Navy coffee
- Tobacco
- Torpedo juice
- Powdered eggs
- Peach preserves

Sight

Images play a major role in our memory bank. Some we would like to forget, some we never shall. The role of the physical surroundings brings description to the writer through his or her eyes.

The scenery from dust trails on Army convoy to the fluorescent sea creatures churned up in the wake of an aircraft carrier all bring physical reminders of the military world we experienced.

Movement and color together can create memories. One of my favorite Harley Wedel stories is about the ballet of the flight deck, the movement and colors of the "Bright pull-over shirts and cloth helmets of reds, yellows, browns, greens, blues, even blacks and whites." My favorite movie of all time, *Top Gun*, reinforced the color kaleidoscope on an active flight deck.

Movies and photographs can open windows in our memory and contain small details we might have forgotten. What images do these thoughts bring to mind?

- Meeting your Drill Instructor for the first time
- Colors of the walls in the gas chamber
- Linoleum floor in the barracks
- Quonset hut

How To Write Your Military Stories

- Basic training graduation ceremony
- Tank school obstacle course
- First convoy
- Flightline at dusk
- Navy battle group on the move
- Boarding a freighter looking for drugs
- Bombing
- Jungle canopy
- Historic ruins
- Agent Orange drop
- Sea Stallion Chopper
- Gunny
- First foreign country
- Hauling ass
- Showers in tents
- Showers out of a helmet
- Camp
- Base
- PX, BX or Commissary
- Refuel location
- Medic tents
- Buddy's favorite car
- Rain, sun, sand storms, typhoons, waves, air pockets, snow
- Enemy dead
- Our dead
- Wounded
- Home
- Golden Gate Bridge
- Your driveway

These details of what you saw create that word picture we talked about at the beginning of the book. A story needs to be filled with snapshots of the senses, so the reader can relate to what the veteran experienced. An amazing book about Vietnam is called, *Requiem: By Photographers Who Died in Vietnam and Indochina*, by Horst Faas, Tim Page and Tad Bartolimus. This book contains photos by photographers killed in Vietnam. It shows the great emotion, clarity and attention to detail these slain men and women captured in their lenses.

Another book, *They Drew Fire, Combat Artists of World War II*, by Brian Lanker and Nicole Newnham memorializes the work these artists did to capture the sights and visions of war. They put on canvas and paper what they saw with their eyes. From their work it is evident they also saw with their hearts.

Before I move onto another topic related to the senses, I wanted to close with a quote from a former student's book. Raymond Goody finished his war stories, about being a Marine in Korea with The Chosin Few, shortly before his death. I quote one passage from his book, *Korea, Shadows In the Night*.

> The bitter cold winds are freezing our weapons. I try to keep the rifle free by sitting on my rifle as I ride in the rear of the wire Jeep. With a lull in the fighting, all the sections weapons are frozen up. I yell to TJ, "We have to get these weapons opened up, any suggestions?"
>
> "Hell, lets put the rifles next to the Jeep's exhaust pipe, Ray," replies TJ.
>
> 'Sounds good to me TJ, if that doesn't work, I'll try peeing on the bolt! I'm so damn cold though, I don't know if I will pee hot or a stream of ice."

One snapshot of war using the power of description with senses.

So you see, bar fights are perfect lessons in using the senses to write. Sight is involved with flying fists or bottles in dim lighting and the taste of blood or beer will definitely be a part of the events. Then hearing shouts, breaking bottles, and the military or shore police whistles combined with bruised knuckles, sore ribs, or sticky clothes all combine with the smell of cigarette smoke, leather upholstery, sweat, cologne and perfume. At least, that is what I have been told about bar fights.

Chuck also told me the destroyer crew used to fight the submarine crew when they were in port. That was until the carrier crew showed up, then the destroyer and sub crews joined up to fight the carrier crew. Teamwork at its finest. And supposedly many of the bar fights are started about sex or the possibility of sex – at least that is one of the stories.

Military Sex

Now that I have your complete, focused attention, let's discuss sex. I figured including it with senses is the best spot for this topic, since we use all the senses for sex. The same as with the Clint Eastwood school of writing, there is good, bad, and ugly sex. When I refer to military sex, I mean how sex impacted you in the service.

Sex includes stories of being with prostitutes on R&R, not being with prostitutes, men and women recruits losing their virginity, or not. A story read in class one night concerned the last night an Infantry grunt spent in Nam, getting drunk at the club. Revealing all his warts, he also let his readers know he was still a virgin. It made me wonder how many virgins are on the Vietnam Veterans Memorial Wall.

Good sex can come from being with the one you love for a lifetime or a night. Meeting your mate or "love the one you're with" as the old song goes. Sex is part of living and life. Considering many states don't allow soldiers to drink until age 21, it seems sex is one of the few true legal stress relievers.

No judgments. Write about the wild R&R parties, shore leave, and the USO shows. I think USO shows fall under teasing, but I could be wrong. I also encourage writers to read some romance novels. Suzanne Brockmann writes a wonderful series involving Navy SEALS and women in uniform. A note to readers: romance paperback books make up 54 percent of all paperback fiction sales in America, a 1.2 billion dollar industry as reported by Romance Writers of America in 2004.

But the best news is women who read romance books have more active sex lives. So heterosexual men, get out there and buy those books for your women! Hell, buy three! The joy I get from reading romance novels is very simple: happy endings.

And not to be outdone, the new online Romantica publisher, Ellora's Cave, is doing a booming business in women's and gay men's erotic romance. I've been enjoying reading several of their latest books. Isn't writing research fun? There are definitely all types of happy endings.

But the best happy ending I know of is coming home from war or military service to the ones you love. So, in actuality, we are all fighting and defending our pursuit of life, liberty and happy endings.

The Ugly

On the other hand, there is the ugly side of sex. Men and women recruits raped and sodomized in basic training or at permanent party. Ritual hazing which gets out of hand. The added trauma of homosexuals in the military who were raped and discharged, not eligible for veteran's benefits. Women who entered the Army to escape abusive homes and were then victimized again. Women from solid, stable homes such as myself who encounter sexual harassment. It happens. It's ugly. It's part of the military story.

Write about it. The truth may not set you free, but it can heal. But most of all, everyone abused or attacked in a sexual manner while in the military needs to know they are not alone. This is another reason to write, to let other veterans know they are not the only victim.

At a Department of Veterans Affairs PTSD Conference I attended, it was estimated 12 percent of military women serving in country were raped during Desert Storm. My advice, get thee to a Vet Center! Counseling services are now available for all veterans who have been sexually assaulted. It's time we all dealt with these attacks by helping those who served and were wounded this way in the line of duty.

Domestic Violence

While we're at it, let's talk about the ugly parts of war or the military we may bring home. We have already buried spouses and significant others of Iraq and Afghanistan veterans. Let's not make more victims of war at home. If you are having anger and violence issues, get to a Vet Center and get help. If you have taken out your anger on your spouse or children, get help now. This is not acceptable behavior. Period. Get assistance. Macho my ass. We don't hurt our own loved ones. Get help from your unit, chaplain, the VA, a crisis hotline or a trusted family member. Get it.

Gender and Sex

Each writer will decide how explicit they want to be in their sexual descriptions. Men and women will also write differently about sex. Perhaps the clearest explanation of the sexual differences between men and women I have read is in Edo van Belkom's book, *Writing Erotica*.

> On a more basic level, women's erotica tends to be about making love and experiencing erotic and sensual pleasure, while men's mass-market erotica is about fucking and coming.

Vive La Difference! Sex can be funny or sad, terrifying and exciting, all at the same time. Think of sex and the senses: smell, hearing, touch, taste and sight. Now there's a homework assignment I wouldn't have any trouble getting folks to do.

Homework Assignment Ten

The next chapter is about the power of God, spirit, or The Force in your life while in the military. Everyone has different religious and/or spiritual beliefs. The next chapter is designed to touch on how that element might enter into your writing.

For assignment ten write down two incidents that happened during your military service where you felt an angel, force, or protective presence helped you out.

1.
2.

Now, think about how you can explain what happened. Can you?

Resources:
Any fiction book written by Suzanne Brockmann or Janet Evanovich. See how they use detail and senses to create complete worlds.

www.tootsie.com/veterans.html
www.hersheys.com/discover/history/rationD.asp
www.hersheys.com/discover/history/hershey_bar_stalag.asp
www.hersheys.com/discover/history/hersjey_hellion.asp
us.mms.com/us/about/history/story/

Chapter 7

The Warrior's Sixth Sense

"Two of the three hydraulic systems are leaking," said the loadmaster. "Arizona is under a severe thunderstorm warning and San Francisco is fogged in. We're heading back to McChord. Rig for crash landing."

These are the kind of words which put a crimp in any aeromedical evacuation training mission. They also tend to test your belief in God, or The Force, however you see the world. Short of taking a cab ride in New York, having a crippled plane that day caused me to lean on my faith and say a few prayers as the loadmaster used the hand crank to lower our C-141B landing gear.

As we slowed to a stop on the main runway, the belly of our aircraft full of hydraulic fluid, I watched the firefighters rush onboard the aircraft in their silver suits. I felt like a Glamour magazine demerit. I preferred one of their snappy silver fashion ensembles to my green flightsuit with the completely washed out fireproofed longjohns underneath.

We were towed off the main runway, since we couldn't turn, and no egress was necessary. I thanked my guardian angels once again. I do believe in miracles.

One veteran working on his stories geared his book toward how his faith in God got him through the war. He was a Huey door gunner in Vietnam during the Tet Offensive. Enough said.

There is the famous cliché that there are no atheists in foxholes. But there is another fallout of belief during war. Many soldiers, airmen and sailors believe God or The Force deserted them during war and in times of need. Those too are stories.

Let's face facts. Men and women who have been brought up in a faith which says "Thou shalt not kill," go out and kill. Some veterans feel they are defiled, made unclean. Others feel they are damned and cannot be forgiven. Counselors say this results from something very deep inside that person having been violated, their ethics deep within.

Do only veterans face these challenges? No. The same Vet Center counselors estimate 75 to 80 percent of clergy have unresolved trauma. We are all in this together. One of my favorite Christian writers, Liz Curtis Higgs, said an amazing thing at a recent writing conference.

"You cannot out sin the grace of God," she said. A simple, but powerful statement. Liz has written many books, one of her most successful? *Bad Girls of the Bible.* Perfect? None of us are.

The role spirituality, religion, or The Force plays in each of our military lives is a story unto itself. Perhaps that is a journey you want to write about, perhaps not. It is an option open to all veterans to explore.

Listen to the words of a veteran who has been there.

Steven Tice, a consultant, writer and public speaker on PTSD issues is a Vietnam combat veteran who fought as an infantry man with the 101st Airborne Division in 1968-69. He was catastrophically wounded when hit by a rocket-propelled grenade in the waning days of the battle for Hamburger Hill in May, 1969, losing his right arm and shoulder as well as receiving multiple wounds resulting in over a year of direct hospitalization and a lifetime of compromised health.

His article *From Trauma to Enlightenment: The Survivor's Journey* discusses the role of religion and/or spirit. I include a part here with his permission.

>The healing from the trauma of war is a journey which encompasses the mind, body and spirit. To attend one and ignore another is to embrace a detour...
>
>I believe war is about loss and that those who have not successfully embraced a healing from war are experiencing profound loss. That loss may be tangible—the loss of body parts or their functioning, the loss of friends to death, wives or husbands to divorce—for intangible losses such as a belief in one's immortality, or youth, or self-esteem.
>
>For many veterans one of the greatest losses they feel they have incurred is the loss of God...which is often camouflaged with anger ... The Reverend Bill Mahedy, who served as a chaplain in Vietnam stated that "teenaged soldiers...had been lead to believe that God would never let them down, that he would always lead them to victory over evil and preserve them in battle against the foe." (Mahedy, *Out of the Night*, p.5)...
>
>Yet eventually, with support, the veteran may work through a grief of tremendous proportions. For once the veil of anger is

removed, a tremendous sadness wells forth. It is here that the heart opens and the healing begins.

When I speak to veterans of spirituality, they often confuse it with religion and thus institution and the reaction is anger. I've asked veterans I work with to reframe this perception, to try on a new interpretation. I ask them to sit still and visualize where they last felt small and the world large: where they knew that there was a larger force at work and that they were not in control; and, importantly, that this condition was all right. Many veterans have told me that this occurs when they are in the woods or on the beach ... For others it is on a clear mountain lake or hiking in the desert, and for some, it is prayer or meditation. I ask the veteran to try on the concept of spirituality in this context-that these methods are vehicles to ... a higher power of whatever name they wish to utilize, that religion is such a vehicle as well which may or may not work for them. I encourage them to embrace a vehicle which will allow them to be still and to lead them into their hearts as that is where the healing lies.

I had the pleasure of hearing Steve Tice at the Department of Veterans Affairs PTSD Conference in Portland, Oregon. He is inspiring for the rest of us who came out of our military service with our bodies and most of our mind intact.

In the military world a normal day can turn into the abnormal quickly and miracles still do occur.

The story of Pilot Shane Osborn in the July 2002 issue of *Guideposts* tells in his own words how prayer and his faith helped him and his crew after a Chinese F-8 Finback fighter jet collided with their Navy EP-3E reconnaissance plane on April 1, 2001.

> "We had survived a midair collision with a big, heavy fighter almost the same size and weight as the powerful American F-4 Phantom of the Vietnam War.
> Standing in the sweltering heat of the Lingshui taxi ramp, I realized I was looking at a miracle."

For those who might not believe in a faith or The Force, whatever you want to call it, I offer up my own story of trying to get this book written. It seemed like such a simple project to begin with, right? Next is the article I wrote for a contest about part of my journey.

Watch Out For The Burning Bush

God has trouble getting my attention. This frustrates him no end, so he goes to great lengths to get my butt in gear when times demand action.

I've known since age 10 that I was a writer. It's like a disease. I can't stop writing. Until last year. I stopped. Cold. The writing project was very important to me. A book on how I taught military veterans to write their war stories.

A veteran myself, I hoped to give this gift to other veterans who wanted, and perhaps needed, to write their stories. The class was my way to honor all veterans and help them heal. We all knew we were doing group therapy, disguised as a writing class. The three years teaching the class had healed my emotional wounds when I didn't even know I was hurting.

But now, for the first time in my life, the words did not come. I became afraid and discouraged. God wasn't real happy either. He took matters into his own hands.

Two friends, Kathie and Carol, are my spiritual bookends. Kathie had spoken to Christian Women's Groups about her journey of faith. Carol had recently been baptized and began working at her church. They both tried to encourage me and offered advice and support. It seemed like whenever I missed God's original message, he would use Kathie or Carol as spiritual voicemail to bring writing to my attention.

"Veterans really need this book," Kathie assured me. "This book is so important." Still no words.

"It will come in time," Carol suggested. "God will help you out."

Little did I know God was ready to initiate a full court press, as they say in basketball.

Autumn 2001 found me grumpy and word stuck. The need to write the book was pressing on my heart. I joined a non-fiction writer's critique group to help me along. The old words from the first draft made their way to critiques, but still no new words.

Then the messages started. I began noticing little coincidences. I've always paid attention to the rule of three; if I see or hear something three times, investigate.

This rule of three taught me to notice details after my first and second wake-up calls from God. The first occurred when I was leaving the Army. The standard out processing physical turned up potential kidney problems. Hospitalization and a kidney biopsy later, the doctors told me at age 21 I had a 70 percent chance of kidney disease. I was devastated. I had to wait three weeks for the final results.

Do Bar Fights Count?

I vividly remember walking across the parking lot at Fort Carson, Colorado, after getting the test results. I spotted my friend Jan across the street.

"I'm normal!" I yelled.

"Bet me!" she shouted back.

I had my life back. I could travel and not be hooked to a machine. I proceeded to pack as much into life as I could.

The second time God grabbed my attention, I was mobilizing my Air Force Reserve Squadron for Desert Shield. My vision started acting up. Working 18 plus hour days, I figured it was fatigue, but I had my civilian eye doctor check. He couldn't find anything after practically crawling in my eyeball.

I was supposed to go to Germany with the fifth wave of Squadron members, but my Commander pulled me from my designated mobilization slot. To say I was mad would be the understatement of a lifetime. Four weeks later I was mobilized anyway to Scott Air Force Base, Illinois. My Chevrolet Sprint and I were rolling East into Twin Falls, Idaho, when the radio announced the ground war was over. I worked at Scott Air Force base for one week, then drove West.

After being discharged from active duty status, I again went to the eye doctor. Two days later I had emergency surgery for a 50 percent detached retina. If I had been sent to Germany, I probably would have lost my sight before I knew what was wrong.

I figured God decided the war wasn't enough to get my attention, so he snapped my eyeball out to make me want to write. But, I had been happily writing for years until I tried to work on the book.

Messages kept coming. I paid attention.

I saw the movie *Pearl Harbor*, and it reminded me of my first oral history interview with a Pearl Harbor survivor when I was in high school.

At a writing conference in Tacoma, Washington, I took a break and walked over to a used book store. I found a book published in 1919 about Verdun and the Argonne-Metz area where my grandfather served in World War I.

On September 11, I was grateful so many lives were saved in New York. The Pentagon was shattered, but kicking back. I felt gratitude in my heart to the military men and women who were in harm's way at that moment. Now there would be even more veterans who might need the book I was trying to write.

A friend from Washington, D.C., was in town for lunch. We talked about the book. A Navy medic during Vietnam, he too knew the importance of writing to process healing.

In early November 2001, a church billboard on my way to work said "God Bless Our Veterans." My count now topped 20 messages. There are four churches on my one and a half mile drive to work, but this was the only church with a message for Veteran's Day.

Carol and I drove up the Columbia River Gorge to Hood River one Saturday and stopped in a Christian Book Store. I overheard a woman raving about a book.

"Oh, you just have to get it," she told the woman next to her. "It's amazing."

A writer always wants to know what book someone is gushing about. Without appearing like a stalker, I casually wedged my way around her and saw the little book, *The Prayer of Jabez*.

I met Kathie for lunch the next week and we both had gifts for each other. We presented each other with copies of *The Prayer of Jabez*. Two days later, a big article appeared in *The Oregonian* newspaper about the book. I figured if I didn't pay attention to the call to finish my writing, it wasn't because God wasn't pulling out all the stops.

But, I was beginning to get a little creeped out and scared. Anytime soon someone was going to walk on water, I knew it. The little Jabez book wanted me to expand my boundaries. With more than 25 million veterans in the United States alone, plus veterans around the world, I became frightened of what my finished book might require of me.

I held out one last hope that all God's "signs" were a big coincidence, when Carol invited me to go out for the evening.

"Let's go to a golf movie," she said. "It will take your mind off all these messages." We went and saw *The Legend of Bagger Vance*. A GOLF movie which deals with post traumatic stress disorder from World War I. I put up the white flag and surrendered. God wanted me writing the book, no ifs, ands, or buts. Besides, I had to protect my other eye.

So when the following note showed up in my Fortune Cookie at a Chinese Restaurant, I was finally able to laugh. "God has given you special blessings." When was the last time anybody got a message from God in a fortune cookie?

At the next reading of one of my chapters written a year earlier, I took a courageous step for an independent woman such as myself. A warrior woman. I asked for help. "I can't write," I said. "I have never had this problem and it's becoming painful."

Do Bar Fights Count?

Jim Petersen, a fellow writer and retired minister, came to my rescue. "I'm pretty good at helping people work through some of these things," he said. "Why don't you come over and we'll spend an hour sorting it out."

Several days later and after two hours of his time, Jim helped me see part of my problem. I am motivated to accomplish things when people tell me I can't do them. I feel it comes from going into the Army as a woman at age 18. Everyone was telling me I had to write this book, even God was telling me to write it. I was digging in my heels, fighting everybody.

Jim suggested maybe the signs were not messages at all, I thought they were messages. Then he told me what I needed to hear.

"You can't write this book," he said. "I don't want you to do any writing."

My inner writing muse stood up and yelled, "Bet me." My mind also told me all this book had to do was honor one veteran, help only one veteran heal, and my work was done. The pressure came off. The millions of veterans I carried on my shoulders after reading *The Prayer of Jabez* changed into only one veteran. My boundaries were now small enough to let me grow into expanding them later, at my own pace. The lesson I had learned after three years of teaching veterans to write came back to me again. The only veteran I had to heal was myself.

I felt God was by my side once more, not shoving me from behind. Four days later I wrote chapter five. The log jam was broken. The critique group raved about the chapter. On my way out the door that night, Jim gave me a stern look. "Now remember, no more writing. Not one word!"

I gave him a silent smile in return.

I believe God has used attention getters, alias miracles, for some of us not paying attention for quite awhile. Parting the Red Sea, Jonah and the Whale, the Ark. Imagine his challenge today with cell phones, e-mail, the World Wrestling Federation, and movie special effects. What would he have to do today to get our attention?

When Kathie told me about the *Guideposts* writing contest, then asked me if we should both enter, imagine my thought process.

"Let's see," I said. "You suggested it. The deadline is my birthday. Plus, last night I realized my first *Writing War Stories* class was taught on September 11, 1997, four years to the day before the terrorist attacks.

"We have to enter this contest. God might think I wasn't paying attention again. I don't want to have to explain the burning bush on my front porch to the neighbors."

I'm paying attention and writing, God. Really. Together we will get this book done. But just in case you don't think I'm listening, I'm ready. The fire extinguisher is in the kitchen.

Resources:
The Legend of Bagger Vance by Steven Pressfield. Pick this book up and read the dedication and "A Note to the Reader." You will be hooked. Then rent the movie.
Taking the High Ground: Military Moments with God by Colonel Jeff O'Leary
Vision of Ghost Armies: Real-Life Encounters with War-Torn Spirits from the files of FATE Magazine
The Faith of the American Soldier by Stephen Mansfield

Chapter 8

Build a War Zone

The August sun beat down on our backs as we leaned over the cement railing. The sea gulls flew about Depoe Bay harbor while we watched the expertise of the filet team cutting the fish from the morning's catch of deep sea fishing charters.

Running feet clattered down the metal dock, causing us to look in the direction of the Coast Guard Station. Guardsmen jumped on the boat and the powerful engines roared to life.

"Whoa, they've got a call out," my sister said.

Their boat horn shrilled the air and the 40 foot rescue boat came charging out of the dock house like a race horse out of the gates. Two fishing boats and a canoe scrambled to get out of the way of the fast approaching boat.

"What the heck are they doing?" I asked. We all watched the boat race to the middle of the narrow 20-foot channel to the sea and stop. We gawked in amazement, standing under the highway bridge underpass, we had a prime view. The boat then began to turn in an arc. Everyone around, ourselves included, uttered our shock.

"Is he nuts?" came cries from the onlookers. "He won't fit" another onlooker yelled. We all crossed our fingers as the long rescue boat turned around under the highway bridge, not more than three to four feet of clearance off each end of the boat.

When the boat was turned, a miracle in itself, the ship's captain cranked the twin diesel engines into frenzy, creating a wave. As we all watched in amazement, around the curve of the rock channel to our right, in came a small green fishing boat coming over the bar, adrift.

We all collectively held our breath as the wall of water ricocheted against the far wall of the channel, just in time to push the small green boat away from the rocks. A perfect rim shot if I'd ever seen one.

The floundering boat swung back into the main part of the channel. The Coast Guard boat roared to its rescue, throwing a line and securing it from a certain dashing against the black seaweed covered rocks. It is one of the finest pieces of boat piloting I have seen in my lifetime. We all gave the crew a mighty round of applause, but I don't think they could hear us.

The ocean is a war zone even without bullets flying. Using the physical surroundings in a story enhances the experience for the reader and can create another character as part of a story. Important descriptions in your stories are lost if the snow in Korea, jungle rains of Vietnam, high-altitude mountain passes of Afghanistan, and the sands of Iraq are not mentioned.

Building a war zone means to write about the physical descriptions of the settings you encountered. From weather to humidity to natural disasters and changing cultures. What season was it when your story happened? Or perhaps there were no seasons. When did the monsoons come? The trade winds? When were mudslides prevalent? Did animals migrate? What do camels do in wind storms? All of these details add to the character and flavor of your story.

Details count. Color, the brightness or lack of light, an odd cloud formation, the clearness of the night sky and rainbows or stars. What elements do you remember to better add life to your writing? In the senses we talk about details, but now consider the countryside as a character.

What does a sunrise look like from the flight deck of an aircraft, the deck of a ship, a foxhole, porthole, or a Humvee? What type of light changes inside a submarine while on a long deep dive? What character comes with the ship, sub, truck, aircraft, chopper or deuce and a half you rode in? We all know those mechanical transports had their own set of quirks and became human to us. Describe how they changed temperament on the course of your journeys.

When thinking about those modes of transport, what images come to mind when you remember:

Duct tape
Oil
Hydraulic fluid
Flat tires
Malfunctioning electrical panels
Wires
String
Bungee cords
Coat hangers
Batteries
Tow trucks
Bilge pumps
Windshields
Seat cushions
Armor plating

Hauling gear
Ammo
TV sets
Camcorders
Folding chairs

Though the modern military is quite high tech, there is always a place for duct tape and WD-40. What memories can you describe for your reader about these daily details to maintain your equipment and accomplish your mission? Make the setting a character.

Clichés
There comes a time in every warrior's writing life that they use the war cliché of all time. In fact, veterans in the class got used to waiting for the FNGs to use it. They knew I would be pouncing soon. A cliché is defined as a "Trite, stereotyped expression," according to *Webster's College Dictionary*.

Examples include water over the dam or a bone to pick. I have seen every beginning writer use the war cliché sooner or later. What amazes me is many practicing writers still use it today. So what is it?

"And then all hell broke loose."

Don't get me wrong. I am sure that happened. But I haven't been to hell recently, so the writer must tell me what hell looks like and how it breaks loose. Details! Description! It is not enough to say all hell broke loose. It doesn't really say anything and everybody uses it.

Now comedian George Carlin put a spin on that cliché which is masterful. "I never worry that all hell will break loose. My concern is that only part of hell will break loose and be harder to detect."

Watch your writing for clichés. If it reads stale, it probably is. Think of another way to describe what you are trying to convey. Then the reader will know what hell is really like. To refresh your memory about setting, go back to chapter two and re-read examples number one, twelve, thirteen and fourteen. Notice how setting details add to the reader's understanding of the world into which they are venturing.

Active Verbs
Another part of building a war zone is action. In this case, active verbs. To keep the reader in the midst of the moment and to feel the tension of the situation, use active action words, alias verbs.

Verbs are words which express action or a state of being. Writers love verbs. There are two ways to describe any action or event; active or passive. Verbs in the active voice give greater force to a sentence than passive verbs.

	ACTIVE VOICE	PASSIVE VOICE
PRESENT	I save	I am saved
PAST	I saved	I was saved
FUTURE	I shall save	I shall be saved

Now, before your eyes glaze over, there are some occasions when it is preferable to use a verb in a passive voice.

Sergeant Pyle WAS PRESENTED with a medal.
PFC Cutter IS CONSIDERED the authority on Patriot missiles.
The B-17 bomber IS no longer USED.

The reminders about active verbs are examples to keep you on your toes. DO NOT OBSESS about verb tense, punctuation and grammar. Write first. This is technical information for later reference.

Here is an example of the use of active verbs in a portion of the story, "Grogan's War Surplus" by Patrick McManus from his book, *A Fine and Pleasant Misery.*

> "You know," he said, "it seems like only yesterday that you an me was crouched in the mud in some Godforsaken place using our bayonets to roast a couple hunks of Spam over some canned heat."
> "Yeah, and heatin' our water in a steel helmet," I said, sinking suddenly into the morass of reminiscence. "And lyin' awake night after night in a pup tent, listenin' for the first sound of attack..."
> "...and half our gear riddled with bullet holes," Retch put in, shaking a tear off the end of his mustache.
> "Yep," I said, "we really had some great campin' when we were kids."

Gotcha. Patrick built a war zone, then moved it to every boy's backyard. It can be done. So, when you finish building your war zone, you have a complete picture for the reader. Then you can move on to the real action in the war zone. One excellent reminder of how things go so smoothly during military campaigns is the ever present "Murphy's Laws of Combat

Operations." The latest version I found on the Internet was up to 114. I list a few of my favorites here.

1. Friendly fire - isn't.
5. A sucking chest wound is Nature's way of telling you to slow down.
24. Don't look conspicuous; it draws fire. For this reason, it is not at all uncommon for aircraft carriers to be known as bomb magnets.
25. Never draw fire; it irritates everyone around you.
46. If you can't remember, the Claymore is pointed towards you!
63. The most dangerous thing in the world is a Second Lieutenant with a map and a compass.

Speaking about Second Lieutenants, now it's time to discuss forced marches. Or in our case, how not to go on a forced march. Press on, Scout!

Resources:
Watch any movie with the sound off. Notice how the scenery plays a character role in the film.
The Elements of Style by William Strunk Jr. and E.B. White
Any eighth grade grammar book. Really. I still use mine.
Thesaurus
Dictionary
Murphy's Laws of Combat Operations – www.swcp.com/~russo/laws-o-combat.html

Chapter 9

Forget Forced Marches

Rat a tat tat. The rounds of an M-60 machine gun fired off and I dove into the ditch from the dirt road. Landing with an "umph" on my stomach, my feet and head were up, my stomach the lowest part of my body.

The high dry weeds poked in my face and sweat trickled down my back. A cloud of white smoke wafted across my position. I wrestled my gas mask out of the bag and donned it in record time. Nothing like a basic training field march. We had just finished going up Agony Hill and down Suicide Hill, both perfectly named.

October 1975 at Fort McClellan, Alabama, it was our forced march test. Seven miles in full gear waiting to be attacked at every turn. I took advantage of the break to rest in my ditch, my body a perfect imitation of Snoopy sliding on the ice, stomach first. My breathing in the black gas mask offered me comfort. I was still alive.

Then I heard it. A rustle in the bushes. Shit. Don't tell me some critter or worse yet a snake was visiting my location. The hair went up on the back of my neck and I strained to hear the noise in between the bursts of gun fire. Wind or snake?

The bullets stopped. I was positive I heard it again. A rustle in the high weeds directly in front of me.

"All clear!" came the command from the sergeant. To this day I am convinced I levitated straight up to get away from whatever that was, because suddenly I was back on the hot, dusty road, grateful to be marching again.

Many writers think they have to write their stories the same as a forced march—direct from point A to point B. Wrong. There are as many different methods for compiling stories as there are writers. In this chapter I will outline four different ways to structure your story writing and revisit one method we discussed earlier.

The four different methods are:
- Key events of your military service
- Mind Mapping from the book by the same name
- Chapter by Chapter
- Using 3x5 Index cards

Another method we already discussed in Chapter Four is the Hero's Journey framework.

Key Events of Your Military Service
This method of constructing stories is a cross between chronological order, starting at the beginning proceeding through to discharge or retirement, and picking out the highlights. When you look back on your military service, not every event of every day probably stuck out in your mind. This method allows you to look back over your entire service and form a timeline.
For example:

```
X_____X_____XX_____X_____X
Training   Deploy to Iraq   Baghdad Falls   IED Blast        Back Home
```

Make a timeline across a page and put in dates and important events. Then, indicate with an X an event you want to write about. Use this as a framework or outline for your stories. Also, you don't have to write these stories in order. Perhaps writing about the Humvee being blown up by a land mine is the story your write last.

I tell veterans to write the story that calls to them most for their first assignment. In class we kidded about how this usually always turned out to be the bloodiest battle or worse situation the person experienced. For some veterans, writing the hard story first seems to free them up to write the rest of their stories or they just need to get it down on paper to help get it out of their psyche.

What most veterans found after writing their "blood" story, it was a first draft. A beginning effort to try and describe what happened. Many veterans went on to write other stories and then would come back to this main story to change, rewrite, update and add details and memories which came back to them over time.

Some memories will return, some will not. Two veterans in my class had experiences of memory blackout. A Marine could not recall a 12-hour period during a fierce battle in Vietnam and an Army Scout lost several days of memory while battling in Germany. Perhaps this is a sign the veteran and the veteran's memory don't want to go to that time and place and perhaps never will. That is perfectly okay.

As an instructor I sometimes felt like I was telling veterans to stick themselves in the eye with a sharp stick, repeatedly, by writing about certain painful memories. The rule? Don't go there if you don't want to. You don't have to. Remember—no forced marches!

When you have the completed timeline and the events you want to write about, write. It's pretty straightforward, but not always simple.

Another surprising development most veterans discovered after they wrote the big battle scene? The so-called boring days and small moments of peace and quiet or interaction between their buddies turned out to be much more important stories than the big battle or action. It is in these stories of small events, details, and buddy moments that the true military stories come to light. Remember that in the back of your mind when you start to write. Less is sometimes way more

Mind Mapping

Mind Mapping is a creative brainstorming technique described by Joyce Wycoff in her book, *Mindmapping; Your Personal Guide to Exploring Creativity and Problem-Solving.* I describe this method as wild crayons for adults. It is a method to let you tap into your creative mind and memories and color outside the lines, no rules, no judgment.

Get a large piece of white paper, say 11 x 17 inches, or better yet a white board. Use either pen or pencil. I prefer crayons and colored markers. On the piece of paper print one or two words which capture the theme or problem you want to write about.

Example:
Beirut   Barracks Collapse

Now, using this method, draw circles around these two words, and then draw lines out in different directions. On those lines print ideas or thoughts, which flow from those two words. When you get a main thought that relates to those two words, make another circle around that word. The key is to use only one word per line and per circle. Think about the problems, needs and the important factors of the event or day.

There are no wrong mind maps. Let yourself use as many pieces of paper as you want or find the largest white board you can and borrow it for five to ten minutes. This is a quick process. Let your thoughts roam freely and record where your brain takes you. It can also help to play music from the timeframe you are working on to help with the idea flow.

Music is one of the senses which can immediately bring a memory with regard to our military service. We remember the time and place with vivid recall when we hear it again. Give it a try.

When your ideas have flowed across the paper and you feel most of your work is done, take a look at what you have constructed. This method helps bypass the brain's resistance, divides the large subject into smaller pieces and simplifies the process. It's not a forced march either. Try it. For right brains, such as me, it's a blast.

Chapter by Chapter

This method may appear to be the same as a timeline or an outline, but it's not. Use this method after you have written several stories and or around ten chapters. Analyze each story to determine the following elements:

Time Frame
Synopsis of Story
Romantic Conflict, if any
Subplot

After you have this mini-inventory of your stories, or chapters, look for patterns. Which stories all occur in the same time frame? Same geographic location? Same events? Stack them in piles according to their similarities. You may find you are writing a book length manuscript about only one or two events. That is fine. Perhaps your stories are split in two; before being in-country and returning home or basic training and the war.

This method could be called organization by paper weight. When you physically look at the stacks of stories, it tells you which areas you are writing about the most and which are important to you. Think about the results and ponder how maybe you underestimated the importance of this one area of writing, or perhaps you really wanted to write about another time too and you have more work to do.

My novel writing instructor, Dee Lopez, talked about this method in our fiction writing classes. "Most writers don't really know what their book is about until after writing eight chapters," she said. "Then they have to go back and change the first part of the book because what they thought they were writing about wasn't really the book inside them."

The same is true for non-fiction writing. After ten to fifteen stories, try this method of organization. There might be some surprises. I am sure the veterans in my class thought I was using a *Field of Dreams* movie type mentality; if you write it, the structure will come, but that is the truth for many writers. A veteran may not know what he or she is really writing about, but our subconscious does.

Using 3x5 cards

Another organization method which can be used is 3 x 5 cards, commonly used in screenwriting. Cynthia Whitcomb, in her book *The Writer's Guide to Writing Your Screenplay*, discusses this method of using Scene Cards. "As their name implies, these are only for scenes, one card per scene." Different than using them for a screenplay, do put a snatch of dialogue, an event or weather on the scene card to jog your memory.

While an average 120 page screenplay will end up with perhaps 60 scene cards, who knows how many you will need for your stories. An advantage with using the cards is their portability, ability to easily change the order of scenes or stories, and being able to lay them out on a diningroom or kitchen table.

Cynthia has tried both Post-It Notes and larger 4x6 index cards and does not recommend them—the stickiness drives you crazy and the larger size cards are harder to handle and lay out on a table. I tried using colored cards for different sub-plots for my screenwriting class with Cynthia and ended up going back to white. It was easier.

Put a story or scene on each card. Lay them out and use the same method mentioned earlier to get a physical look at where your story writing interests are. Do you have a lot of basic training cards and no advanced training stories? Where are there gaps in your military service?

When you have ten to fifteen stories and/or scene cards, lay them out and see where you are missing certain events or things you want to add. Make another card. Keep making cards as long as you need to, perhaps even over years of working on your writing. Contrary to popular belief, it takes time and effort to write stories and definitely books. But a book is only a bunch of stories piled together—just like scene cards.

Another big advantage of these little index cards? You can carry them anywhere in case you get a story idea to jot down. They stay together with a rubberband, and are much easier to haul around than a whiteboard. It's a different kind of card game than we played in the military, but still fun.

Structure

Another way to break down structure into smaller pieces is to look at the classic patterns of:

Goal
Conflict
Disaster

Reaction
Dilemma
Decision which leads to a new Goal.

Pretty much the proverbial rat on a wheel if you think about it. What was the goal of the military operation? What conflict happened? What was the disaster—there's always something. What was the reaction? How did this create another dilemma? What new decision was made based on the intel which led to another goal?

I'm sure special operations and special forces veterans lived in this wheel of misfortune for days on end, heaven knows regular troops do. Think about these elements of structure when you look at your writing and how you want to arrange your stories.

Hero's Journey

Remember, you can use the Hero's Journey we discussed in Chapter Four as another method of creating structure for both the individual story and an entire collection of stories.

"Structure is nothing more than a way of looking at your story material so that it's organized in a way that's both logical and dramatic," according to Jack Bickham in his book *Scene and Structure*.

None of these methods is the "right" method. The right method is the one that works for you, the writer. Sometimes I use pieces of all of them, depending on what I am trying to figure out.

See, definitely no forced marches in this version of writer's basic training. But, remember how you made friends in the military? It's time to make more friends. Now.

Resources:
Beginnings, Middles & Ends by Nancy Kress

Chapter 10

How To Make Foxhole Friends

The photos brought back many memories. Part of the homework assignment had been for the veterans to dig out a photo from their military days and bring it to class. During class I had them pass their photo to another veteran. Then each wrote what they saw in the other's photo.

An amazing amount of detail springs from each photo. The power of photos also jogs long ago memories. After completing their in-class assignment, I gave the next task. "Your homework assignment for next week is to interview a veteran and write his or her story," I said. "I want you to all become reporters."

The next week they returned with stories of many acquaintances or family members who they interviewed. They discovered not only the commonalities they had across wars and military service, but the amazing little details they had never known about a neighbor, friend or family member.

The secret? The veterans took the time to listen to other veterans. A friend of mine in my non-fiction critique group, Jim Petersen, has a book out called *The Listening Book – A Practical Guide To Better Communication*. In it he says, "The act of listening is an act of unconditional love." Think about that. Who in your life really listens to you?

Not the everyday, "How are you?" "I'm fine," exchanges, but who really listens to you? When veterans listen to each other, they confirm and honor each other's experience. Veterans can also understand the challenge of listening to a story someone has never told to someone else.

With that in mind, Al Siebert, Ph.D., has given me permission to include his *Guidelines for Listening to War Veterans* in this book. Al has done a tremendous amount of work on the survivor personality and is himself a former Korean War paratrooper.

For those who have wondered how to listen to other veterans or loved ones, here is a guide:

> The main problem for many survivors and war veterans is not *what* they went through. Their problem is that very few people have the emotional strength to listen to them *talk* about what they went through. The poor relationships survivors often have with spouses, children,

relatives, neighbors, employers and co-workers are not merely a result of delayed reactions to stress. The feelings of isolation and poor relationships with others are, in part, from having to associate with people who are poor listeners. "People would go weird," one combat veteran said, "when they hear I fought in Nam. I never talk about it now."

People who have survived torturous experiences will usually talk with a good listener who will take the time to hear the whole story. If you are willing to listen to a distressing experience that someone rarely talks about, here are some useful guidelines to follow.

1. *Don't ask about a person's experiences unless you can handle honest answers.* When Vietnam combat veterans returned home they found that very few people had the emotional strength to listen to their stories. Don't open someone up and then "chicken out" when their story gets too rough. Tell yourself that a reasonably strong human being ought to be able to at least *listen* to what another person has lived through. Survivors of horrifying experiences will usually talk to a person who has the courage to listen.
2. *Give the person lots of time.* Vietnam veterans found that the average person could listen for only several minutes. When a veteran is willing to talk to you, it is important to allow him or her plenty of time to talk. Don't interrupt to share your feelings about the war. This is not a time for discussion! Plan to listen for hours. Expect to have some follow-up sessions. When people open themselves up to relive strong emotional experiences, additional details and feelings may flood into their minds in the days that follow. It is typical for combat veterans to have nightmares and periods of emotional turmoil.
3. *Be an active listener.* Ask for details. Ask about feelings. Ask questions when you feel puzzled about facts or incidents.
4. *Remain quiet if he or she starts crying.* It may help to touch or hold the person if it feels right to both of you. Don't tell the person to not feel what he or she is feeling. Don't suggest a better way to look at it. Leave his or her thoughts and feelings alone. Your quiet presence is more useful than anything else you can do.
5. *Listen with empathy, but minimize sympathy.* It is easier for combat veterans to reveal what they went through if they don't have to put up with sympathy. (What a horrible experience! You poor man!") Survivors of horrible experiences talk more easily to a person with

calm concern. Control your imagination and resist letting their feelings become your feelings. Don't make the veteran have to handle your emotional reactions as well as his or her own. If you need emotional support, seek it elsewhere.
6. *Ask if he or she sees anything positive about being in combat.* It is not accurate to think of most war veterans as having post-traumatic stress disorder. Some do. The majority do not. Research shows that many who served in Vietnam became significantly more mature and developed a healthy personal identity. The same extreme circumstances that cause emotional trauma for some people cause others to become stronger.
7. *Discuss why the war was a valuable experience.* Ask each other what you learned from the war. What are the positive ways in which it changed each of you?

I recommend Al Siebert's books and website, www.resiliencycenter.com, to anyone interested in this topic. Also, I encourage veterans to also read Chapter 28 where Dr. Siebert has allowed me to use his information on "Telling Your Survivor Story."

A writer must not only observe, but listen. Through listening to other's stories, it helps us define and clarify our own. I remember one day while working as the Pubic Affairs Officer for the Portland VA Medical Center, the director's secretary called me in to talk with a veteran.

It turned out the gentleman had been at the dedication of the original Portland VA Hospital. He wanted to be invited to the dedication for the new Portland VA Medical Center, some fifty years later. I assured him it would be no problem and took his name and address. The veteran had had throat cancer surgery and used a larynx amplifier.

When he was finished and left, one of the secretaries said to me, "He was so hard to understand. Why did you take so much time to listen to him?"

"Because I would hope that someday, someone would take the time to listen to my military stories too," I replied. That event happened long before I even thought of teaching the writing class. But I remember that gentleman to this day. And yes, he did attend the new hospital dedication.

Homework Assignment Eleven

So sharpen up your pen or pencil and decide who you are going to interview. Use the techniques you have learned from this book. Get the following information for your story:

- Name, rank and maybe serial number
- Years of service, branch and unit and/or ship
- Why they went in the service
- Most memorable moments – good and bad
- Funniest thing that ever happened, saddest also
- Fights? Screw ups? Bad Luck Days?
- A favorite saying or accent of a buddy
- Senses – sight, sound, taste, touch and smell
- Any sixth sense, luck or spirit filled events
- Friends they made and kept or lost track of
- Any animals, children, and civilians they encountered
- What was good about the experience?

You will have an entire story when you get these questions answered and write them up. Use what you have learned so far to create a rounded story which accurately describes the person and their experience. When you have edited and cleaned it up, make sure you give a copy to the veteran.

What a wonderful gift to have someone not only listen to their story, but give them a copy of what you heard them say. A true gift from one veteran to another.

There is also a new type of homework assignment afoot. A wonderful article in the May 2005 *AARP Bulletin* titled "Heirs of War" details how boomers are on fact finding missions. "The children of the 'greatest generation' hit the trenches to uncover their parents' lost stories" says the article written by Suzanne Freeman. I will list some of the resources from the article at the end of this chapter. Do you have a family military story to write? Get to it.

Now, ready to learn about some four-footed veterans? Fetch!

Resources:
www.petersenpublications.com
www.resiliencycenter.com
www.aarp.org/bulletin/yourlife/heirs.html
Dad's War http://members.aol.com/dadswar/index.htm
www.fatherswar.org
www.familytreemagazine.com

Finding Your Father's War: A Practical Guide to Researching and Understanding Service in the World War II U.S. Army by Jonathan Gawne
My Father's War by Julia Collins
Our Father's War; Growing Up in the Shadow of the Greatest Generation by Tom Mathews
Our Mothers' War: American Women at Home and at the Front During World War II by Emily Yellin
The Souvenir: A Daughter Discovers Her Father's War by Louise Steinman

Author's Note: Don't get me started on the whole "greatest generation" label. My parents are members of that time, but I feel every generation which has military members serving is a great generation. We can't compare. One great generation was the Army of 1776. Read David McCullough's book of the same name and see what you think. The military members serving around the world today, in addition to Afghanistan and Iraq, are a great generation too. Let's stop the labels and be thankful we have generations who serve. Including the four-footed vets.

Chapter 11

Corporal Cupcake Wins A Chew Toy

So one night in class we were talking about my ass. Er, mule. Wind River was the last living Army pack mule and I was her handler for several dress occasions. I listened in amazement as several other veterans told wild stories about animals they encountered in the military.

"I'm going to have to write the story about the fucking monkey," Bob said. We all erupted in laughter. He did write it and "The Fucking Monkey" became a classic.

Talking and writing about animals in the veterans' military lives opened a wide window on how these men and women appreciated and reacted to unconditional love. Animals are the few beings on this planet who can love without strings attached. Military dog handlers know this all too well.

The powerful story of the work done by men and dogs in Vietnam, depicted in the film *War Dogs*, haunts me to this day. Those dogs gave everything to protect their handlers and fellow military members and many were left behind or euthanized at the end of the war. That is a legacy which still haunts the two-footed veterans.

By writing down the stories of the handlers and the other animals we work with, dolphins, mules, the bulldog, chickens, elephants, homing pigeons, camels, to name a few we honor our four-footed, feathered and finned warriors.

Now, some were civilian animals, so to speak, but we all have memories. Write about the animals in your military world. One of my favorite *M*A*S*H* television episodes of all time is about Corporal Cupcake.

The chopper lands and the medics rush to help one soldier, but he won't hear of it until they help his buddy. His buddy on the other side of the chopper is a very large German Shepherd, Corporal Cupcake. (I think that was his name)

The television series also showed the importance of a horse to the former cavalry commander, Colonel Potter, and how Radar's animals helped him keep sane in an insane world.

Remember back to the animals. One veteran remembered a lizard in Vietnam who made a sound they we're sure was "fuck." Seemed to fit the surroundings.

Members of my former Airlift Wing flew Keiko, the *Free Willy* movie star, to his home in Iceland. The Wind newsletter explained how that C-17 aircraft now sports a Keiko killer whale symbol above the passenger door. I remember seeing the camels painted in black above the C-141 door which said Sand Box Express after the Gulf War. Gulf War One, that is.

The history of military animals can come in unexpected moments. I remember my first glimpse of that gorgeous stud. Muscled and proud as could be, head held high. I had never seen such a large stallion. Rutger Hauer sat on top of him, in the movie *Ladyhawke*.

The horse, a Friesian, was what the medieval knights rode in Denmark. Looking like a larger black Clydesdale, these amazing horses were bred for battle. This legacy also explains the brilliant white Lipizzaner Stallions, bred for war, who now entertain.

- What animals do you remember?
- What were their names?
- How did they help out?
- Which human were they closest to and why?
- How did they help/hinder the mission?

While out on field training in Germany during Reforger 78, we had to exit the tent to make midnight trips to the bushes. We knew there were wild boar around, so Jan or I never dallied. We were always ready for flight at the slightest rustle of leaves. Not the most restful potty break.

Then there was the German field mouse who almost got me court-martialed, but that is another story. What are your stories?

Our connection with animals does not end with our military days. If we are pet owners, we again experience their role as friend, companion, and playmate. This is also why I believe veterans who lose their pets have a rough time with the grief. For some veterans, the pet in their life is the only one left giving them unconditional love.

Veterans can also use animals as a way to work through some of their past experiences. Kent Anderson, author of *Night Dogs and Sympathy for the Devil*, explained it in a news article by Jeff Baker in *The Oregonian* on March 3, 1998. Anderson talked about how being close to a herd of horses had helped him deal with issues from his time as a Special Forces sergeant in Vietnam and later as a police officer.

Night Dogs recounts some of his recollections while a police officer in the 1970s in Portland, Oregon. Animals were involved in real life and in his fiction book.

War definitely makes strange bed fellows. The plight of the Baghdad Zoo animals was made public, but only after the troops had to figure out what the hell was going on when in the middle of a firefight, a camel came wandering through their lines. They could hear the growls of large cats and monkeys were chattering in the treetops. Never something one expects in the middle of an inner-city fire fight.

Remember the senses when writing about animals.
- Touch – a camel's hide
- Smell – camel dung
- Taste – snake meat at survival school
- Hearing – monkeys in palm trees in Baghdad
- Sight – A parachuting elephant in the movie, *Operation Dumbo Drop*

So, in case you want to read my ass, er mule, story, here it is. It was first published in 1992 in *ARMY* magazine.

Windy, A Grand Old Lady

I stared hard into the large brown eyes of the 1,200 pound retired Army combat veteran and saw my military career crash and burn. My number was up.

The 1977 post retirement ceremony at Fort Carson, Colorado, had started and we were late. "Wind River," the last living Army pack mule, and I, her handler, were supposed to be in the gym. She wouldn't budge. The First Sergeant had decided the 4th Supply and Transport "Packhorse" Battalion should have their mascot present at the ceremony.

It appeared First Sergeant Behnke was the only one in the Battalion who knew we had a mascot and he'd talked me into volunteering for this duty. I thought it sounded like a good opportunity to get out of standing in rigid formation in full combat gear.

Not being reared on a farm, I pictured a nice little BURRO-type mule, not a 15-hand high packhorse. The difference between burros and packhorses appeared to be about 700 pounds, give or take a few sandbags. The top of Windy's ears were above my head, so we didn't see eye to eye from the start.

I looked into the gym and felt my stomach lurch as I pulled on her rope. With her hooves planted firmly at the back door sill, I knew a city-bred 145-pound female Army Sergeant was no match for Windy. Retired from the Army four months before I was born in 1957, Windy had survived 21 days of continuous Japanese field gun fire in the China-Burma-India Theater in WW II, attended John F. Kennedy's inauguration and been lead mule for the Al Kaly Shriners of the Inter-National Shrine Horse Patrols. At age 45, she didn't have to do anything she didn't want to, including entering the gym. She was still spry enough to drag me, black combat boot skid marks and all, right past the Commanding General.

I tugged on her rope. Nothing. I swatted her ample behind. Not a flinch. Begging was in order. Facing her muzzle squarely, I laced my fingers through her halter and brought her eyes down to my level. "Please?"

Inside the gym a sharp blast from a bugle ripped the air and Windy snapped to attention. Seeming to remember such occasions from years gone by, she turned her head toward me and started into the gym at a loping gait, the smell of hay lingering behind her.

Windy's keeper had forgotten to put her booties on so the two of us made quite an entrance as 1,200 pounds carried on four metal horseshoes hit the wood gym floor. I couldn't tell who was more surprised to see her, the audience or Bravo Company standing next to her.

The formation area was so cramped that should she decide to turn around once in a full circle, I knew Bravo Company would go down like dominoes. That was not the worst of their problems though. They weren't even supposed to flinch while at attention, but they got a bad case of mule giggles. Watching Bravo Company turn blue and their eyes bug out was quite a pleasure for me, a member of Alpha Company.

Windy presented a fine silhouette throughout the Retirement Ceremony. Several times she moved from side to side, keeping an eye on Bravo Company. Other than that, she seemed to enjoy all the pomp and circumstance.

When the honored retirees inspected the troops with the Commanding General, Windy received more than her share of attention. One of the retirees had been involved with mules during his Army career.

"Good to see ya, old gal," he said to her and scratched her between the ears. Tears came to his eyes, and I felt a lump rise in my throat. "Thanks for bringing her," he said to me and shook my left hand, since my right was wrapped in a strangle hold with the rein. All I could do was nod.

Do Bar Fights Count?

I looked at Windy. I swore she cocked her head at me as if to say, "Now that's a mule skinner. A man of honor."

The bugle sounded. Windy came to attention. The troops were dismissed. Windy and I filed back out into the afternoon sun. The First Sergeant and I loaded her back into his trailer, and she prepared for her trip back to the Shriner's Mule Train barn. She looked back over her shoulder as the truck and trailer drove off, and I waved at her. Somehow, I expected her to wave back.

I endured the usual "Sgt. Cook and her ass" jokes for several weeks after that, but life continued. Dictionary research on my part defined a burro as a small donkey and a mule as the sterile offspring of a female horse and a male donkey. A packhorse was a horse that carried packs. So Windy was actually a pack mule, not a packhorse.

In January 1978 I went away to Fort Irwin, Calif., for Desert Training for a few months. Word got back to me that Windy had appeared at another ceremony for our Battalion. One of our female truck drivers, a known killer cowgirl who could probably pin a horse, was her handler. Windy dragged both her and another soldier out of the gym. Somehow it did my heart good. I knew better than to treat Windy like a common animal.

Research I did on her soon reinforced my rookie beliefs as I read information about the mules of the World War II Mars Task Force. Nothing came easy for the animals or their handlers.

Just arriving in Calcutta was an effort for them, as evidenced by the 33rd QM Pack Troop which was aboard a ship which sunk off the Arabia coast by an enemy submarine, according to Col. Charles Hunter in his book "Galahad."

The challenges went from bad to worse as related to 1Lt. Dan Thrapp in his two articles, "The Mules of Mars" in The Quartermaster Review in May-June and July-August 1946.

He tells about the horror of war for the mules. A two-day critical forced march saw the mules carry loads for more than nineteen hours at a stretch with no place to rest them. The mules were exhausted and thirsty and unsteady on their feet. "Our battalion lost seventeen of them over the side of the mountain that day and night," wrote Thrapp. Later, a night mortar barrage took its toll.

> No Japanese penetrated our perimeter that night, but enemy
> explosives rained on us until after dawn. The mules suffered most.
> Picket lines snapped by mortar shells, and occasionally in the lurid
> light of that Burma moon we could see animals go down, or sometimes

we could hear heavily wounded mules staggering and falling into abandoned foxholes. The ravine that night earned its soubriquet of 'Dead Mule Gulch.' Twenty-one mules were killed outright or died of wounds as a result of the night's action. Casualties were caused because we could not disperse the animals properly.

Windy was purchased in 1936 by the U.S. Army at the age of 4 at Sacramento, California. Her military career between 1937-1943 is vague. In 1943 she joined the 35th Quartermaster Pack Troop which was activated Jan. 30, 1943 at Fort Bliss, Texas. Records indicate she debarked at the China-Burma-India (CBI) Theater in Calcutta in 1944. By all known facts, she participated in one of the longest pack marches in military history, bypassing towns in Burma occupied by the Japanese and moving entirely over mountains and jungle trails.

Windy assisted the 3rd Battalion, 475th Infantry Regiment while in the CBI Theater. Several units, including Windy's, made up what was the Mars Task Force. This group also included two elephants. I would have loved to talk to those elephant handlers.

The summer of 1978 dawned with the DISCOM change of command ceremony. This was a major event with all the Battalions on the parade grounds, a pass in review by jeep, and other assorted highlights. Windy's presence was requested. After painful deliberation, the brass determined once again that I should be Windy's handler. This assignment brought me the mounting fear that Windy would now have the opportunity to drag me across several football fields, not just out of a gym, if she set her mind to it.

The big day dawned, July 7, 1978, and I went to meet Windy at the parade grounds. My boyfriend was watching from our unit loading dock. He later told me of the expletives he used as I backed her out of the trailer and he saw her size. New to the unit, he was also thinking BURRO. "I kissed our special dinner plans good-bye when I saw her," he told me later. "If you came out of this alive, I figured it would be a miracle."

Windy looked splendid. She had been brushed until her coat shone. She was wearing her special green Wind River blanket and her hooves were manicured. I'd have matched her against any Kentucky Derby winner that day for grace, style, and class.

After my Battalion had marched to their position on the field, Windy and I strolled over behind them to take our place. A small ambulance was off to our right, behind us, to care for any sick soldiers. The beautiful Colorado sun was beating down this hot July day, and heat stroke was often a problem.

Do Bar Fights Count?

The trumpets sounded and Windy snapped to attention. Her interested eyes searched the troops and large grandstand far out in front of her to assess the action. She moved around, but all in all was quite content to be an honored observer. I had been talking to her on and off, making snide comments about our luck at not being in formation and relaying the latest Battalion gossip. She seemed to enjoy the news.

The ceremony droned on. A soldier two formations to our left fainted. The medics grabbed a stretcher and raced for the man. Windy went nuts. She pulled hard on the rein and almost jerked my arm from the socket. Caught off guard, I was pulled several feet before I dug in my heels.

"What's wrong," I asked her. Her big brown eyes were troubled, and her forehead appeared tense. I rubbed her neck. "You're okay, girl. What's up? Nothing to worry about."

She stamped her feet, moved from side to side, and became extremely jittery. She kept trying to head away from the ceremony, and I had to plant my boots, shove my body into her side, and make her pivot. I could only imagine how we looked to the audience, playing do-si-do in the backfield.

A few minutes went by, and she seemed to calm down, but every few minutes she would fix me with those big brown eyes, as if to ask for reassurance.

Another soldier fainted to our far left. The medics took off again on the run. Windy threw her head up and started away from the ceremony. As I looked frantically to my left, I caught a quick vision of what she saw. A young soldier, his M-16 lying on the ground beside him, out cold, being scooped up by medics.

Could Windy be remembering fear from her days in battle? I held tightly to her rein and tried to reassure her that everything was okay. She stopped for a minute and fixed me with a haunted stare. Her eyes looked like a television screen with ghostly figures and memories rushing through her mind.

I was amazed at the possibility she was reliving her combat experience. Because I was in the immediate post-Vietnam military, I had seen that same look when our former First Sergeant used to get drunk. At 27 he was one of the youngest First Sergeants, due to Vietnam. He only talked about Nam when he was drunk. During those moments it wasn't the blank shutdown feelings of combat, the 1,000 yard stare, but the horrible memories which refused to stay behind locked doors. Windy must have had her bad memories too.

As we passed the ambulance on our way to the Post Library, I stood my ground and turned Windy. She stepped on my foot. Since even "Webster's

Dictionary" describes the ass as a "sure-footed domesticated mammal," I knew that wasn't an accident. Somehow I had anticipated that movement by one second and retracted my toes from permanent damage, but my shined boot would never be the same. We had to go back to the formation.

Windy appeared to recon the area. The soldiers who'd fainted were being cared for, and both had revived. There were no more noises, like bullets, artillery, or bombs.

"Let's go back, Windy. You're safe. Really." She must have believed me. She slowly walked toward me and I choked up at the level of trust she had just shown me. Of course, I realized she had also done her own inspection of the area, just in case her stupid handler had a screw loose.

The ceremony was soon coming to a close. Thankfully, no more soldiers fainted. Locked knees will do it everytime. The jeep filled with dignitaries passed in review and Windy kept a watchful eye on the small vehicle as it drove around the troops. One false move from the jeep and I knew I'd be out the front gate, flying behind Windy.

The order for Pass in Review was shouted and Windy came to attention. Alpha Company moved out in front of us. I urged her forward and Windy moved out like a high stepping Lipizzaner stallion. The post Army band sounded wonderful and I swore Windy puffed out her chest.

We made a right turn, then a left turn. The Band started the Army Caisson Song. Windy knew that song. Her ears perked up, her strut stretched out and she picked up speed. Perhaps she was remembering the emotional ceremony December 15, 1956 when the 35th Quartermaster Company (Pack) was deactivated on this same field and the mules received a salute from an Army helicopter, their replacement.

Whatever she was remembering, I realized she was heading straight into Alpha Company's formation in ten more steps. She wanted to strut again. I wanted to survive. I did the old mule donut drill maneuver and turned her in a circle. The commander of Bravo Company gave me a tight smile as we cleared him by a few feet. The guidon bearer was closely watching the end of his pointed pole.

Alpha Company began their left turn at the edge of the viewing stand to pass in review. Windy speeded up again. I threw my body into her and we did the mule minuet once again, clearing the rear of Alpha Company by inches. As we pulled straight behind them, the grandstands were on our right.

Windy slowed down, strutted her stuff, and performed eyes right as if on cue. I could feel the sweat running down my back and was grateful for my place off to her left side, only my legs in view. She received a smart salute from the new Commander and Commanding General, then went on her way.

Just past the grandstand I pulled her off to the right, as I'd been requested to do so the crowd could meet this famous lady. She was gracious and endured the small children and mule remarks from admiring cavalry soldiers.

At the end of the ceremony, the First Sergeant boosted me up and I rode her bare back across the parade field to her trailer. Her backbone stuck up several inches and was not very comfortable. Her 45 degree sloped sides caused me to ride while doing a Chinese split, her body still made to order for the packs she had carried. After a not-so-graceful dismount on my part, our big day was at an end.

I scratched her between the ears.

"Thanks for a great day, Windy."

She looked at me, the former terror filled eyes now replaced by a look of pride. She shook her ears at me and I laughed. I hugged her neck and we loaded her into the trailer. She cut a fine figure as I watched her disappear around the block on her way back to the barn.

November 22, 1978. Four months later I read Windy's obituary in the local newspaper and my eyes filled with tears. The First Sergeant had come into my office the prior afternoon and told me she had died. An era was gone, but I wept for a grand old lady with big brown eyes and a hell of a combat history.

"You get out in December, don't you Cook?" the First Sergeant had asked me after he told me the news.

I could only nod in reply.

"Seems kind of funny she died right before you left the Army and Colorado," he added.

Several weeks later I was told Windy would be mounted and placed at the Fort Carson Museum of the West. It seemed a more fitting end than a burial on the grounds like Hambone, who had gone before her, at Fort Carson. I'd have to come back and see her some day.

December 21, 1988 I was commissioned into the Air Force Reserve as a Medical Service Corps Officer. Many times I had thought of Windy since leaving the Army, but I had never returned to Fort Carson.

In May of 1990 a training flight from my Squadron was scheduled into Colorado Springs. Quickly, I volunteered. I wanted to visit the Fort Carson Museum and see Windy. After a quick call to the Fort, I discovered the Museum had been torn down and all items stored, presumably at the Pueblo Army Depot.

A feeling of great sadness washed over me as I thought of her, packed up in some crate in a warehouse. I decided to try to find out some information anyway, but our flight was diverted to San Antonio, Texas. Windy slipped out of my mind for several months.

In January 1991, I felt an intense need to locate Windy. The Financial Secretary of the National 4th Infantry (Ivy) Division Association identified two members who had helped clean out the Museum and thought most of the items were in their garages.

I was devastated. Visions of Windy, abandoned, moth-eaten and stuffed in a garage, sent me into action. I tracked down one of the gentlemen through telephone information, and his wife answered the phone. She assured me that Windy was not in her garage and said all the items had gone to the Pueblo Depot. I thanked her heartily, my mind at rest.

The next day a letter arrived from the U.S. Army Quartermaster Museum at Fort Lee, Virginia. Quite helpful, Museum Specialist Luther Hanson said he had last seen Windy in 1989 at the Pueblo Depot and assured me she would be taken care of for the future until a new museum was constructed. It occurred to me that I was probably the only person in the U.S. chasing a beloved stuffed mule across the country while war loomed on the immediate horizon, but she deserved to have a proper resting place.

I sent a letter to the Pueblo Depot. Desert Shield became Desert Storm and an additional three groups of Squadron members deployed. After that, those of us still left behind were dealing with constant stress and feelings of separation from our unit members overseas. In late February I was activated and sent to the Patient Airlift Center at Scott Air Force Base, Illinois. Luckily, the number of war patients were much less than expected, and the end of March 1991 found me discharged back to Reserve status and settling in at home in Oregon.

Sorting through a month's worth of mail in early April, I found a letter from the Pueblo Depot Activity. Wind River had been shipped to Fort Leonard Wood, Missouri, to the U.S. Army Engineer Museum. I quickly called the museum and was thrilled to learn she had just been put on display in the Encyclopedic Gallery.

It was quite ironic. My deployment to Scott Air Force Base meant I had driven within 150 miles of Windy.

Since I am on flying status with the Air Force Reserve, I had to track down one last fact about Windy. During my days at Fort Carson rumors had circulated about Windy having been airborne. I couldn't figure out how anyone could have pushed a mule with a parachute out of an airplane, but my research found out Windy might have flown, but not officially "jumped." More than 2,682 horses and mules were flown over the Burma "Hump" in Douglas C-47s, according to Col. Ralph Mohri's article in the September-October issue of "The Calvary Journal."

In the progression of my military career from a sure-footed pack mule to flying C-141B Starlifter, there are more similarities than differences.

Perhaps members of my Squadron who flew patients out of Saudi Arabia cared for a son or daughter, or maybe even a grandson or granddaughter, of someone who served with Windy. Back home now, Squadron member's eyes reflect an emotional toll when they talk about the men and women they transported.

As for me, I go back in time to 1978. I can still see those wise and understanding big brown eyes and remember Windy's fear for falling soldiers on a hot Army parade ground. In my heart, I feel Windy understands and is proud of what her former handler has accomplished. I don't know if I'll visit her or not at the Museum. I dread facing those brown eyes, the life forever gone.

In my memory, Windy will always be alive, proudly strutting across that parade field to the Army Caisson Song, standing tall and eyes right.

Afterword: After the story was published, I found out Windy might have jumped from a plane after all. One of the many letters I got from veterans who worked with the mules was a copy of an oral interview with a pilot who talks about the mission where they air dropped mules.

Think one little mule isn't a story? It all started with my ass.

Resources:
www.wardogsmemorial.org
www.uswardogs.org
Vietnam Dog Handler Association - www.vdhaonline.org (Vets of all eras & active duty)
www.war-dogs.com
Association of Pet Loss & Bereavement - www.aplb.org

Pet Loss Support - www.petloss.com

Chapter 12

The Strategy and Tactics of Publishing

The Army obstacle course. While I remember it, fondly would not be an adequate descriptor. But the blood, sweat, and tears of getting through it did prepare me for the publishing world.

There are tricks to the publishing world. Writing is both an art and a business. While you work on your stories, be aware the publishing business has rules and regulations that would make a Marine gunny proud.

On the other hand, there are times when going at the publishing business with the fortitude and flexibility of Special Forces is the only way to make progress. Because, in the end, we all have to know what we are fighting—er—publishing for.

My first step in this mission is to recommend veterans make a RECON trip to a few book stores. Field trip! Okay, here is what you are looking for in the stacks and piles of military books. Look for a book similar to yours. Check the time frame, characters, like books, fiction, non-fiction. Carefully examine the enemy. Oops, competition.

What many students are usually shocked to learn is their type of book does not exist. Why? Because their story has not been written yet. They also find out there are some published books which are not as well written as their own work. True also.

A lot of publishing is luck and timing, along with preparation and practice. Books are a good way to keep up on what readers are interested in buying, but it's also not the be all or end all of publishing.

Unit newsletters, weekly newspapers, and magazines are also a good place to look. I suggest scanning the *Writer's Market 2006*, either in hardback at your library, or book store, or online at www.writersdigest.com. I believe there is a fee for the online subscription.

Picking up this book will impress upon the student the incredible number of publications in the world. I might also suggest a tactical application when starting a writing career; don't expect to make a successful parachute jump without training and practice. The same is true for a writer.

Before trying to query *Reader's Digest* or *The New Yorker*, start with less known, but more open publications in the trades and local markets. Think of it as a flanking move, not heading straight into a fortified bunker position.

Do Bar Fights Count?

Look up the publication you are thinking of approaching in *The Writer's Market* and carefully look at the requirements. More recon. What is their publication size? What length and type of stories do they want? Does your story meet their guidelines? What copyright do they buy? How much and when do they pay, if at all? Do they accept email queries or by letter only? All of these are important business decisions you need to make about your writing.

This is also the time to bring back the red ink pen. Every piece of writing you submit for publication needs to be error free and spotless. Fully spit shined, so to speak. I remember laughing to myself one night while editing class papers. I wondered if any other teacher was checking the dictionary for how to spell garrote, masturbation, and maneuver all in the same night. Spell correctly when it counts for submission.

Do not trust spell checkers either, as they miss context. Example? Bob could **sea** his boat crew wanted **too** large **fiche,** even with the bad **whether.** Spell check thinks that sentence is fine!

Certain military abbreviations can give you heartburn too. One challenge I had with this book was the LAW. In the Army it is the light anti-tank weapon. In the Navy it is a light anti-aircraft weapon. LAW vs. LAAW. So I guess it depends on who is firing the weapon and what they're firing at. When in doubt, go to a Marine gunny.

In his new book *Mail Call* by R. Lee Ermey, based on *The History Channel* television show, he calls it "the LAW, or light anti-tank weapon." Page 43. Works for me!

Another challenge was aerovac and aeromedical. Most of my manuscript readers tried to change it to airevac. The story in Chapter 28 has a mission quoted as "airevac" in an Air Force publication. It's wrong, but since I am quoting the article, I have to include the error. I belong to The AeroMed Evac Association with our www.amea.us home page.

I hope to visit the Aeromedical Evacuation Museum at the Brooks City Base. I'm thinking the name originated with the fact we transport patients on aeroplanes, but somebody will fill me in, I am sure. If I get it wrong will a reader tell me about it? You bet your aerovac butt they will.

So let me say right now, the spelling of "fuze" in Chapter Two is straight out of the Soldier's BCT Handbook, PAM 21-13, May 1969, page 57, Section 1, paragraph 26. Trust me.

What have we learned from this? Watch every detail when proofing your work. And now you know one more reason why most writers drink. This also explains why no matter how many readers I had and how hard I tried, I bet there are some typos in this book. I'm human. It's my computer's fault.

Depending on if you are submitting to a newspaper, magazine or book, the styles are also different. What do I mean? Many newspapers use *The Associated Press Stylebook.* This book tells you that in a newspaper article, book titles are put in quotation marks, except for the Bible. In reading *Windy*, you may have noticed the story was published in a magazine so quotation marks were used for magazine titles. In a book, titles are put in italics.

Know the rules for each type of publication so you don't look like a slick-sleeve private to the editor who reviews your work. A little recon can make a big difference. There are also some fascinating tid-bits in *The Associated Press Stylebook* ranging from how to correctly abbreviate military titles in newspaper articles to knowing bra is acceptable for references to brassiere. Who knew?

As a query example, I will use the process I went through to get my article *Windy* published in *ARMY* magazine in April 1992.

I checked out the *Writer's Market* in 1991 and found my story fit their guidelines. I then drafted a query letter. What is a query letter?

Query Letter = Pop A Smoke

Part of the yearly *Writer's Market* contains some of the best guidance on how to break into the publishing arena using the proper tools. I highly recommend *The Query Letter Clinic* chapter. This explains the Standard Operating Procedures for walking point into the publishing business.

In helicopter terms, think of it as "Pop A Smoke," seeing if your story idea is on target with what the publication wants to publish. Not only is this the professional approach, it also saves both you and the editor a lot of time and frustration.

This is the exact query letter I submitted in 1991 to the magazine.

June 30, 1991

James L. Binder
Army Magazine
2425 Wilson Blvd.
Arlington, VA 22201-3385

Do Bar Fights Count?

Dear Mr. Binder:

> "I stared hard into the large brown eyes of the 1,200 pound retired Army combat veteran and saw my military career crash and burn. My number was up."

So begins my article about Windriver, the last Army mule. This approximately 4,000 word feature article describes how a young city-bred female Army sergeant ended up as her handler. The article also details Windy's historic 46 year life, information on the mules who served in the China-Burma-India theater in World War II, and culminates in my search for Windy after I returned from Desert Storm as an Activated Air Force Reservist. A copy of her obituary from the Colorado Springs, Colorado newspaper in 1978 is attached.

My publishing credits include 18 months as a feature section editor for a weekly newspaper in Newport, Oregon, three national awards for writing and a recent publication in "The Officer" magazine in April 1991. I would like to send this article in for your review, but I am only willing to sell First Serial Rights to the article, since it is part of a future book.

I believe this article would be of great interest to your readers, and I have specifically slanted it for "Army" magazine readership. Thank you for considering this query. A self-addressed stamped envelope is included for your reply.

Sincerely,

Moi

Looking at it some 15 years later, I cringe, but only because we can all improve our writing by editing again and again. Some style changes have also occurred since this version. But, the letter did the trick at the time and I got a very nice letter back from Mr. Binder in August. He asked me to send the article, along with any photos I had.

Photos are a gold mine, especially for historical stories. If not your photos, make sure you have legal right to use the photos and permission from the people in the photos, unless they were taken in public areas.

A nice letter arrived from Mr. Binder in September. He liked the article but needed fixes in three areas. He needed me to cut 1,000 words. They normally buy all rights, but they would reassign book rights to me and they needed the original photos. Worked for me. He also recommended where I could cut, keep the hands-on dealing with Windy parts, he said, and he would pay me $600 for the article. Whoa.

I cut the article and shipped the photos registered mail. A Christmas card arrived from the editorial staff of Army magazine in December. I was thrilled.

I received a letter back in January 1992 that the fixes worked, they loved the article and they needed a short biography. The second paragraph was one any writer would kill to hear from an editor:

> You have a nice touch. I enjoyed following through your "pass in review" travails and reading your sensitive observations. Having such insight into the mind of a mule bespeaks considerable creative talent and I hope that whatever you are doing in your post-military life includes much writing.

Okay, at this point I am ready to marry this wonderful man. Then in March 1992, a check for $650 arrived, $50 for the photos. I must say, Mr. Binder was a light of hope and joy for a young woman writing about her mule. Have I had another publishing experience like this? No, but after that one, who needs Paris?

The article appeared in the April 1992 issue of *Army* magazine. Then another amazing thing happened. Mule mail.

I heard from China-Burma-India Veterans association members, one being Edward A. Rock, Senior, "Rocky." He and I send cards today. He sent me more mule information, plus pictures. One very important item was an oral history about how they did try to parachute mules. Another was Corry Mordeaux a former MOS 006 Animal Driver who worked with mules in the 666 FA Bn (Pack) at Fort Carson, Colorado. He sent me information and personally knew Hambone.

Randy Colvin of the Btry C, 612th FA, BN Pk also checked in from the Mountain Artillery Association. Then I got a letter from John I. Ladd of Pueblo, Colorado, the former commander of the 66th FA BN Pk. He included stories and a beautiful photo of him astride Windy in her Al Kaly Shrine Mule Train gear. She looked marvelous!

Next came a letter from S.A. Glass DVM, author of the book *Who Stole My Mule?* about his days as the American Liaison Veterinary Officer serving with Chinese combat troops in the Burma jungles. I bought two copies.

Then a friend forwarded a specialty publication called *Mules and More*, to see if I could submit the article. Next came a letter from Professor Melvin

Bradley of the University of Missouri. Not only was he writing a book about CBI packers, he was going to check on Windy at the Engineer Museum in Fort Leonard Wood, Missouri. He even sent me pictures. (Windy is stuffed.)

The outcome? Windy and I ended up in the book, *The Missouri Mule: His Origins and Times, Volume II*, published by Melvin Bradley with the Extension Division, University of Missouri-Columbia in cooperation with The Missouri Mule Skinners Society. A referral to my article is on page 478 in the *Some Special People and Special Mules* chapter. My favorite picture of Windy at the stunning age of 42 is on page 479.

I tell you all this to prepare you for unexpected happenings in the universe. Little did I know the small story of one girl and her mule would set off mule mania in my life. I do have enough for almost an entire book on Windy! Who knew there were mule groupies just like me?

That was a perfect publishing experience. Trust me, it is rare, but it happens.

So what do you do when things seem to go wrong or no one seems to want to publish your work? Publish it yourself. Just like I decided to do with this book. The age of Print-On-Demand and e-books are leveling the publishing field. Do your research, figure out how much money you are willing to invest and go for it.

Nobody tells a former pack mule handler she can't do something!

Resources:
The Writer magazine – www.writermag.com
Writer's Digest magazine – www.writersdigest.com
Writer's Digest Book Club – www.writersdigestbookclub.com
Maui Writer's Conference – www.mauiwriters.com (Can't get to Maui? Buy the tapes, CDs or MP3s! Many writers' conferences sell the presentations, including Romance Writers of America at www.rwanational.com)

Chapter 13

Certificate of Achievement

Every writing effort deserves a thank you. When the first term of *Writing War Stories* approached the end, I felt I needed to make a point of honoring each writer's commitment. I decided to award Certificates of Achievement to each veteran who finished the course.

I went out and got official certificate paper from the office supply store, complete with gold seals. The veterans might think it was hokey, but I wanted to do it. I used my "From the Desk of" embosser and imprinted on the gold seals.

Then I drafted the following language for their certificates:

"Presented to _____, on completion of the *Writing War Stories* class, given at Mt. Hood Community College in Gresham, Oregon on _____.
"In recognition of your writing contributions to the class, support of your fellow students and your military service to your country. Thank you for your efforts, past and present.

Kim A. Cook, Class Instructor"

At the end of the last class for the first term, I told them I had something for them. Given my practice of food tasting and homework assignments, they were a little worried. Then one by one, I read their certificate and had them come up and shake my hand.

It amazed me. The certificates seemed to mean something to them and they didn't think it was hokey. In fact, some of them said it was the first time they had ever been thanked for their military service.

Each term after that, the advanced students would know what was coming at the end of the term, but the newbies were clueless. Each time we celebrated another veteran completing the course, it was an unofficial party for all of us.

So now that you have come this far, you too have earned your certificate of achievement. I will let you fill in your name, the date, and where you completed this part of the book. Writing is not an easy profession or journey, so bravo to you for sticking it out with me and slogging through.

Don't be bashful. Fill in the spaces and make sure you write in ink. This is important.

Certificate of Achievement

Presented to _____, on completion of the *Writing War Stories* class, the book version, at _____, _____ (location) on _____. (date)

In recognition of your writing contributions to the book class, support of your fellow veterans and your military service to your country.

Thank you for your efforts, past and present.

Kim A. Cook, Class Instructor

The beginning goal of the class was to write a 12-page double-spaced story. Perhaps you have written more or less. It doesn't matter. It's the effort I want to acknowledge.

So what if you haven't written a word? What if you're reading and have not put a word on paper at this point? It's okay. Perhaps you are not ready to write stories. Maybe a journal is more your speed right now. A journal is nothing more than a place to write down your thoughts.

When a friend of mine lost his partner to AIDS, I suggested writing to deal with the grief. He told me months later how much keeping the journal had helped. He was able to look back and see where he had come from and to recognize that he was moving on in his grief.

I've written some journals, but I probably need to shred and burn them soon. Some of my most intimate thoughts are probably not for accidental public exposure. Or maybe I will put them in fiction and make a mint!

You don't have to write a story or a book to feel completion or have the writing bug move you along in your life. In 1997 I started keeping a Gratitude Journal. Yes, I saw it on *Oprah*. Sarah Ban Breathnach had come out with *The Simple Abundance Journal of Gratitude*.

Each day you write down five things you are grateful for that day. That's it. A list. Pretty easy to do. I am still keeping my daily Gratitude Journal, nine years later. I am convinced keeping these journals helped me to come out of the depression I didn't know I had after Desert Storm.

The magic of this task is each day you start to look for five things to put in your journal. Here are some of the things from that first year. A sunset. Chocolate chip cookie. Laughter with friends. Sleeping in. Flannel sheets. Spring night air. Pajama day. Cuddling my cat Amber. Coffee with Mom and

Dad. A hot shower. Reading in bed. Squirrels. And one which showed up a lot – my veteran students.

My Gratitude Journal has traveled with me on camping trips, to Hawaii, on a Panama Canal Cruise and weekend trips to the beach. It is the second to last thing I do before I go to bed each night. It helps me wrap up my day and go to bed with pleasant memories of what has been great about that day.

What has surprised me over the years is the impact of the small and simple. Most of the things in my journal cannot be bought with money. They involve slowing down and appreciating the day. For a writer, paying attention to details is required. The journal is one way to reinforce my ability to look for the good each day.

So, maybe you can write down five things every day instead of writing a book or a story. That's okay too. It's all writing. It's all good.

Now that you have these stories or books, what might you do with them? If you want to be published, refer back to the publishing chapter. It is another quest. But I also want you to consider some other options.

There are places beyond your family and your local Historical Society that are interested in your stories. Some have paperwork requirements, but they do want your stories. Here are a few to consider:

Veterans History Project
Library of Congress
(888) 371-5848
Email: vohp@loc.gov
www.loc.gov/folklife/vets/

The Vietnam Archive
Texas Tech University
Box 41045
Lubbock, Texas 79409-1045
(806) 742-3742
Email: Vietnam.center@ttu.edu

Department of the Navy
Naval Historical Center
805 Kidder Breese SE
Washington Navy Yard
Washington, D.C. 20374-5060
(202) 433-3224

Do Bar Fights Count?

www.history.navy.mil/branches/nhcorg10.htm
They have a web page titled *Creating a Personal Memoir of Your Naval Service*.

National Museum of the Marine Corps and Heritage Center
To open in 2006 next to the U.S. Marine Corps Base at Quantico, VA
www.usmcmuseum.org

The U.S. Army Center of Military History
Collins Hall
103 Third Avenue
Fort Lesley J. McNair, D.C. 20319-5058
www.army.mil/cmh

National Museum of the U.S. Air Force
1100 Spaatz St.
Wright-Patterson AFB, OH 45433
(937) 255-3286
www.wpafb.af.mil/museum

Air Force Historical Web Sites
www.af.mil/history/links.asp

Coast Guard Museum
c/o U.S. Coast Guard Academy
15 Mohegan Avenue
New London, CT 06320-8511
(860) 444-8511
U.S. Coast Guard Historian's Office
www.uscg.mil/hq/g-cp/history/collect.html

Coast Guard *Oral Histories, Memoirs and other First-Person Accounts of Coast Guard History*
www.uscg.mil/hq/g-cp/history/OralHistoryIndex.html

DoD Web Sites
www.defenselink.mil/sites

American Merchant Marine Museum
U.S. Merchant Marine Academy
300 Steamboat Road
Kings Point, NY 11024
(516) 773-5515
museum@usmma.edu

WIMSA
Women In Military Service For America Memorial Foundation, Dept. 560
Washington, D.C. 20042-0560
(703) 533-1155 or 1 (800) 222-2294
www.wimsa.org

Directory of Veterans Service Organizations
www1.va.gov/vso/index.cfm

    This is just a start. There are historians from your units who need your stories. Go to the reunions, swap stories and get the details down on paper. Not only do families need to know, but everyone in the United States needs to know the price of freedom.
    And time keeps marching on.
    It has taken me four years to complete this book. Not that I am an especially slow writer, but the act of writing this book became a journey in itself. Having 9/11 and the Afghanistan and Iraq wars start up while writing it, added to the book's length.
    One can never tell where writing will take you. So it is with me on this day. Books don't write themselves in a chronological order. This is the last chapter of the book I am writing. Who could have known chapter 13 came after chapter 32, but that is how it worked out.
    Perhaps I wanted to award myself my own certificate of achievement, which I will do Thursday. Tonight is a Monday night and I meet with some of my veteran alumni students on Thursday. After ending the class in May of 2000, we met off and on for reunions, usually around Veterans Day.
    Then about a year and half ago, I let the guys know I needed help to stay on track with the book. We started meeting again about every other month in book store cafes. We catch up for about an hour, then critique each other's work, just like in the class. Except they get to edit my work now too. Oh joy for them.

They all have books in progress. Big books. Now they are enjoying the fun of editing. Another journey which I am one day away from starting on this book. I am giving myself tomorrow off. Then I will get started on editing the entire manuscript. And so it will continue to go.

This morning at work (my day job) I opened up my email to learn a friend from my past had died. It was a shock since I didn't know she was ill and had been fighting an inoperable brain tumor for the last two and half years.

Jennifer Sears was a joy. She is the only person I know who was taken to be a human exhibit at a Humor in the Workplace conference in Japan. She loved to laugh and eat chocolate. A fellow writer, she served in the U.S. Army as a photographer. We are close in age. Jennifer was taken too soon from us, but I am so glad she passed through my life.

She moved to the Oregon coast with her husband a couple of years ago and we lost touch, but she stayed connected with another writer friend in my Oregon Press Women group. When two-by-fours like this hit you upside the head on a Monday morning, it reinforces the point that we only have so much time to tell our stories.

So, in that vein I will tell you Jennifer is the only person I know who came out of anesthesia and asked the nurse a question which almost gave the poor woman a heart attack. That was Jennifer. She and I shared the desire to not have children. My favorite Jenniferism of all time was her joke, "I love children. They taste just like chicken."

In Jennifer's honor tonight I threw myself off my diet and ate a box of Goobers. Jennifer would approve. Chocolate. And I bought a pint of Haagen Dazs Rocky Road Ice Cream to celebrate finishing the last chapter in this book and to salute Jennifer.

And I know tonight there will be a list of five things in my Gratitude Journal:

    The joy of knowing Jennifer Sears.
    Finishing the first draft of Bar Fights.
    Beautiful sunset I saw coming out of the grocery store.
    The gift of writing.
    Scoring the last box of Pillsbury Easter Bunny cookies.

Life is in the details. And small things are very large indeed.
Thank you for taking this writing journey with me.
Your efforts fill me with joy.
To be followed pronto by Rocky Road Ice Cream.
Keep writing.

PART II

SPECIFIC VETERAN GROUPS

Chapter 14

POWs/MIAs

The images flickered on the late night television screen. I kept watching as the men walked slowly down the airplane steps.

"Are you coming to bed?" my mother asked.

"Just a few minutes more," I said.

She smiled and nodded her head. It was a school night in March, 1973, and it was very late, but she left me there in the living room. And then, there he was, his name on the television.

Captain Gerald Venanzi.

I had worn a silver bracelet around my wrist for months, with his name on it. A Vietnam Prisoner of War, he was coming home. I touched the band on my arm and a few tears slipped down my face.

I couldn't imagine the elation his family was feeling or the long journey they would all make to bring him truly home, but for now, he was safe.

Some twelve years later I had just been notified I was the new Public Affairs Officer for the Portland Veterans Administration Medical Center. Thrilled at my new job after spending the last eighteen months as a newspaper reporter, I was taking a shower to go buy my new wardrobe to begin work on the next Monday.

I got another call from the VAMC and my mom threw the phone over the top of the shower.

"They have to talk to you, now," she said.

I had the presence of mind to turn off the water and heard the following words.

"We need you to start tomorrow instead of Monday," the EEO Manager said. "Can you do that?"

"Sure," I replied, wondering what was going on.

"Good," she said. "By the way, the Deputy Administrator of the VA will be there and we need you to get the newspaper to interview him."

Forget that I'm standing dripping naked, I have my first assignment to get news coverage before I'd even stepped foot on the grounds.

"Oh yes," she continued, "it's also the Rose Festival Wheelchair Parade tomorrow and the newspaper said they can't send any reporters."

"Can I ask who the Deputy Administrator is," I queried.

"Oh, that's right," she said. "You don't know him at all. His name is Everett Alvarez, Jr., and he was the longest held POW in Vietnam."

And that is how I spent my first day as the new Public Affairs Officer for the Portland VA Medical Center, meeting Mr. Alvarez and helping to escort him around the grounds. The Army taught me well and smoke and mirrors came to my rescue, since escorting a deputy administrator is no mean trick when you don't know where you're going or where the bathroom is. Somehow I managed to follow and lead at the same time. I think.

Mr. Alvarez was most gracious and my Hail Mary phone call to Norm Maves at *The Oregonian* that morning resulted in an interview. I knew Norm was the only reporter covering any military issues in those post-Vietnam days. I am still grateful to him for the interest and respect he showed Mr. Alvarez.

Years later when I was being processed into the Air Force Reserve, I found out my recruiter was a member of the aeromedical evacuation crews that went in to retrieve the Vietnam prisoners of war.

"We painted up the insides of those C-141s with white paint and we stowed every comfort on board we thought they would need," he said. "We sent extra planes, just in case there would be more prisoners than they told us. Our plane didn't land, but that is still a flight I will never forget."

A few months later I heard one of the Vietnam prisoners of war talk about those flights. "We kept thinking it was a hoax," he said. "Until I was walking across the tarmac and I saw an Air Force flightnurse, a roundeye. Then I knew it was real and we were going home."

POW/MIA rescue and recovery missions like these are the greatest calling for military members. The men who rescued Jessica Lynch from Iraq will never forget what it felt like to bring home one of their own. There is no way to easily explain this commitment to our fellow prisoners of war, missing in action, our buddies.

Perhaps the best is to say we are family. Many times we are closer than blood family, shaped by the triumphs and tragedies we experience together in the military. **Writing down these stories begins to illustrate the small details which explain the commitment military members have to each other and to defending the United States.**

One of my instructors in the Air Force Reserve, John Simpson, was a former loadmaster who became an Aeromedical Evacuation Operations Officer. One of his most memorable flights was the mission to transport MIA remains to Hawaii for identification.

"I knew their names and I carry them in my flight pouch at all times," he said. "It was an honor to bring them on their journey home." It doesn't matter what service, which branch and from which war, we have to bring all our family home.

In these days of DNA identification and research, finding and identifying the dead and missing is a science, but also painstaking, backbreaking work. We have lost military members on these retrieval missions too. But still, we search.

As the POW/MIA patch says, "You Are Not Forgotten."

If you knew of a military member who was listed as Missing In Action or a Prisoner Of War, your stories might help the current hunters have a better chance of finding remains. Or your stories can bring enlightenment and comfort to family members still waiting for closure for a son or daughter who never knew the funny stories and little quirks of their father or mother.

Writing down the stories of those we have lost honors their memory and brings them alive again, to live on paper, forever. I can think of no greater honor to their memory.

Articles I read on the www.pownetwork.org web site quoted Gerald Venanzi when he left the "Hanoi Hilton."

> "I was among the group of prisoners that was released on March 4, 1973. I did not look back at the camp. I said a prayer that went something like this:
> Dear God, We thank you for taking care of us for such a long time. We now ask that you give us the courage to face the future and to accept the changes that have taken place."
> Gerald Venanzi was shot down September 17, 1967.

Also listed on the same web site, was an interview with Everett Alvarez, Jr. by the *Washington Times* on May 31. "Vietnam is in the past, but it's attached to me whether I like it or not," he said "It's like my shadow."

He went on to say, "Most of us POWs are too busy to sit down and look back at Vietnam. But let's never forget the thousands of men who will never return."

Everett Alvarez, Jr., was shot down Aug. 5, 1964 and released February, 1973 along with 591 other American POWs.

Alvarez mentioned in one article that his "proudest achievement is raising a family."

Which makes the following story even more poignant and illustrates when bringing our POWs and MIAs home – it is never too late.

I include this article from the United States Army Central Identification Laboratory in Hawaii published on the web in January, 2003. The unit is now called the Joint POW/MIA Accounting Command (JPAC).

Sons Return Father's Remains Home from Vietnam after 34 years
By Maj. Jessie Massey

Like many young men of his generation, Evert overflowed with enthusiasm. The tall Lanky youth – known as Jerry to friends and affectionately called Big Ev – excelled at sports, especially basketball. At some point Evert developed a fondness for airplanes. But more importantly, Evert loved his country. That love would guide his decision to join the Army National Guard in 1955 when he was a senior in high school.

In 1958, while attending Brigham Young University, Evert's unquenchable desire to fly airplanes led him to transfer to the Air Force Reserve Officer Training Corps. Program. That same year he met Wanda and soon after, the couple married. The following year their first child Daniel arrived. The future looked bright. In 1960 Evert graduated from BYU and enthusiastically accepted a commission as an Air Force pilot. And while the war in Vietnam quickly escalated, Evert became consumed with his flight training and keeping one step ahead of his growing family. Following his training, Evert moved his family to Chandler, Ariz. He now had three children with another on the way.

In April 1967 the inevitable call for duty came. The proud F-105 pilot shouldered a bag, said goodbye to his family and flew out for a tour of duty over the hostile skies of Vietnam. Only 29 years old, it would be the last time his family would see him.

"My father was shot down on November 8th, 1967," said Dan Evert, eldest of the Evert children. "He had just received permission to come home for the birth of his child and was to return home a few hours after the completion of his mission."

Elizabeth, the couple's fourth child, was born 5 days after the tragic incident.

Sadly, details surrounding the events that day would elude the Evert family for over three decades. Only recently did the final chapter of this tragic story come to light. In a twist of fate, President Clinton played a role. The ordeal, though, took a toll on the deeply religious family. "I remember coming home from school that day," said Dan, then eight years old. "I saw an ambulance and several blue cars in front of the house. I knew something was wrong but I didn't know what it could be." An alert neighbor of the Evert's saw Dan and pulled him into her house.

"I stood at the window in their living room watching my house. Eventually some people in uniform came out of the house with my mother. I was able to cross the street and find out what happened. The only word I remember is missing," Dan said. The Air Force had little information to report. Evert's aircraft was backup for a bombing mission on the outskirts of Hanoi. During the mission's approach, one of the primary aircraft had difficulties and had to break away. Evert – call sign Bison 4 – got the nod. Flying nearby, it did not take long for him to respond. Lieutenant Colonel (Ret.) Marty Scott, then Captain, was flying in position number three at the time. Scott and Evert had roomed together during flight school and became close friends. Scott remembers the events of the day all too well.

"When Evert pulled up beside me, he gave me an A-OK hand signal, and we flew off to our target. During the bomb run, I heard a short radio transmission that was too fuzzy to understand. Evert was about 50-100 feet behind me as we dove for the target. As I pulled off the target, someone radioed that they had seen an F-105 go down. I called Jerry (Evert) to join me but got no reply. Our flight circled around the target again. But all we could see was a spot on the ground where an airplane had gone in," Scott said.

Because of the target's proximity to enemy territory, the Air Force could not launch a search and rescue mission. Scott and the remaining pilots returned to their base in Thailand. For the next eight years the Department of Defense officially listed Evert as Missing in Action. It was a difficult time for the Evert family. "My mother always kept my father's memory alive in our house," Dan said. "His pictures always had kiss marks on them. We had MIA posters and MIA bracelets. I remember putting together the care packages that were sent to Vietnam for prisoners. They were always returned."

Tamra Evert, the eldest Evert daughter, remembers her mother's efforts to keep their father's memory alive. "My mom had a box of my dad's personal things," she recalls. "On some family nights she would bring out one of the boxes and let us try some of his things on. My dad's shoes were so large. This was one of my favorite things to do." In 1973, during Operation Homecoming, the North Vietnamese released their American prisoner's of war. The Evert family received news that Evert's name was not on the list of returnees. Still, because of the family's deep religious faith – The Church of Jesus Christ of Latter Day Saints – they held onto hope of seeing Evert again. "When the POWs started to come home in 1973 we watched the TV very closely as each man came off the plane," recalls Dan. "We sat together as a family late into the night on my mother's bed, hoping that someone would look familiar. We saw the last plane land and let the last POWs come off. The realization that he wasn't there was a very difficult time. I remember my hope for him to be alive turning to hope that he never had to suffer." In 1975 the Department of Defense officially reclassified Evert as: Dead, body not recovered. Dan and his younger brother, David attended the hearings.

"I was in high school when they held a hearing to declare my father dead," said Tamra. "I wished that my sister and I could have been there. Our father was such a big part of our lives even though he was not with us."

Evert's military records were eventually transferred to the Joint Task Force – Full Accounting (JTF-FA) and the U.S. Army Central Identification Laboratory, Hawaii (CILHI), organizations with responsibility for the search and recovery of Americans missing as a result of the Vietnam conflict. Birthdays came and went. Christmases passed with no news. Then, in the fall of 2000, the Evert family received an interesting phone call.

"I worked in Europe for most of 2000," said Dan. "I came back to Arizona in the fall for a short visit. In October, Dr. Kay Whitely, (Director of Family Support Services for the Defense Prisoner of War/Missing Personnel Office), informed us of a crash site in Vietnam that may be associated with my father's case. We set up a meeting with her at our home."

At the meeting, Whitely brought along a notebook containing a map and photos of the suspected crash site. The Evert family was aghast. For the first time in thirtysomething years they actually had information regarding the loss of their father. Whitely also informed the family that the Central Identification Laboratory along with Joint Task Force – Full Accounting planned to conduct an excavation of the site within the next month. What she said next caught the family completely by surprise.

"Dr. Whitely said that the same presentation was given to President Clinton," Dan said. "She said the President would be in Vietnam at the same time as the excavation and they wanted to know how we felt about him visiting the crash site."

The Evert family had no problem with President Clinton visiting the site. The family conveyed their feelings to Whitely but added one request.

"We want to go, too."

Whitely departed with the promise that she would relay their concerns to the White House. No one in the family expected anything to come from the request. Dan had to return to work in Europe. Within a few days they received a second phone call.

"I was driving down the road in Belgium when my cell phone rang," said Dan. "A very excited Kay Whitely was on the other end. She said the family was approved to travel to Vietnam. President Clinton invited us and the invitation included a visit to Washington, D.C. on Veteran's Day. Myself, Tamra, David and Elizabeth would all go to Washington. David and I would go to Vietnam." Dan cut short his business trip and returned to Arizona.

For the Evert family, the events of the next few weeks were a blur. They flew to Washington and had breakfast at the White House with hundreds of other families of personnel missing in Southeast Asia. They participated in the ceremony at Arlington National Cemetery, where the president laid a wreath at the Tomb of the Unknown Soldier. President Clinton even acknowledged them at the ceremony.

"It's hard to describe my feelings as I looked at all the grave markers in that beautiful place," said Dan. "They announced that the President was entering the grounds and the 21-gun salute began. That was a great moment in a great place." Following the events in Washington, Dan and David headed to Vietnam.

Months before the visit, members of the JTF-FA and CILHI conducted investigations of the alleged Evert crash site. Maps were analyzed, officials consulted and elderly witnesses interviewed. Following several detailed investigations of the area, local and U.S. officials believed they had pinpointed the crash of Evert's F-105 in a rice patty adjacent to the national railway line. A specialized CILHI team departed for Vietnam.

Following the pomp and circumstance of the visit, Dan and David traveled with the president's entourage to the site. The CILHI team was hard at work on the excavation.

"I remember my first glimpse of the blue tarps used for shelter," said Dan. "It was a very emotional and draining moment and I couldn't hold back the tears as we stood at the edge of the crater and watched the work in progress. Americans and Vietnamese worked side by side. They scooped mud into a bucket and passed it to a station where others would search through the mud for wreckage and human remains."

The brothers were cautioned not to expect too much from the initial excavation. Although the team had discovered small pieces of aircraft and even a few fragments of what appeared to be human remains, this was by no means conclusive. They were told that it would take several excavations of the site to recover sufficient information to lead to a positive identification.

The excavation ended a month later but the evidence was not conclusive. A second excavation was planned for February 2001. This time, Dan was accompanied by all of the siblings, including Elizabeth's husband. The CILHI team worked feverishly to reach the bottom of the crater, but a subsequent trip would be necessary to complete the excavation. On this trip however, large sections of aircraft debris were unearthed that could lead to an aircraft identification. More promising, however, was the significant amount of human remains found in the crater.

"They asked us if we wanted to see the remains. We told them we wanted to see anything they had," said Dan. "We were taken to a private viewing area. For Elizabeth, who has never seen our father, this was the closest she had ever come to him."

In June 2001, a CILHI team returned to the site for the final time. During that excavation, Dan was able to bring his wife and two sons. They quickly became part of the team and before long Dan and his sons were in the crash crater, moving mud with the rest of the workers. It was the highlight of their trip.

The final excavation of the site proved what they had suspected all along. As they reached the bottom of the crater, the team found Evert's wallet, identification tags, religious emblems and other personal items. They had found Evert's crash site.

Evert's remains and personal effects were returned to Hawaii with full military honors. The entire Evert family was on hand for the solemn occasion. At last, the family could put to rest the questions that had surrounded Evert's death. On July 6 the family lay Evert to rest in a cemetery in Mesa, Arizona.

"I don't have the words to describe how valuable that experience has been in my life," said Dan. "I know my father loved us, and we all loved him. He was lost, and this was the fulfillment of a childhood dream. That we could go to Vietnam and help bring my father back."

Do you know stories about POWs and MIAs that need to be told? There is no time like the present. We had prisoners taken in Desert Storm, Somalia, Bosnia, Afghanistan and Iraq. And we still have MIAs. Every single story counts. Especially for the loved ones left behind.

Resources:
Soldier Dead: How We Recover, Identify, Bury & Honor Our Military Fallen by Michael Sledge
Chained Eagle by Everett Alvarez, Jr.
Code of Conduct by Everett Alvarez, Jr.

She Went To War by Rhonda Cornum as told to Peter Copeland
We Band of Angels – The Untold Story of American Nurses Trapped on Bataan by the Japanese by Elizabeth M. Norman
In the Company of Heroes by Michael J. Durant
Glory Denied: The Saga of Jim Thompson, America's Longest-Held Prisoner of War by Tom Philpott
No One Left Behind: The LT. Comdr. Michael Scott Speicher Story by Amy Waters Yarsinske

Web Sites:
www.jpac.pacom.mil
www.pownetwork.org
www.pow-miafamilies.org
National Prisoner of War Museum – www.montezuma-ga.org/chamber/pow.html
Andersonville – National Park Service – www.nps.gov/ande

Chapter 15

Special Operations, Special Forces, and Military Intelligence

Fall 1990.
The back of the C141B was piled high with gear. I looked around. This could not be the right aircraft, I said to myself. One of the first jobs for an Aeromedical Evacuation Operations Officer of an Aerovac unit is to go out and check the aircraft and make sure the cargo bay is set up correctly.

This can be no easy trick when maintenance moves the aircraft on you at 0 dark thirty. I went back outside and checked the tail number. Yup. Right aircraft.

I surveyed a group of what appeared to be black parachutes along one wall of the cargo bay. Along the other side were a group of what looked like bulky green parachutes. Usually on a training mission the Aerovac crew has the entire cargo bay. An uneasy feeling raised the hair on the back of my neck.

They'd done it to me again. This had to be another goat rope mission. (Ever tried to rope a goat? Exactly.) I thought something was up when my operations officer asked if I could take a three-day training mission to Las Vegas. We rarely did three day trips. Especially to Vegas.

Two hours later it became clear to me I was a partial ringmaster for a three-ring circus.

"Take the incubator back to the Squadron," I told the med tech. "It won't fit."

About that time a group of Army paratroopers came on board. The medical crew director hunted me down.

"Who are they?" she asked.

"Passengers," I said. "Don't worry, I understand we're going to throw them out the back troop doors when we get close to Vegas. We're giving the Army a lift."

She raised an eyebrow at me. I shrugged my shoulders. The Army guys settled in and appeared quite happy to be on the aircraft. They also seemed to notice the majority of our crew was female. Who says Army guys are slow?

Then another group of Air Force passengers came on board. When they walked on the plane they seemed miffed. They did not look like the type of folks who were used to sharing anything with other military pukes.

The group sidled over to their equipment and began plugging themselves into their CD players. The medical crew director beat a path to my location.

"Air Combat Controllers," I said to her raised eyebrow. "We're going to throw them out the back of the aircraft when we get close to Vegas."

She was not impressed. For those of you who have not worked with military nurses, especially flight nurses, let me tell you a little secret. I'd put a few of them up against a battalion of Marines anyday. They'd win.

There was enough tension in the cargo bay to make the stand off at the OK Corral look like a tea party. The medical crew was barging into and over the combat controllers, the controllers were not giving any ground over the fight for equipment storage and the Army guys were watching the med crew vs. combat controllers duel.

I checked in with my contact with the combat controllers and made sure they had enough space for their needs.

"No problem," he said.

We were all a little jumpy about being on alert for a possible Gulf War. I wondered how they were handling the lockdown on critical positions. "Think you'll be going to Kuwait?" I asked.

"We just got back," he said.

"Right," I said. "Let me know if you need anything." I knew when I was out of my league and beat a hasty retreat.

Another two hours later, I looked up from my in-flight duties running chemical training checks and the 1,000th message to the flight deck and realized the groups had reached détente. It appeared the combat controllers had realized the female content of our crew too. What appeared to start as a turf air war was quickly becoming a cocktail party at 37,000 feet.

Only problem, the medical crew was actually trying to train and the Army and combat controllers were trying to get dates for Vegas. Add in the extra amount of flight crew and the cargo bay turned into a flying ant hill.

When we got near the drop sites, we stopped our training and buckled in for safety. One of our Squadron photographers had brought his camcorder. Show time! The breeze was a bit heavy as the troop doors popped and the Army guys jumped out on the static lines. The loadmasters stood by with knives to cut the jumpers loose if they got tangled.

Not to be outdone, the combat controllers waited on the back ramp as the clam shell doors opened and the ramp went down. Not used to an audience, with camera rolling, they put on a show for us jumping out the back of the aircraft. The last two even did a piggyback kind of jump, to which we all gave a very loud round of applause.

Do Bar Fights Count?

That is those of us who were not puking, due to the corkscrew combat flying we were doing to simulate setting down in a hot landing zone, gave them a hand.

Later that night we bumped into some of the air crew at dinner and got to discussing the day's events.

"Did you see those jumps off the back?" the major asked. "Those are some crazy bastards."

"I'm just glad they're on our side," I said.

That was my second brush with members of the special forces. To my knowledge, that is. If the military is a tight family, Special Operations and Special Forces are Siamese twins. We ask an incredible amount from our Navy SEALS, Army Rangers, Snipers, Green Berets, Recon, Delta Force and whoever else I may have left out. We train them for harrowing, soul killing missions and their deeds go mostly unknown.

When the going gets beyond tough and moves into completely shitty, these are the amazing folks who go where no one wants to tread. While many of their stories cannot be told due to classified information, they can be written as fiction until such time as they can be declassified.

Richard Marchinko's *Rogue Warrior*, series is an excellent example, as well as Chuck Pfarrer's *Warrior Soul; The Memoir of a Navy Seal*. More and more books are being written by special forces personnel and SEALS. Do things always go well for them? No. Do they do their best and push the limits? You bet.

Would you ever catch me jumping out of a helicopter or aircraft into water in a scuba suit? Not this girl. The jumping part would probably be okay, but I'm not real big on the plummeting into water thing. I'm very glad there are men and I bet some women, willing to do it. (See, I'm just assuming some women are doing it and it is so secret no one really knows about it. It's a girl thing.)

My first possible brush with Special Ops Forces? My work study at the VA Medical Center. Jack showed up the night after I attended a Chippendale's Men's Revue. My co-workers were convinced I swiped him from the show. He was out of active duty, in the reserves, and going to college on the G.I. Bill.

"You know if I disappear one day," he said without much fanfare.

"I know," I said. He felt comfortable with me because of my Army background. He talked a little about SEAL training, but when someone else came in the office he clammed up and I could see the shutters go down in his eyes.

His silence intrigued my co-workers, but I told them he was just shy. This theory was tested the day he wore shorts to the office. I could hear hearts breaking all over the hospital grounds and I had a constant parade of women visitors into my office. They talked to me and looked at Jack. Or to be more specific, Jack's calves.

One day he did disappear. Shortly thereafter the trouble with the oil rigs in the Persian Gulf was in the news. I got a call from him a few weeks later. Long distance, not sure from where, but the connection was not great . He said he'd let me know when he got back. He did and I got to check out his new job as a bartender. Can I prove he was a SEAL? No. Did he look different? The shadows in his eyes were a little darker. That's all I really know to this day.

Military Intelligence
Okay, all the jokes aside, let's discuss these folks. I know nothing about them. When I was in the Army, military intelligence ended up breaking folks for drugs and chasing idiots trying to sneak on base (we were trying to get off base) and people stealing weapons. That was all I heard about.

While on the *Run For The Wall* biker trip in 1998, I met a police officer who was in MI in Vietnam. Seems he signed this piece of paper that said he couldn't talk about anything he did for thirty years. Bummer, big time.

Meeting several members of the Marine Navajo Code Talkers while on the motorcycle run, gave me an even greater appreciation of their sacrifice. Not only could they not talk about what they had done, they were not even nationally recognized until 1969 – 24 years after World War II.

A marvelous book entitled *Warriors - Navajo Code Talkers*, by Kenji Kawano offers a marvelous photographic essay of the Code talkers after the war. It is an amazing story of the true contributions of the "first Americans" to this country during World War II and how they kept their secrets long after the war.

The 400 code talkers used their own Navajo language to develop a secret code to be used in the Pacific. Japanese cryptographers never broke their code. The entire program was classified as top secret from the beginning.

There are many stories about tricks of the trade and how deception saved lives. A recent book titled *Secret Soldiers*, by Philip Gerard explains *How a Troupe of American Artists, Designers, and Sonic Wizards Won World War II's Battles of Deception Against the Germans*. As we say in public relations, talk about using smoke and mirrors. These guys did it when it really mattered.

Do Bar Fights Count?

And don't think to leave the women out. The book *Sisterhood of Spies*, by Elizabeth P. McIntosh relates how the women of the Office of Strategic Services during World War II put themselves at risk without any uniform and still served America. These women numbered Marlene Dietrich and Julia Child among their ranks.

Are military women in intelligence now? You bet. Will we read their stories? Maybe one day. I bet they have some beauts.

Or read a CIA cleared intelligence story in *Spy Dust* by Antonio and Jonna Mendez, about *Two Masters of Disguise Reveal The Tools And Operations That Helped Win The Cold War*. There is also a new book I am waiting to arrive in the mail titled, *Blowing My Cover: My Life As a CIA Spy* by Lindsay Moran.

How about you? Got some sneaky stories? Want to get some special ops out of your system? Fire up that computer and get cracking! I've got some books to read!

Resources:
Warrior Soul: The Memoir of A Navy SEAL by Chuck Pfarrer
Shooter: The Autobiography of the Top-Ranked Marine Sniper by Donald A. Davis, Jack Coughlin and Casey Kuhlman

Web Sites:
Naval Special Warfare Foundation – www.nswfoundation.org
Navy Seal Museum – http://navysealmuseum.com
www.navyseals.com
www.specialops.org
U.S. Army Ranger Association – www.ranger.org
www.armyranger.com
www.amea.us

Chapter 16

Disabled and Paralyzed Veterans

The team leader for the brand new VA Veterans Outreach Center looked at the woman applying for the vacant secretary position. "So, how did you come to be in the wheelchair," he asked. "I think I heard the Human Resources person swallow her tongue," he said with a laugh. "She jumped right in and changed the subject and gave me a look like my hair was on fire."

"I wasn't sure what I'd done," he said. "The woman applicant gave me the dirtiest look too. When we hired her for the job, I explained myself. When disabled or paralyzed vets come in, the first thing a counselor asks is how did you get your injury?

"The vet tells us how they were injured and we move on," he said. "We don't try and act like they don't have an arm or leg or eye missing. We acknowledge it and move on. That way we can deal with what issues are really bothering the vet. It may not be the injury or amputations at all."

He told me that story about his early days as a new team leader in one of our conversations. Sometimes I wonder if all this "political correctness" doesn't make life more difficult for veteran amputees and veterans who use a wheelchair. Kind of like the elephant in the room nobody talks about.

Kids don't have a problem asking how someone got hurt. They are generally curious and not looking for gory details. I think they figure this person has one big owie. We ask people how they break their legs and arms, but asking how a person was burned or lost a limb or ended up with PTSD, doesn't seem right?

One of our local television stations, KATU, did a series on recovering local soldiers at Walter Reed Army Medical Center by reporter Anna Song. The transcripts are on their web site at www.katu.com under Casualties of War.

"At first, everyone would stare and I hated it," said Sgt. Lucas Wilson. "I would actually yell at people for staring at it. Then, as time went along, it got a lot easier."

"I've got two messed up legs, but if you look around here, there is always someone worse, so I'm actually very fortunate because I have two good arms and my head still works," said Sgt. Mike Buyas.

Wilson said he didn't look at his amputation the first month. "I was hoping it would magically grow back." His challenges have been both mental and physical. "There were days when I'd wake up and I just wouldn't get out of bed," he says. "There were other days when I'd go to sleep and hope that I'd never wake up. To help me get out of that rut, I went and got Buddy (my dog) and he's been instrumental in helping me."

The series also featured Major Tammy Duckworth, a Blackhawk pilot who lost both her legs while on a combat mission in Baghdad when Fallujah was a hot spot. A fireball hit her at knee level and she couldn't move the rudder pedals. She didn't know that not only were the pedals gone, so were her legs. "Her right leg had been torn off at the hip and her left one was gone below the knee. Her right arm was also broken in three places."

Due to major advances in battlefield medicine, she was saved and flown to Germany, then to Walter Reed within 60 hours of the explosion. Her goal now? "I want to stay in the Army and I want to fly helicopters for the Army again," she says. "I'm not letting some guy who got lucky one day in Baghdad decide my future."

See? Pissing off a warrior woman is never a good idea.

I need disabled and paralyzed veterans to write or dictate their stories so I know how they feel about the questions we are too polite to ask. Just like the rest of us, I imagine their answers are as individual as each one of us. Some will want to talk, some won't. But ignoring the elephant in the room seems a little like the story "The Emperor's New Clothes" – the politician was naked, folks!

Perhaps some of the greatest challenges are for veterans who have Post Traumatic Stress Disorder (PTSD) or Traumatic Brain Injuries (TBI). I heard a Marine Iraq veteran say on a television program that he wished he had an amputation or shrapnel injury so people could physically see his wound. Stress or brain injury wounds are just as real and debilitating as visually physical wounds – they impair everyday functioning.

A favorite quote of mine says, "We all fight our own secret battles." This is true of everyone. Veterans are the same. Whether suffering from PTSD or the result of a concussion, these closed body injuries are ticking time bombs if not treated. PTSD and traumatic head injuries will impact a veteran and his or her family for the rest of their life.

Will they be non-functioning? Probably not. To what extent will each veteran be affected? That's between the veteran, his or her doctors and a higher power. Do we want to hear these stories? Absolutely!

Do we want to read about the triumphs and the challenges? You bet. We need to realize that just because someone comes with wheels, prosthesis or scrambled synapses, they're still a whole human being. I think of these folks like a Christmas toy that got jumbled in a car wreck. Some assembly required and batteries not included. They have to provide their own batteries and they accomplish amazing things.

Anyone who has seen the Department of Veterans Affairs National Veterans Wheelchair Games or National Disabled Veterans Winter Sports Clinic comes away with a great deal of respect for these athletes. They have powerful, self-made batteries motivating them. I hope they will write down or dictate their stories to let the rest of us know what to do when we are lucky enough to meet them.

If nothing else, we can ask them what happened and then move on. Just like they did. I would really like to know what the amputees would write to those medics who saved their lives and worried they didn't want to be saved, because they were missing an arm, leg, or eye. Those medics need to know too. Because no one can see the medic's secret battles either (See Chapter 25). We all fight our own secret battles, visible and invisible.

Got stories about losing your body parts or parts that quit working? Get them down on paper.

Author's Note: Update from the recovery trenches. Major Tammy Duckworth is running for Congress for Illinois District Six. Check out her web site at www.duckworthforcongress.com That's what we need in Congress, more Black Hawk pilots! Lock and load.

Resources:
Back In Action: An American Soldier's Story of Courage, Faith and Fortitude by David Rozelle
The Long Road Home – One Step at a Time, A Doonesbury Book by G.B. Trudeau
Born on the Fourth of July by Ron Kovic

Web Sites:
Disabled American Veterans – www.dav.org
Paralyzed American Veterans – www.pva.org
Wounded Warrior Project – www.woundedwarriorproject.org

Amputee Coalition of America
http://mentalhealth.about.com/library/h/orgs/b12916.htm

Chapter 17

Native American Veterans

The welcome overwhelmed me and my eyes filled with tears. In this desolate but beautiful golden land of the Navajo Nation, myself and my fellow veterans were greeted with open arms. My tears did not spill over until Suzanne Sigona looked at me and said, "This is for you too, lady."

Those words sent a torrent of healing tears to run free down my face. It was day two of the *Run for the Wall* and we had arrived at the Navajo Reservation outside of Gallup, New Mexico. We were offered pieces of fry bread and waited for the main group of bikers to arrive behind us.

Once we were all together, a procession of Native Americans led us through the reservation to the Veterans Memorial at Window Rock. This natural monument overwhelmed my senses once again. Between the large greeting crowd, the speeches and hearing actual code words used by several Navajo Code Talkers, it is a memory I will remember all of my days.

I escaped outside the bounds of the wood fence which enfolded all the riders, veterans and the bikes and stood apart on the hill, watching the Native American children playing on the rocks. The warm welcome by the tribal elders touched me deeply.

A people who had their land stolen by our forefathers welcomed us to their land as the veterans we were and the warriors we rode to honor. I took pictures and managed to compose myself.

"Can I take your picture?"

I turned to see a small Native American girl with a camera. "Me? I asked.

She nodded. I smiled and she took my picture.

"Can I take a picture of your patch too?"

"Of course," I said. I turned around and let her take a picture of the patch on the back of my vest. Designed by my next door veteran neighbor Mikel Mathews, there were only about 40 of them made. It made my heart sing to know a young Native American girl thought the patch was important enough to take a picture. And it floored me to know she thought it was important to take a picture of me too, I guess, since the back of my vest said in large letters, NAM VET SUPPORTER, then in smaller letters under Mikel's patch, Desert Storm Veteran.

Do Bar Fights Count?

Taking my picture that young girl started my healing on the bike trip – I realized I could not be an invisible veteran anymore. When the young acknowledge you, you know what you did mattered, no matter how small it seemed.

When we first arrived at the gathering place on the Navajo Reservation, Suzanne's bike had been up on the trailer. Another young Native American girl was admiring her bike.

"Do you want to sit on it?" Suzanne asked. The girl's face lit up. Suzanne helped her climb up on the bike. I took a picture of them both and it is one of my favorite photos from the entire trip. We were a bond of female intensity across a chasm of age and cultures, all over a Harley. Amazing.

Window Rock affected me on our short visit that day. I still feel the need to go back and spend time there. Not only to acknowledge the Navajo Warriors honored at the site, but to also experience the peace and grace of the natural vista. I know it is a healing place, for I felt the healing touch while within its grasp. It is truly a sacred place for many reasons.

Perhaps it should not have surprised me so to find such peace from the open arms of another culture. In the fall of 1997 I made contact with Dick French, President of the Northwest Indian Veterans Association, Portland/Vancouver Chapter. My mother gave me his name as a veteran I might be interested in contacting.

I had a wonderful visit with him and he asked me to submit an editorial for their newsletter. I did so and thanked him for his time and he let his readers know about the writing classes. The editorial titled, *Indian Veteran Stories Important To Capture*, appeared in the Fall 1997 edition of the newsletter.

Soon after the publication of the newsletter, I got several calls asking if the editorial could be read aloud at Pow Wows. Overwhelmed once again, I immediately gave my permission. A month after I returned from the biker ride and my visit to the Navajo Nation, I made a note on my calendar on July 21, 1998 to call Dick. Before I was able to call, I heard of Dick's untimely death at age 59 on July 21. A member of the NIVA honor guard, he buried many of his fellow veteran members and they were there for him at his funeral.

A veteran of the U.S. Army, Dick worked for 35 years as a forester for the Bureau of Indian Affairs with the Blackfeet, White Mountain Apache and many other tribal groups. Shortly before his death in an interview he gave an answer for how he wanted to be remembered. "I tried to open a door for Indian people," he said.

He definitely accomplished that with me. He related stories to me of how more than 10,000 Native Americans served in World War I. Citizenship was not granted to all American Indians until 1924, six years after the war was over. Yet, they still volunteered, relayed Dick.

Native Americans are also victims of the warrior stereotype. One article in that same newsletter illustrated the fact. "If you are an Indian, you are supposed to be good," said Harold Barse. "We had one Navajo guy who was born and reared in the city. And he had no conception of making his way around in the woods, or anything. And yet, he was put on point, because he was an Indian."

With a largely oral storytelling tradition, the war stories of Native Americans have been passed down by verbal story. I hope Native American veterans will write down as many stories as they can tell themselves or remember others told to them. All the stories are a part of the Native American experience and need to be recorded.

Or to put in it the words of Harold Barse once again, "Indian people have always respected their vets. It's never made any difference with the politics of war. They recognize these people who done a sacrifice for them. When they serve they are serving for their people. And that's who they do it for. And Indians recognized this. So when they come home, they come home with honor and dignity. Not like many of the non-Indians who came home to outright hostility. Yet, that does not keep you from having the problems. Indian people have recognized that war changes people. For centuries and centuries, they've known this."

Maybe that is what I felt in my soul at Window Rock. Understanding that war changes all of us, just as military service also changes us. What are your Native American military stories?

Resources:
Strong Hearts Wounded Souls; Native American Veterans of the Vietnam War by Tom Holm

Film – *Navajo Women Warriors: Sani Dez-bah*, Director Alice Carron

Chapter 18

Women Veterans

"You have got to be shittin' me," I said, looking down at the sergeant standing at the back of the deuce and a half.

"I'm not, Cook," he said. "You and the other two women can't go to the range. The LAW is a combat weapon and they won't let you fire."

"It took them a day and a half of classroom training to figure that out?"

He nodded his head, shaking it from side to side. "Come on, let's go," he added. "You can go through shotgun training."

I grimaced at him. Who wanted to fire a shotgun when a Light Antitank Weapon beckoned? Not me.

I jumped down out of the back of the truck. I was mad. The rest of the troops loaded up and the truck left with the familiar low voiced growl of the gears and the rumbling sound only an Army truck can make.

The other two women and I stood there frustrated. "Why in the hell didn't they tell us that before we took the training?" she asked.

"Welcome to the new all-volunteer Army," the other troop said.

"Well, for me, I know how to use the damn thing," I said. "If some day I need to fire the damn thing, you bet I will. What's the first thing the enemy hits anyway? Supply lines!"

We sulked around the battalion the rest of the day, mad and with no place to direct our anger. When the guys returned from the range, we heard how one troop almost became a crispy critter. Seems he let his Parka hood fall over the back end of the LAW. Not a good thing. Flash zone is about 40 feet of pure flame from the projectile. Luckily, an instructor saw him right before he fired and prevented the barbeque.

I walked up to the sergeant. "I would not have let my parka hood fall over the back of the LAW," I said.

He nodded in response. "I know. Don't kill the messenger, Cook."

That was the one main episode which made me mad the Army treated me as a second-class citizen. There were other indignities like being issued men's long underwear to wear and cleaning urinals we only used to wash our boots off in, but those didn't really count. When you enter a male domain, you learn to adjust.

But damnit, I wanted to blow up a tank! Note to the Army: Feel free to invite me to fire a LAW. How many times in your life do you get to fulfill a woman's fantasy?

One night while teaching class I got the question I knew would come.

"What do you think about women in combat?" asked Ward. "I think women are too pretty to be shot."

"Well, Ward, you have to look at it from my perspective," I answered. "Why is it okay to say, hey, you have a penis, we get to shoot you. Hell of a birthright if you ask me. I think you guys are pretty good looking yourselves. I think if the person can do the job, let them. It's my country too."

Women have been killed, raped, tortured and brutalized in the military and during wars. Sexual discrimination happens to women and men. Those stories are important to write down for historical purposes and hopefully some healing.

There are also crazy fun situations which can only happen in the military. Being in the Army during the buildup of women in the mid-1970s, sometimes I actually pitied the men. But I must say, the majority gave us a chance to show what we could do. A far cry from some of the things I experienced later in the civilian job market.

Women served in the military unofficially from the beginning of this nation. Some women dressed as men and served. Others were camp followers, supporting the troops. The only woman recipient of the Medal of Honor, so far, is Dr. Mary Walker, a surgeon during the Civil War.

Women Marines were telephone operators in World War I in Europe. Nurses served and died in tent hospitals in Normandy after D-Day. Nurses pumped frozen blood with their hands into wounded troops during the Korean War. Vietnam War nurses triaged the wounded and decided who would live and die, and then some died themselves. There are eight women's names on the Vietnam Veterans Memorial.

In the mid-1970s we started getting into jobs as truck drivers, tank retrievers and supply sergeants. The number of women who served during Desert Storm showed how women were being utilized from flying cargo aircraft to a flight surgeon being taken a prisoner of war. Whether in Beirut, Panama, Grenada, Haiti, Somalia, Bosnia or the Iraq war when women Navy pilots flew their first combat missions, women are there, working alongside the men.

Every woman veteran's story is important to record and keep. From the trials of sexual harassment to the "firsts" women keep breaking on the planet and in space, women's history needs to be recorded.

Do Bar Fights Count?

It is incredibly easy for a woman veteran to become invisible. No one even thinks to ask if we are veterans. So, ladies, time to put pen to paper. Let's get those tales down to educate and make proud the women warriors who will come behind us.

I always found it strange for some men to think women could not be warriors. In nature, one of the scariest situations any hiker will ever come across is getting between a mother bear and her cubs. Why would anyone think it is any different getting between women and our families and country? Add in PMS and menopause and heaven help the idiot who takes on us "girls."

One of the few things that gave me comfort after September 11th was realizing I was Osama Bin Laden's worst nightmare; a college-educated weapons trained woman veteran warrior with PMS. I also knew the current batch of woman warriors were out kicking butt. Gives a whole new meaning to "The Powderpuff Girls."

Want to know some more fascinating facts about our warrior foremothers? Here are a few:

- From 1898 to 1901, twenty-two women died as a result of service in the Spanish American War. Twenty-one were Army contract nurses and one a volunteer. More than 1,500 women served in the states, overseas, and on a U.S. Hospital ship. The women's deaths were from Typhoid Fever, except one death from Malaria.
- 1917 – The Navy Department authorized enrollment of women in the Naval Reserve.
- "Legend has it that the first woman Marine was Lucy Brewer who supposedly served, disguised as a man, on board the frigate *Constitution* in the war of 1812. While there is no evidence that Miss Brewer ever wore a Marine uniform there can be no question about Opha Johnson, who on 13 August 1913 enrolled in the Marine Corps to become America's first woman Marine." *Women Marines in World War I.*
- In 1942 the Women's Air Force, Women's Army Air Corps, the Navy Women's Reserve and the Coast Guard Women's Reserve were born.
- Approximately 40,000 women served at Air-WAC bases all over the world – they included nearly half of all the women in the Army during World War II.

- 21 Army nurses escaped from Corregidor before it fell in May, 1942, but 66 of them and 11 Navy Nurses remained in Japanese prisoner of war camps in the Philippines for 37 months. Another five Navy Nurses captured at Guam were interned in a military prison in Japan.
- In 1943 a bill passed to establish the Women's Army Corps with full military status.
- In 1944 the first WACs arrive in Australia to go on to New Guinea, Hollandia, and then to the Philippines, arriving in Manila four days after enemy resistance ended.
- In 1944 the Women Air Service Pilots were disbanded, but had flown 77 different types of aircraft including the famous P-40 Flying Tiger and the B-24 bomber. A total of 38 WASPs lost their lives in the process.
- In 1951, a year after the Korean Conflict started, the Army Nurse Corps had grown from 3,500 to nearly 4,500. Between 500 and 600 served in the War Zone supporting combat troops during amphibious landing on the East coast as forces pushed toward the Yalu River.
- Eighteen women died during the Korean War from the Navy, Army and Air Force Nurse Corps.
- In 1964 at the start up of the Vietnam War, Marine Corps women's strength expanded by 70 percent and previously closed skills opened to women, with assignments to additional bases.
- In 1965 General Westmoreland insists a small group of WAC officers and enlisted women take over desk jobs in Saigon, South Vietnam.
- In 1967, Army Nurses served in Southeast Asia handling unprecedented injuries with dedication, courage and patience in the face of grave danger.
- In 1973, six Navy women become the first to win their wings and be designated Naval aviators.
- In 1974, Lt. Sally Murphy became the first female helicopter pilot in the U.S. Army.
- In 1975 the Army requires women to participate in individual weapons training. Those assigned to combat support units learned to use Light Antitank Weapons, M-16 rifles, grenade launchers, claymore mines and M-60 machine guns.

- In 1975 President Gerald Ford signed P.L. 94-106 allowing admission of women to the military academies at West Point, Annapolis, Air Force Academy and Coast Guard Academy.
- In 1976 Captain Charlotte Green flew a C-141 from Frankfurt, Germany to Charleston, South Carolina.
- In 1977 women were assigned as permanent crew on Coast Guard high endurance cutters, USCGC *Morgenthau* and USCGC *Gallantin*.
- In 1978 President Jimmy Carter signed P.L. 95-485 and the Navy began to send its women down to the sea in ships on non-combat vessels. Women can also serve on combat ships on a temporary duty basis not to exceed 180 days.
- In 1979 the Department of Defense officially recognizes the WASPs as military pilots and grants them full military benefits and privileges, May 23, 1979.
- Sally Ride is picked as the first female astronaut to go into space aboard the Space Shuttle.
- NASA Astronauts Judith Resnik and Christa McAuliffe are killed aboard the Space Shuttle Challenger on January 28, 1986.
- Sixteen women were killed during Operation Desert Storm, the majority from the Army. Sixteen percent of Gulf War veterans are women.
- There are 1.7 million women veterans in the United States.
- Women military personnel have been killed in the Iraq War. And as is befitting our warrior sisters, they are listed as fallen soldiers. Not counted by gender, but by their job and their commitment. Female blood is the same red as male blood when it spills. It is warrior blood.

Grenada, Beirut, Panama, Bosnia, Haiti, Afghanistan, Somalia, Iraq? Peacetime?

What are your stories? They ARE important. Write them down for your warrior sisters.

Resources:
They Fought Like Demons: Women Soldiers in the American Civil War by DeAnne Blanton

Nurse and Spy in the Union Army: The Adventures and Experiences of a Woman in Hospitals, Camps and Battle Fields by S. Emma E. Edmonds
Women in the Military: An Unfinished Revolution by Jeanne Holm
Our Mothers' War: American Women at Home and at the Front During World War II by Emily Yellin
American Nightingale: The Story of Frances Slanger, Forgotten Heroine of Normandy by Bob Welch
Home Before Morning: The True Story of an Army Nurse in Vietnam by Lynda Van Devanter with Christopher Morgan
She Went To War by Rhonda Cornum as told to Peter Copeland
Love My Rifle More Than You: Young and Female in the U.S. Army by Kayla Williams and Michael Staub
Women in Military Service for America Memorial Foundation (WIMSA) www.womensmemorial.org

Film – *Navajo Women Warriors: Sani Dez-bah*, Director Alice Carron

Chapter 19

Minority Veterans

"So what does it mean," I asked.
Candelario looked at me and smiled. Then he got a shy grin and wiggled his eyebrows. "It means give me a kiss," he said.
"Don't think I am going to need that to help me get around," I replied and we all laughed. Candelario was one of several Puerto Rican soldiers who worked at the Class two and four warehouse with me. They were earning their United States citizenship by serving in the Army.
"Teach me some Spanish I can use," I said.
"You can use that!" he said and everyone laughed. We had gotten into this discussion about what Spanish phrases I should learn. They felt asking for a kiss was all I really needed.
The Army in 1975 was a vast melting pot of different cultures and people. With the increase in women in the Army, everyone coped with realizing they were not in Kansas anymore. In my platoon there were Puerto Ricans, Blacks, Hawaiians, Southerners and Yanks. An occasional Native American, Eskimo, Korean, Filipino, and Asian, and some foreign transplants also added to the mix.
A long way from my white northern Yankee upbringing, it was like getting thrown into a wild stew. The culture shock which started in basic training moved along with us all to permanent party, our duty station. Women were a given minority in the Army at that time. Black women an even greater minority.
Somehow we all managed to get along. Most of the time. We learned about different cultures, dialects, food and how to swear in many different languages. Perhaps the biggest education for me was to stretch my own personal boundaries of what I thought the world was like by seeing it through someone else's eyes.
I don't know what it is like to be black, Asian, Native American, Puerto Rican, or a white man. But I do know what it was like to be a white woman in the U.S. Army in 1975. It was a ride. But I want to know what stories are out there for all minorities.
Stories like the ones about the Japanese-American troops who fought during World War II, while their families were interned at home. The Code

Talkers. Black Americans who endured before and after segregation in the military. Puerto Rican and Filipino soldiers who could not even vote in United States elections, but could die in a war for their adopted country before becoming citizens.

These are important stories which only those who lived them can tell. Plus I am sure there are many minorities I have overlooked, either because I am ill-informed or the stories are not out there to read. One newspaper story I read about an African American Native American soldier is one such tale.

On one of my many book store prowls, I came across a book titled, *Autobiography of an English Soldier in the United States Army*, by George Ballentine. A paragraph from the preface is what prompted me to buy the book to add to my treasures.

> "The text is the autobiography of George Ballentine, a Scotsman, who emigrates to America expecting to use his skill as a weaver. Unable to find work in New York City, he enlists in the United States Army and in less than two years becomes a part of General Winfield Scott's invasion force that lands at Vera Cruz and fights its way to the Mexican capital and the war's end. Ballentine, who had previously served in the British Army, provides excellent descriptions of the incredible hardships and privations of peacetime and wartime army life, particularly for the enlisted man."

Ballentine served in the U.S. Army from Aug. 12, 1845 to Aug. 13, 1850 and re-enlisted in 1851. He wrote the book in 1853. Hello! 1853. A Scotsman comes to America, joins the Army and fights a war in Mexico. How's that for travel and a mixing of cultures?

His first chapter is titled "Strange Acquaintances in New York." I bet. In chapter two titled, "First Experiences as an American Soldier," he describes his first morning as a new recruit.

> "We were roused next morning by the reveille, which is always beat a little before sunrise." Having got up with the assistance of a good-natured recruit who happened to glance into our tent, we rolled up our mattresses and folded the blankets according to regulation, and then, falling into the ranks formed in front of the tents, we answered to our names as they were called by the sergeant who had charge of us. All hands were then distributed in separate parties,

each party in charge of a corporal to 'police' or clean round the garrison."

Police call in 1845. Who knew?

How many other millions of stories are out there by Scotsmen, Australians, Canadians, and anybody else who might have served in the United States military to earn their citizenship? Like Eric, one veteran in class, who survived being interned as a British child with his family for three years during World War II when Hong Kong fell. He later came to America and served with the Air Force. Then came to class and wrote his stories.

What are your stories? Write them!

Resources:
Bloods: An Oral History of the Vietnam War by Black Veterans by Wallace Terry
We Were There: Voices of African American Veterans, from World War II to the War in Iraq by Yvonne Latty and Ron Tarver
American Patriots: The Story of Blacks in the Military from the Revolution to Desert Storm by Gail Buckley

Chapter 20

Gay and Lesbian Veterans

I was nineteen, a virgin, and confused.

"We fell in love with each other," Sara said.

"How did this start?" I asked.

"Remember when you fell in the river up on the Continental Divide and we put you in the truck cab to thaw out?"

"Yes."

"Well, we slept together in the truck bed to keep warm all night and one thing led to another."

I stared at my two Army women roommates. It wasn't a huge surprise. Sara and Angela had been sleeping in Sara's room since the trip. Angela had hickies on her neck and I knew she hadn't seen her married boyfriend since we got back from camping.

"This will all work out," Sara said. "Your boyfriend can move in and it will work."

Our fourth housemate had moved out and we needed another to be able to pay the rent.

This episode was my first known encounter with a lesbian relationship. It was quite difficult to sort it all out since I was still learning about my own sexuality.

"This sounds odd, even to my ears, but I feel like our friendship has been broken," I said. "Not because you two are together, but because I will never have as close a relationship with the both of you like we had before. You're a couple."

We all looked at each other and they nodded their heads in agreement.

This was 1976.

Don't ask, don't tell wasn't even a homophobic idea in some top brass's scurvy brain. After we decided to all move out of the house, I somehow ended up being the one to break the news to Angela's married boyfriend, another Army sergeant. You just never know what life is going to throw at you.

According to the 1990 census approximately one-sixth of one percent of the United States population is gay or lesbian. Apply that statistic to the 1.5 million active duty troops and at any time we have about 2,500 homosexuals in the military. Same percentages for Guard and Reserve. Given I'm a writer and not a mathematician, that number might be kinda close. Or not. Since the United States population was about 297,755,670 on Nov. 27, 2005, that would mean one percent would be about (2,977,556 divided in half would be) 1,488,778, plus that other one percent. I don't like story problems. Don't quote me on the math. Basically, lots of people are gay or lesbian in the United States.

In the Air Force Reserve there was a saying, "What goes TDY, stays TDY." TDY meaning temporary duty away from base. Whether people cheated on their marriages or had affairs, the bottom line in the military is everybody knows what everybody else is doing. That usually includes who is gay, who cheats on their spouse and who is a *Star Wars* geek.

We are a family, dysfunctional at best, but a family. Thinking gays and lesbians should not be in the military makes me crazy. They have been, they are, they will be. Get over it.

Anybody who reads security reports knows the biggest threat to leak military secrets are heterosexual men. I think if we increase women and gays to 52 percent of the military, we improve that security issue.

With the advent of AIDS, being gay or lesbian in the military carried increasing risks, not only of career-ending exposure, but deadly health risks. We aerovaced some military patients with AIDS, mostly from drug use. But this is an equal opportunity killer disease which now counts middle-age heterosexual women as one of its major new targets.

Personally, I have no idea what it is like to be gay or lesbian in the military. Being a heterosexual woman was challenge enough for me. That is why those veterans need to write down their stories. Gays and Lesbians will always be with the military and they have stories to tell. Write 'em!

Resources:
My Navy Too by Beth F. Coye, Commander, U.S. Navy (Ret.)
Secret Service: Untold Stories of Lesbians in the Military by Zsa Zsa Gershick

Web Resources:
www.usnaout.org - U.S. Naval Academy Out
SAGALA – Service Academy Gay And Lesbian Alumni
www.academygala.org

Chapter 21

Biker Veterans

"You should go on the run," Mikel Matthews said to me as I stood in his driveway in August 1997. He and Big Dave were tinkering with one of their Harleys. We were discussing why I had quit my job to write about veteran issues and to teach veterans to write their war stories.

"What's The Run?" I asked. Matthews, my next door neighbor, told me the *Run For The Wall* is to honor and raise awareness of the POW/MIA issue. He made sure I saw the 1991 videotape. I was hooked.

Nine months later at 4:15 p.m. on May 7, 1998, I got the call from the hospital. "They're going to let him go," Cindy Matthews told me, her voice holding as much surprise as she felt. "Can you still go?"

"You bet," I answered. Mikel had been diagnosed with lung cancer in November. We had continued making reservations for The Run, but at the end of March it didn't look like he would make the trip.

My goal was to write about the other veterans on The Run, but it turned into my own journey as a woman veteran. I felt honored to be included with Mikel and Cindy as we threw things together and headed down the road from Portland, Oregon to Los Angeles. The love in their close knit family was evident in those hurried two days. Cindy, Lindy, 17, and Nick, 14, worked under Mikel's instructions to build a trailer to haul the Harley-Davidson Fat Boy.

Mikel drove the van out of Portland at 5 a.m. on Sunday, May 10. "Let's get the gross stuff out of the way," he said to me. "Sometimes I get sick in the morning from the chemo and I throw up."

"Doesn't bother me," I replied. "Been in medicine for eight years. Besides, if you don't mind if I fart, we're okay."

"You fart and he will throw up," Cindy laughed. So the tone for the trip was set. I found out they hadn't told anyone they were coming. It would be a complete surprise when we hit Ontario, California.

Mikel and Cindy told me tales of The Run, the Black Sheep, and different riders as we drove toward California. Mikel was coping amazingly well with not being able to do the things he normally did and Cindy had picked up the task of being even stronger than normal.

Do Bar Fights Count?

We arrived in Ontario on Monday afternoon. Mikel was greeted with open arms and hugs. Everyone was glad to see Mikel, but some didn't recognize him. The normally bear-sized man with hair down his back had been replaced by a warrior once again fighting a battle with chemotherapy as his weapon. But Mikel's quick wit still snapped in his eyes.

Every once in awhile he would nail one of us with a pithy comment.

The day spent visiting friends on Tuesday was probably the highlight of their trip. Mikel drove the van out of Ontario on May 12 behind the RFTW bikes. The days of riding in the van soon took a toll on his strength.

"We want you to ride with the pack tomorrow," Cindy said that evening. "Perhaps we can get you a ride in the chase truck. And you might ask around if you could get a ride with someone else, because we might be turning back."

"I don't like to run with the pack," Mikel explained. "We are called the Black Sheep because we ride ahead of the pack, then greet them at the next stop."

Pops Borskey of Louisiana, a World War II Seabee, came to my rescue and agreed to haul me in his red chase truck to D.C.

It became clear I was on an important quest myself. I hadn't realized I had allowed myself to become invisible as a woman veteran. I still didn't think my stories were important. The Run changed that for me.

When Mikel and Cindy turned around before Cimarron, N.M., I felt I was completing the trip for the both of them. My emotions were all over the board with the fast takeoff of the trip and then suddenly being in the company of strangers. But they weren't strangers, they were veterans.

When I went into the post-Vietnam Army in 1975 as a private, I served with men who only talked about Vietnam when they were drunk. They had old soul eyes.

People asked me what it was like to be a woman veteran back then. I told them I met great people and made some wonderful friends.

And, yes, there were times when I was scared. Like the time I awoke at 3 a.m. while on Reforger in Germany to find a man standing over my cot. Since my other roommates were away for the weekend, I was alone. I knew who he was.

Doing my best to sound mad, wearing only a t-shirt, I summoned up my command voice and told him to "Get the hell out of here. What do you think you're doing?" He left, begging me not to report him. I didn't, but I did booby trap the door with empty pop cans and my mess kit.

When a woman ventures into a man's world, she realizes she will not meet all princes. I picked my battles. On the other hand, I got to travel, use the G.I.

bill, and get two home loans. Plus I rode in helicopters, cargo aircraft, drove a deuce and a half and Jeep, and rode in armored personnel carriers and a tank. How I missed a motorcycle I am still not sure.

The majority of my Army memories are good. The friends I made I've kept for a lifetime. And the Army always gave me a worse situation to compare anything I've bumped up against since. After you've hung your butt over a slit trench dealing with diarrhea in the pouring rain, praying your shaking knees won't give out, the rest of life's accommodations appear pretty good.

Ten years later I entered the Air Force Reserve in time for a little thing called Desert Storm. I worked five and a half months deploying my Aeromedical Evacuation Squadron out of McChord Air Force Base to Saudi Arabia, Germany, England and Texas. Handing out chemical gear, atropine syringes and weapons to Reserve friends took an emotional toll I am now just able to reconcile. The Run took me by Scott Air Force Base.

Due to low casualties, I was back home from Scott AFB in a month and spent four more months demobilizing my unit. But when I told people I was a Desert Storm veteran they always asked where I served. "Stateside," I replied. "Oh," was their answer. Like it didn't count. I quit telling people I was a Desert Storm veteran. I became invisible.

On The Run, when the kids in Rainelle, West Virginia asked me to sign their books, t-shirts and shoes, I was honored. They didn't care where I served, they just knew I was a veteran. And that was enough.

By the time we got to Washington, D.C., I bought a VET patch to sew on the new vest I would buy to replace the one I threw together for the trip. I wear the 1998 Run bracelet every POW/MIA Day to reconnect me to the Run and the POW/MIA cause.

When I met up with my new biker family at Rick and Shirley Whiting's Sturgis RFTW Reunion in August, I showed them the stories I had started to write. Rod "Bungee" Coffey told me to expand them, then challenged me to write about myself. So now I am.

But on Saturday, Aug. 8, 1998, I walked down main street Sturgis, South Dakota, with my new vest on, sporting Mikel's POW/MIA patch with Desert Storm Vet added underneath and my unit patches on the front. It was an important statement to make for myself, plus I felt Mikel was there in spirit.

I flew back from Sturgis on Aug. 9. Mikel Matthews died the morning of Aug. 10, 1998 at age 46. The RFTW riders were at his family's side and attended the funeral and procession to the Willamette National Cemetery.

Our presence was a comfort to Mikel and Cindy's families—they said so. Their daughter, Lindy, slept in her dad's leather vest. I talked to Nick and said we would have to get him one. Suzanne Sigona is taking care of that for her "brother" Mikel.

Suzanne's words when she introduced me to the rest of the Black Sheep in the hotel in Ontario, California, still ring true. "These guys taught me how to hug," she said.

I will always be grateful to Mikel and Cindy Matthews for inviting me on the run and to the Black Sheep button brigade for adopting me along the way. I won't ever be an invisible woman veteran again. I think Mikel would approve.

****

I wrote that story in 1998. It was one of the few things I ever read of mine in the *Writing War Stories* classes.

I kept a personal diary, pictures and pieces of that ride. There is a book there too, I'm sure. Some impressions from my journey?

Some of Kim's Favorite Run For The Wall X Quotes

Cindy: "When we pull up to a stop sign with the Harley, people either dive for the door locks or love it."
On the road to Ontario, CA, May 11.

Hawaii Mike: "Do you have any Earl Grey tea?"
At T.G.I.F. Restaurant in Ontario, Tuesday May 12.
(Can't tell you how comforting it was to know there was a fellow tea drinker among the bikers.)

Pops: "Don't want no skinny woman. A man wants a trampoline girl he can bounce on."(This is a wonderful thing for a full-figured woman to hear.)
On the way to Gallup, N.M. in the chase truck on May 14.

Kathy, whose daughter worked at Angel Fire, (I met her in the parking lot): "The Indians say if you find a home and work, then the mountains have accepted you. We found both, so I guess they have."
Angel Fire, May 15.

Jerry: "If I had a nickel for every time that dog's picture has been in the paper, I'd be a rich man."
After leaving Cimarron, N.M., about his dog, Dawn's, picture in the Albuquerque newspaper, May 16.

Big Dave: "Well, today's Sunday. The paper costs more on Sunday."
His comment after I complained I couldn't get the stupid newspaper machine to give me a paper for 50 cents. I didn't know what was wrong with it.
SUNDAY, May 17 in Limon, Colorado.

Iron Mike: "Shall we dance?"
In response to the loud music coming from the grandstand.
Salina, Kansas on May 17.

Beanie: "I bet they'd give up two ceiling tiles so you could leave your butt prints at the Red Hiney Bar."
To me on the morning of May 18, Salina, Kansas.

Rick/Papa Smurf: "Well, I bet you've got something to write about now."
Usually said after some catastrophe or weird happening. Averaged about once a day.
This time after the LONG Harley Shop stop in Salina, Kansas on May 18.

Claudia's Mom using the C.B. to communicate with some crude truckers: "If you were my sons, I'd wash your mouths out with soap."
Not a sound was heard on the airways after that.
Going into Wentzville, MO on May 18.

Crash: "The first time I went on the run, I wanted to do the cross country trip. Then the guys became like mentors to me. These guys are my heroes."
May 19, in the chase truck on the way into Corydon, Indiana.

Vince: "This used to be a pilgrimage, now it's an event."
In the food tent, May 20, Huntington, West Virginia.

Squirrel: "Hey, I'm not doing too bad. I can see Bungee's helmet now."
Heard over the C.B. radio going into Rainelle, West Virginia, May 21.

Do Bar Fights Count?

C.B.: "It helps me to talk about it. But I can't talk about certain things for 35 years."
In Rainelle, West Virginia, May 21.

Jerry: "I love the Wall, but I hate to visit it."
In Rainelle, West Virginia, May 21.

Duke: "I put 5.7 gallons of gas in my tank. I think I have a five gallon tank!"
In Washington, D.C., Fairfax, Alexandria and wherever the hell else we were that day. This was the gas stop on the way to the D.C. Ramblers Club House, that we never got to. May 23.

Big Dave: "We made that u-turn and started up that freeway. I said, 'We're fucked.'"
On the above mentioned lost sheep run in D.C., May 23.

Cisco: "Being in the original Black Sheep meant we supported the mission of the run, but disagreed with the management."
In the Comfort Inn pool, May 23, Fairfax, Virginia.

Squirrel: "Rick don't care if you piss in his Cheerios."
On the grass in Washington, D.C., eating lunch after Rolling Thunder, May 24.
I didn't catch the first part of the comment, but the ending was great.

Duke: "The only thing I can do six times a night is go to the bathroom."
On The Mall, Washington, D.C., May 24.

Wizard: "My counselor told me that if I wasn't a painter, sculptor or French pastry baker, I couldn't be sensitive all the time. Artists are the only ones who get away with being sensitive all the time."
After visiting the Korean War Memorial, on The Mall, May 24.
(I was glad to find out as an artistic writer I could now be moody. What a different Run it would have been for you all.)

Bungee: "This is what I like. Relaxing with a cup of coffee, a smoke and good conversation with these turkeys."
After Rolling Thunder 1998 at the D.C. Ramblers Club House, May 24.

There is a legacy between Harley Davidson motorcycles and veterans. While Harleys were first used by police officers starting in 1908 in Detroit, Michigan:

By the time the United States entered the First World War in 1917, H-D machines had already seen action in skirmishes against the forces of Pancho Villa, the Mexican revolutionary. Under General "Black Jack" Pershing, machine-gun-toting Harley-Davidson's proved themselves ideal for border patrols in rough terrain. From *The Ultimate Harley-Davidson* by Mac Mcdiarmid.

The book goes on to state that some 20,000 motorcycles were used in World War I, the majority Harley-Davidsons. More than 90,000 Harley-Davidson motorcycles were used in World War II. John E. Harley also trained Army motorcyclists at Fort Knox, Kentucky.

And how about women and motorcycles? According to a documentary from Harley Davidson on women riders, women served in World War II, also riding Harleys. I am still trying to track that story down.

All I know is there is nothing like the sound of a Harley. Especially when it is the rumble of 150 or more starting up at dawn to ride across the United States to honor Prisoners of War and those Missing In Action.

That's just one reason why on the Sunday before Memorial Day in Washington, D.C., you hear *Rolling Thunder*.

Harleys and veterans, together again.

Got biker stories? Get it in gear!

Afterword: On Dec. 18, 2004, I had the joy of attending Lindy's wedding reception. Suzanne flew in from Denver and Big Dave and Carina drove up from California. We were all thrilled to learn the rider who bought Mikel's bike brought it into the studio and Lindy had pictures taken in her wedding dress with her dad's Fat Boy. The wedding photographer was a Harley guy too.

We all felt Mikel was there with us. And we knew he wanted to be blowing up firecrackers in the parking lot!

Web Resources:
www.rollingthunder1.com
www.rftw.org

Chapter 22

Incarcerated Veterans

I had to buy a new bra to go to prison. At least I thought I did when I was told no underwires were allowed. The occasion was an invite from the Oregon State Penitentiary Veterans Association to come and speak to them about the *Writing War Stories* class.

The process involved finding out which of my students wanted to go, then getting full names, addresses, social security numbers and birth dates. The staff had to run police checks on us to make sure we were okay to visit prison. Somehow this hit me as funny. I think I got into the Army by breathing.

With a car pool chain we were off on the Monday night drive to Salem in a howling rain and windstorm. Meeting up at Wendy's in Tualatin, Dave Hammond drove us all down. We joked and laughed in the big red suburban, but my nerves were on edge.

We pulled into the prison parking lot and tried to figure out how to get into the place. A gentleman in a rain slicker came over and told us the guard was waiting for us. We killed time until Mike, our fellow writer who counseled the veteran inmates for PTSD, showed up to help us find the entrance. Built in 1869ish, the concrete and steel structure looked like a cross between a prison and a Spanish hacienda. Even yellow in color.

The corrections officer, Ms. Brownley, welcomed our group and signed us in. Being the only "special visitors" that night, we were our own group. We put our things into lockers and hung up our wet coats. After we signed in and showed her our picture identification, it was time for the mandatory stripping.

The OSP metal detector is about a trillion times more sensitive than the one at the airport. Pre-September 11, 2001, that is. For good reason. I ended up taking off my shoes, earrings, watch, vest and glasses. I passed. No wonder the underwire bras were out.

After we were all through the strip and re-dress phase, she moved us down a hall to the first set of gates. White bars. Very clean place. This was master control. When they opened the gate, we came into the little room, surrounded on three sides by bars and the other wall a glass cage with dark windows. It looked a lot like the flight operations center at the Air Force Operations building.

We were instructed to put our right hand in a slot in the door with our driver's license, then wait to get our hand stamped. The young corrections officer checked our names, and then stamped our hands with invisible ink. At least I think that is what he put on my hand.

We were given a red visitors badge in exchange for our driver's license, which he kept. (I didn't realize this until I panicked three-fourths of the way through the evening and realized I didn't have my license. My vet students laughed because they had all done the same thing.)

Next came the opening of the bars and we were led down a long cold corridor to another set of bars. The walls were light blue and the floor the most highly polished tan linoleum I have ever seen. Obviously there were buffer fiends amongst us.

We came to another little walled dark glass cubicle, perhaps secondary control. Each of us had to walk up to the dark glass and show the number on our red badge to verify our visitor status. Since the red badge was clasped on the top parts of our bodies, I was once again shoving my flat boobs in someone's face. (Let me explain flat boobs. Sports bra without underwires plus gravity equals flat boobs. Nuf said.)

While we waited we could see inmates being walked through what looked like a main traffic hallway beyond the bars in front of us. Lots of inmates. As the doors opened for us to walk in, my nerves were a little shot. They weren't going to wait for them to pass. Three corrections officers stood to our left, evenly spaced out. They were strac, shined and spit polished to the max, with uniforms pressed into creases. (I have learned those creases are actually sewn in these days. Who knew?)

One or two of the inmates spotted me and said something like, "Whoa, look at that" or some sort of comment. I moved closer to the corrections officer, picking a large one, and in amongst my students. Of course, everybody had figured before hand they were probably talking about Dave. Not me. I'm thinking it might have been my biker vest. After all, I had flat boobs.

We marched across the wide open interchange area to another locked gate, where we went upstairs to the activities room.

"Wow, I didn't think they were going to walk us right in with the guys like that," Dave said to me as we climbed the stairs.

"Yeah, imagine how I feel about it," I replied.

Dave started to laugh, then proceeded to howl. Glad I could lighten up the moment for him.

Do Bar Fights Count?

We walked into a large room closely resembling my grade school cafeteria. Wood stage, linoleum floor, light blue paint and white perforated ceiling tiles cris-crossed by black pipes. A large mural on the far wall depicted Mount Hood and had many interesting items hidden in it – kind of the Where's Waldo theme. I liked the raccoon best.

One inmate told me to go over by the brooms to their office. First thinking he might be referring to me to ride the broom, we soon realized it was their work space for the veterans organization. Dave and Doug and I filed in.

"That corner belongs to the lifers, and this is our space for the veterans association." We nodded and I tried to figure out why they had a desk area for folks retired from the military. Then it dawned on me. Not military lifers, prison lifers. Duh.

I chatted with the inmate and answered questions about how we wanted the room set up. I felt it was fine with the podium and microphone, though a bit formal. But with the size of the room and expecting 50 to 60 inmates, we would need the PA system.

"Could you move a round table up to the front for us to sit at?" I asked. I wanted to make sure the inmates could see our reactions to the readings – considering some of the content.

Drinks were brought over, lime green Kool-aid in white paper cups with light blue designs. Amazing stuff, really. Inmates began to file in. Some came up and chatted with us, others milled around or sat down.

Mike introduced me to a couple of members in his PTSD veterans group.

"I don't much believe in this stuff," the one veteran said. "There are some places that are just too hard to go." I agreed with him that everyone has to write at their own pace, but I thought it was really the only way to heal, to lance the boil.

There was a tentativeness about the inmates approaching us and us them, but not for long. I was always talking to someone and knew the guys were busy too – I could hear them conversing behind and around me. Their blue shirts and blue jeans were the definite uniform, but they all had different shoes. Somehow I guess we thought they would have military issue uniforms, shoes included.

The vice president of the association introduced me and I was on. I gave a little talk about how important it is to write their stories down, how it helps not only them, but others. Then I talked about the challenges of writing the hard stuff and the truth – swearing included. Phillip was on point, so he read his "This is it" piece about the first day he was committed to action in World War II Germany as an Infantry scout.

He was well received and looked for other World War II vets, but they were not there. Only about seven were in the prison, he was told. The corrections officers later said by the time the inmates reach into their late 40s and early 50s, they usually quit coming back – they've finally learned they don't want to be there.

Chuck was next up with his story about wet socks. Thankfully he read slowly and the guys started to chuckle. We were concerned how they would take a story about the mad masturbator, but they were laughing in all the right places, and some quite loudly. We knew we would be okay.

Next came Dave who read about his last day in the Vietnam bush, plus letting them know he was the coordinator for the Americal Division.

Then Doug read his cocoa scene and some of "The Bantam." He read very well and held their attention with his quiet intensity.

Last but not least was Bob. "The Fucking Monkey" hit a high point with them and we ended on laughs. Next we had a reading of two poems from one of the veteran inmates. They were wonderful poems.

We took a break and then everyone wanted to talk to us. Topics and questions ranged from how to get started writing, to how to help a son on the outside having problems, to how to get the VA to reopen a claim. All of them were polite and respectful. And one was a little nuts. Many thanked us for coming and wanted to know if I would teach at the prison.

"I didn't go to work tonight to come to this," said one inmate. "I'm really glad I did. It lifted me up."

While I was told how long a term they had left on their sentences, one with 20 years and one with two months, Bob was being told who was in for murder and child molestation. I felt better not knowing who was who. After the break we reconvened for more questions.

Questions ranged from "Why didn't you kill the Fucking Monkey" to "Will this be offered as a correspondence course?" I was also given copies of poems, the vet's newsletter, and return addresses. Then I had to surrender them all to one of the correction's officers to be mailed to me. Could only take out what I brought in. We were only supposed to stay until 8 p.m., but it was 8:30 p.m. before we left.

Back down the stairs we went, out the locked gate to the main hallway; very little traffic this time. A correction's officer asked me about the Warrior Tales patch on my vest, as I waited for the rest of the group to clear secondary control. Seems he served 17 years with the Army. We passed into the long hallway and noticed the ORKIN bug man being escorted into the place. Bugs, huh?

Back to another gate, then master control. Hand the visitor badge with my right hand, have my hand stamp checked, then get my driver's license back. Back in line to be let out of master control.

The steel bars slid along their path and we walked up the inclined gray carpeted hall to the visitor processing room. Along came Ms. Bradley who let us back into the reception area to retrieve our goodies.

"So, how did you like your first visit to prison?" she asked.

"It reminds me a lot of the inside of a ship," Chuck replied. "They even serve the same Kool-Aid."

A sigh of relief and some giddiness pervaded the air as we packed up and headed back out into the pouring rain.

"I don't mind the rain now," said Dave. "They don't get to experience it."

Back in the big red Suburban, we joked and kidded about the event, the different inmates and compared notes. I drove Doug back to Mt. Hood Community College, then headed for home. A quick stop at Albertson's produced Rocky Road ice cream and peanut butter cookies. My treat for the day.

I came home and watched the *Ally McBeal* television show I had taped and ate away. Then off to bed and a good night's rest. Thankful I wasn't behind bars.

And realizing the thought of strapping on my underwire bra the next morning was a new kind of freedom I didn't even know I had.

How must it feel to live behind bars? Those are stories only those who have walked that path can tell. If you have served time or are serving time now, please, let writing set you free. Write those stories!

Resources:
Dancing to the Concertina's Tune; A Prison Teacher's Memoir, by Jan Walker

Chapter 23

Corrections Officers

You never know who you're going to meet at Alcatraz. I turned the corner into the former barracks to see the introduction film. Outside the gift shop, Frank Heaney, Alcatraz's youngest guard, was signing his book.

"I worked here from 1948 to 1951, until the Korean War" he told the man in front of me. Veteran alert!

Standing in line to get my copy of his book signed, I read about his having served in the Coast Guard at the end of World War II. The book didn't say anything about his Korean War service. When it was my turn for his signature, I asked him.

"Yes, I served in the Navy on a destroyer in the Korean War," he explained. "Dropping depth charges, it wasn't much fun." I thanked him for his service, both times.

His book, *Inside the Walls of Alcatraz*, written with coauthor Gay Machado, chronicles what it was like to serve at "The Rock," back in the day and before the Sean Connery and Nicholas Cage movie of the same name.

> "I was the youngest guard ever to serve at Alcatraz, and I saw *first-hand* exactly what happened. I know that many of the horror stories had no basis in fact. But I also know that Alcatraz was indeed a living hell for many of its inmates – a hopeless, deadening end of the road. In a way I think it might have been worse than the stories the public *was* fed.
>
> The story of Alcatraz, the federal prison, is one of drab, lonely waiting, sudden bursts of violence and, yes, some harsh solitary confinement. It is also the story of some extraordinary people."

Because Frank Heaney and Gay Machado took the time to write down his stories, we have a correction officer's view of Alcatraz. Corrections officers face different challenges and threats than patrol officers. I remember one display at a Romance Writers Convention where U.S. Marshals had a display of shivs seized in federal prisons.

Do Bar Fights Count?

Inmates had made knives, shanks or shivs from a variety of items – coat hangers, Styrofoam cups, utensils, the variety was amazing. Inmates have time on their hands and corrections officers have to be aware at all times.

I've heard stories from folks who work at our county jail that would curl your hair. They range from the bizarre to the deadly. From suicides to repeat offenders who come in to get their medical care. The public rarely sees inside these institutions and we are both repelled and attracted to them.

One writer, Ted Conover, who let his curiosity get the better of him, wrote *Newjack: Guarding Sing Sing*, a book about what it was like to work at Sing Sing prison for a year as a rookie guard, or "newjack." The book explores "the harsh culture of prison, the grueling and demeaning working conditions of the officers, and the unexpected ways the job encroaches on his own family life."

Corrections work is a tough and demanding field. It is also a field where the balance of power and abuse must be carefully monitored to prevent the inevitable power plays of jailer versus incarcerated.

My one occasion entering a military stockade was to attend a Military Police graduation. Okay, so only the Military Police would hold a graduation in a stockade, guess it had the biggest room. It was Fort Carson, Colorado in the late 1970s. One of my many roommates had completed the sergeant school and I was invited to attend.

After getting cleared and escorted through the air lock, or whatever they call it, we entered the main cell block. As the large metal door slammed into place behind me and the sound actually reverberated, just like in the movies, I had two distinct and opposite reactions.

I had an overwhelming urge to yell, "You'll never take me alive, copper!" like a bad James Cagney movie, and at the same time confess to every crime ever committed on the planet. And I was just there for a graduation ceremony. I knew I was leaving. Most likely.

Perhaps that is when it occurred to me that the corrections officers who worked there probably had longer sentences than the inmates, in most cases. They and the support staff were locked up for years. How does that affect your psyche?

Those are other military stories which need to be written down. How do military corrections officers maintain order, both stateside and during war? I remember during Desert Storm when so many Iraq soldiers were surrendering, the military police had quite a challenge on their hands. How to contain, search, feed and figure out the real bad guys from the run of the mill troops given the large numbers of prisoners they suddenly had on their hands.

What was that like? How do veterans who work in corrections today deal with the daily challenges? What are the stories? Write them down! Enquiring minds want to know. Trust me.

There are more than a million visitors to Alcatraz each year. When on the boat ride over and walking around the grounds, I heard British and Australian accents, and Italian, Chinese, Vietnamese and Spanish being spoken. People all over the world want to know about The Rock.

The same is true for your stories. Get busy. You never know where something can be used. The recent *Code 7 Cookbook* created as a fundraiser for two Clackamas and Grant County deputies shot in the line of duty included a recipe submitted by my friend, Joyce. Her mother, Dorothy, had received the recipe while on a visit to the Oregon State Penitentiary with Joyce's father, Jim Brouillette, former Deputy Chief of the Portland Police Bureau. Her mother so loved the bread, she had to get the recipe.

The bread? Jailhouse Rolls. And yes, you can also get a collection of the Alcatraz recipes at either gift shop on The Rock.

The Rock started out as the first lighthouse on the West coast and was an important military fort in 1853. In 1861 the island began receiving military prisoners from the Civil War. In 1934 the military closed their prison. Within a month, the rock became a federal penitentiary until it closed in March, 1963. In October, 1972, the rock became part of the Golden Gate National Recreation Area and is operated by the National Park Service.

One account details how the military showed up at the rock again in May, 1946, when six inmates attempted to escape Alcatraz. They took nine guards hostage and refused to surrender when their plan went awry.

"U.S. Marines shelled the cell house, and five Coast Guard ships and a Navy destroyer circled the island," according to Ernest B. Lageson's book, *Battle at Alcatraz: A Desperate Attempt to Escape the Rock*. After the three-day siege, the inmates shot the hostages to eliminate witnesses. Ernest Lageson Sr. was one of the guards shot and left for dead. He survived, testified at the trial, and his son wrote the book in tribute to his father.

And guess what? Ernest Lageson Sr. served in the Navy during World War II. His son also served in the Navy and was the newspaper boy at Alcatraz.

You never know who you might meet at Alcatraz. Do you have correction officer stories? Get them down on paper.

Resources:
Inside the Walls of Alcatraz by Frank Heany and Gay Machado
Battle At Alcatraz by Ernest B. Lageson
Alcatraz by Richard Dunbar
Alcatraz at War by John H. Martini
Newjack: Guarding Sing Sing by Ted Conover
Code 7 Cookbook 2004 by Clackamas County Sheriff's Office Cookbook Committee, Oregon City, Oregon

Web Sites:
Golden Gate National Recreation Area
www.nps.gov/alcatraz

Alcatraz – History, Archives, Links
www.notfrisco.com/alcatraz

CCSO
www.co.clackamas.or.us/sheriff

Chapter 24

Law Officers

July 1997. I sat on the stairs in my nightgown holding the loaded Colt 45. Two a.m. in the morning, I heard the running footsteps outside on the street. Moving to the open window, I peered out into the dark and saw the officer running behind a German Shepherd police dog.

"Over here," I yelled. "In my backyard."

The officer stopped and turned to run into my back yard. "Rocko!" he shouted. The dog turned and ran in front of him, into my backyard where a fleeing felon had impaled himself on my cyclone fence.

I moved to my bedroom window and watched in the darkness as Rocko stopped behind the 12 foot hedge.

"Up Rocko, up," I heard the officer command and they were off through my neighbors' backyard. I sat back down on the steps and waited. I had been awakened by a loud crash. Perhaps a large tree falling. When I looked out my front windows, a man ran into my backyard. I knew it wasn't my neighbor Mikel. Rushing back to my bedroom windows, I saw him dash headlong into the tall arborvitae hedge. He tried to run through it, unaware my dad had tied it with strings. He seemed to boomerang around in the bushes then must have fallen onto the low cyclone fence.

"I'm hurt," I heard coming from the bushes.

Enough of this, I thought. I locked and loaded Grandpa's gun. If he had any idea of crashing through my patio door, it would be target practice from my perch on the stairs. I called 911.

Turns out the police were pursuing a man who rolled a car on the busy street close to my house. He ran from the accident and they were in hot pursuit. I laughed to think how much smarter Rocko the police dog was than the perp. Rocko knew to stop at the fence before he went over.

While I waited, police and sheriff cars moved through the neighborhood. Area dogs barked up a chorus and I sat and said a prayer for all the officers. One week before, Portland Police Officer Thomas Jeffries was shot and killed not ten blocks from my house. He had been chasing a suspect accused of shooting a 7-year-old-boy, running through the neighborhood, just like tonight.

Do Bar Fights Count?

The suspect had fired at Jeffries and shot him right above his flak vest. He died quickly, leaving behind his wife, pregnant with their first child.

This was only the second time I had called 911 in my life. Still the officers responded. Even after the death of one of their own, not more than a week ago.

Several years later, I worked for Clackamas County in video production. We were shooting a new program introduction for the County's very own *Most Wanted* show for the government television channel. Deputy Andrew McVey was shadowing the current Public Information Officer at the time, Sergeant Damon Coates. I found out Andrew had been in the military and asked him how he thought being in the military was different from being a deputy.

"One of the deputies at the Jail, a former Marine, describes it best," he said. "When you're in the military you usually go to a place and that is the battle zone. When you're in law enforcement, you live and work in your combat zone. So do your family and friends."

It is an excellent description of the differences faced by law enforcement personnel, who of course include a lot of former active duty and current reserve and guard members. That discussion took place before Sept. 11, 2001.

It was before Sergeant Damon Coates was shot in the face in the line of duty on Jan. 9, 2003. When the news first came over the television about who was shot, not only did I gasp watching my television set, but the on-air reporters gasped also. Everyone knew and liked Damon. He was our own Tom Selleck of Clackamas County and a nice guy with a great family.

Damon and his family are still working their way back. He was not expected to live, but he fought the odds and is now actually beginning to walk again. It has been three years and still he and his wife, Tammy, work toward him coming back to work.

Since the day Andrew said those words to me, they have echoed in my mind many times, especially the night Damon was shot. Deputy McVey is Damon's brother-in-law. It suddenly became a very real war zone for all of them that night, right here in Clackamas County, Oregon.

Combine the toll of law enforcement service along with or in addition to military service, and one begins to get a glimpse of why law enforcement personnel and their families are a very tight knit group. They live, work, play and sometimes die in their war zones, right here on United States soil.

What about those Military and Shore Police stories too? How about getting those down on paper? To this day I'm sure I traumatized a young MP for life at Fort Carson, Colorado. They were clearing us through military customs to go to Europe for Reforger in 1978. The large trunk I had painstakingly taken three days to pack had its contents spewed across the gym floor.

Since there were only two women out of the 52 Army folks on the flight, my contents were quite colorful. The young MP began to carefully squeeze frisk each one of my Tampons. I was not amused. It must have been my Sergeant tone when I said, "If you keep that up I won't be able to use them," that made him drop the current victim like a hot potato. To this day I wonder if he knew what they were. He did blush a nice shade of red. Hopefully he did stay in law enforcement.

Like firefighters who rush into burning buildings, law enforcement officers run toward shootings. I am thankful we still have women and men who have the courage and compassion to put on the uniform every day.

Because some day a fleeing felon hopped up on meth may be in your backyard and the only thing between you and him is Rocko the police dog and his officer. And they do come when you call for help.

Law enforcement stories? Write em, Dano. (For those of you too young to have seen the television show *Hawaii Five-O*, ask one of us old veterans what that means.)

Resources:
I Love A Cop; What Police Families Need To Know, by Ellen Kirschman, Ph.D.
Closely Watched Shadows; A Profile of The Hunter and the Hunted, by Ronald Turco, M.D.

Web Sites:
www.tributetohonor.org

Chapter 25

Emergency Medical Personnel and Firefighters

The Washington, D.C. bar was noisy all around us, but Doc and I had been sitting there for three hours.

"I don't know why I'm telling you all this stuff," he said.

"Maybe because I'm listening," I replied. Doc was sipping on his third beer and I was pounding down 7Ups with cherries.

It was a night in May 1998. We had finished all the *Rolling Thunder* events and gone out to dinner at a restaurant near the hotel. Doc was a medic in Vietnam who rode with us in the biker parade. Don't know his "real" name to this day.

"I had to make life or death decisions every day over there," he said. "Who I would save and who I had to let go. So many guys with legs blown off."

"Have you ever met anyone you saved?"

"Hell, no," he answered. "Wouldn't want to."

"Why?"

"I couldn't face them telling me I should have let them die instead of coming back without their legs."

Welcome to the daymares of medics and medical personnel. Improvements made in medical practice in the Korean and Vietnam War have moved on to make sure more soldiers are brought back alive, but with major wounds. The current aerovac patients from the Iraq war are coming home quicker and being transported on aircraft with very serious injuries. It takes a toll on all the medical crews who care for them at every step of their journey and at journey's end.

"The part that's hard is, we never hear what happens to them," I remember one of our flight nurses telling me after Desert Storm. "We haul them out from Kuwait or Germany and then we never know if they're okay or not. There are always a couple patients who stay with you."

The military tries to prepare medical personnel for the harsh realities of war, but the real thing involves all the senses. In Medical Indoctrination Training with the Air Force Reserve, medical officers were given two weeks to try to get ourselves up to speed. One way they trained us was to have us watch movies of the battlefield surgeries done in Vietnam.

I can get through regular war movies because I know it's all special effects. This was the real deal. As an administrator, not a nurse, I figured I was at an immediate disadvantage, but some of the nurses were having a rough time too.

We could hear the noise and voices, and watched as doctors and nurses pushed fingers into bullet wounds to clear them and tried to sew up soldiers blown apart. At one point I had to look away when they showed them peeling the burnt skin off of a soldier. All I could think of was, thank goodness they haven't included the smells on the film.

Those five senses can wreak havoc with what medical personnel see, but smell will bring a memory back in a heartbeat. As Bob Morris said in class one night, "Blood has a smell all its own."

Medical personnel also have a wicked sense of humor. It helps when needed. The television show *M*A*S*H* was actually telling the story of Vietnam but set it in Korea to make it more politically palatable. The medical hijinks were and still are real.

My friend Janice loved to tell the story of how the nurses at Fairchild Air Force Base would get back at the fighter jet pilots who thought they were hot stuff.

"You wouldn't believe the look on a pilot's face when I'd come in to give them a shot with a cardiac needle." Those things are about the size of a horse's leg.

We always knew we had the ability to scare the crap out of the Air Force pilots. While they will fly to the edge, dodge flak and missiles, medical personnel are some of the few people who can ground them from flying. Very scary indeed.

Or the little initiation rites when you join a medical unit. My operations officer got quite worried when he realized I was going on the one-week mid-Pacific training flight with the three biggest jokers in the Squadron, including my training officer. I managed to sidestep the first two attempts, but they suckered me on the third.

It took the entire medical crew and flight crew to get me, but they did surprise me when they had me play a patient who goes into code. Suffice it to say it was all an elaborate ruse to pump two bags of saline IV solution into the seat of my flightsuit; much to the amusement of the space available passengers I had to walk by for the next hour.

Hijinks are one way to blow off steam and cope with the grisly world of medical reality. Use writing to record your medical stories, your interactions with medical folks, or to say thank you to that medic who doesn't think you wanted your life saved. Or perhaps you can recall joint exercises that involved working with medical units from other countries.

There was one instance where we played with the Republic of South Korea on a big exercise. We were to staff AECEs, the small units where patients are first put on C-130s. We trained and flew on C-141Bs, so this would be good field training for us. Several days long, 24 hours a day training.

"We've got a problem" said Jody, my OIC. "They don't have someone to staff the brigade medical office." She looked at me.

"I'll do it," I said.

"Great," she said.

"What do I do?"

"Got me," she replied.

The Brigade guys were very nice and we were having quite a jolly time until we started getting our butts kicked on the battlefield. We ran out of hospital space. Since I was in charge, I decided to activate the Navy's hospital ship the U.S.S. *Mercy*.

"Can you do that?" one of the Brigade staff asked me.

"I don't know," I said. "They need beds, I'm giving them a hospital ship."

Since this exercise was played largely in a huge computer room, I soon heard the gamers were not happy about the hospital ship showing up. What did they expect me to do? Let the patients stack up? I think not!

Ground forces ran out of hospital beds again, so I shipped out the U.S.S. *Hope*. The commanders were happy, the gamers were pissed. It appears the hospital ships were not in the computer. Guess they had to put them in. They needed to use the F word like we did in Aerovac. Flexible at all times.

I hadn't thought of my shipping out the hospital ships for ages until I heard on the news they were deploying the U.S.S. *Mercy* to help in disaster recovery for the Asian Tsunami. Those hospital ships are old, but mighty. I would love to read some stories by those who served on them.

Unfortunately the medical and military personnel on the ground in the disaster areas now will have stories to tell which their hearts may not be able to hold. Those are the stories we all need to read to honor the dead and those who lost a part of their own heart helping the living.

So, I guess as one of my favorite heros would say:

"What's up, Doc?"

Firefighters

I loved those lime-green fire trucks that would stand by while we loaded patients into the aircraft for an Aerovac flight. Being responsible for ground operations, I always felt they were my guardian angels, our ace in the hole if the shit hit the fan.

They were always there while we loaded and unloaded the patients. They would then follow the plane while we taxied, to make sure they were as close as possible in case something went wrong. When there are patients strapped down in litters, newborn babies riding in airborne incubators, and oxygen lines everywhere, firefighters are our saviors.

It takes a special breed of man or woman to run into a burning building or aircraft while everyone else is running out. I first got a lesson in firefighters when covering a story for the *Newport News-Times* on a controlled caboose burn with the Depoe Bay, Oregon, volunteer firefighters. The experience stayed with me, as part of the column I wrote in March 1984 demonstrates:

> As smoke started to billow out of the caboose, Jay called to me from the open door. "Kim, come here," he yelled. As he beckoned me with his hand. I turned around and looked behind me. Must be a firefighter named Kim too. Looking at Jay again he kept yelling at me. Finally I did the old, "Who me' trick and pointed at myself. "Yes," he yelled, "come here."
>
> Casually I strolled over and received the following instructions. "Now just crawl down low on the floor here and I'll show you what fire does." The man had obviously lost his mind. Firefighters outside were wearing probably 20 pounds of protective equipment and he wanted me to go in a flaming caboose with a highly flammable purple quilted coat on.
>
> I can see the headline now, Trend Editor Goes Up In Smoke. Well, I figured, they won't let me burn up. It's bad for publicity. As I carefully duck-walked into the caboose, not too far, black smoke started to drift over my head. "Now see how the heat and smoke is all at the top," Jay patiently explained. "That is why people need to stay close to the floor in a fire. If they stand up, the heat will burn their lungs and the smoke will asphyxiate them."
>
> Carefully I listened, expecting to dash from the scene at a moment's notice. Jay was quite content to explain to me firefighting techniques and I was quite interested until I noticed the orange flames creeping up the far wall.
>
> "Well, I guess we better get out of here and let them at it," Jay said as I sprinted for the fresh night air, not needing further urging. After becoming known as the "blonde at the fire" to the firefighters, I was honored to be invited to their annual firefighter awards banquet. There I found out just how dedicated these volunteers were.

According to the wife of one of the firefighters, when a call came in reporting a woman had fallen in the shower, the immense turnout of helping males was a truly remarkable showing of volunteer spirit.

Spirit is also something we will never forget after losing 343 firefighters on September 11, 2001 in New York City. We saw the devotion of firefighters to each other from across the nation and the world. But it is the details, the small things, which illustrate the story of such a large and tragic loss.

My students met for a class reunion on Veteran's Day in 2001. One of my students, Tom, was dealing with the impending death of his son, a firefighter with terminal cancer. His son talked to him about a memory that haunted his comrades in arms from Boston who responded to 9-11 in New York.

"He told me the firefighters have these beepers they wear," he said. "When the firefighters are down for a certain amount of time, the beepers go off, so they can be located. My son told me that sound haunts many who responded that day. The firefighters knew those beeps were downed firefighters. They sound off for thirty minutes."

Later I read an article with quotes from one of the medical workers who responded to the World Trade Center Towers, trying to find survivors. "I heard all the beeping and I didn't know what it was," he said. "When they told me later, I couldn't believe it. I was walking over those firefighters."

Those beeps were the sound of death. Imagine how a 9-11 New York firefighter feels now when he or she hears a beep that sounds similar? Details and small memories make up the pieces of each of the 343 killed firefighters' lives and tell a part of the overwhelming loss that day.

We know these small details because someone tells someone else or writes it down. Firefighters rescue people, cook meals, live together, and fight flames. Whether they are in the military or in the civilian world, they are brothers and sisters of the flame, united by very large hearts.

Do you have a firefighter story? Fire them up! So to speak, that is.

Resources:
"Casualties of War – Military Care for the Wounded from Iraq and Afghanistan" by Atul Gawande, *The New England Journal of Medicine*, December 9, 2004

Heart of a Soldier by James B. Stewart

Chapter 26

Australian Veterans

The sun beat down and the warm ocean breeze blew the smell of salt across my skin. I seemed to be standing on a desert at the edge of an ocean. Behind me in this peaceful place lay the graves of hundreds of Australian and New Zealand Army (ANZAC) soldiers in a place called Gallipoli, Turkey.

If not for happening to see a 1981 movie by a new young actor named Mel Gibson, I would have had no idea about the story. The movie made me realize the importance of this location to my fellow travelers from Australia and New Zealand on this day, Aug. 4, 1983.

Behind us were rows of markers with the names of the dead lined up like soldiers once again, staring out over the sea, back toward the home they never returned to in 1915. The plaque at the Ari Burnu Cemetery and Beach Cemetery tells of the British, French, Australian and New Zealand armies on April 25, 1915, to start phase two of a planned three phase attack.

Unable to make more than a kilometer of progress with heavy losses, the troops were bogged down in trench warfare until the troops were withdrawn Dec. 19-20 and Jan. 8-9 in 1916. A sadder tale is told by the inscription on the plaque:

> "Under the terms of the Armistance with Turkey the British Army re-entered the Peninsula at the end of 1918 and cleared the battlefields of the bodies still unburied. In the nine months of this bitterly fought campaign the Commonwealth lost more than 36,000 dead. The 31 war cemeteries on the Peninsula contain 22,000 graves but it was possible to identify only 9,000 of these. The 13,000 who rest in unidentified graves in the cemeteries together with the 14,000 whose remains were never found are commemorated individually by name on the Helles Memorial (British, Australian and Indian names) the Lone Pine Memorial (Australian and New Zealand names) and the Twelve Tree Copse, Hill 60 and Chunuk Bair Memorials (New Zealand names)."

This experience opened my eyes to truly consider the suffering and sacrifices of our Australian and New Zealand allies. As we walked along the grounds, we knew we could be treading on soldiers' remains. I also picked up the disparaging comments from the Aussies and New Zealanders against the British for how the ANZAC troops were used during the campaign. Even 68 years after the battle, the memories of these descendants were bitter.

I heard they consider Gallipoli their greatest defeat and their greatest triumph as ANZAC troops fought hard and long during the nine month battle. The white walls etched with soldier names carries an inscription which many military people today would find hard to fathom:

> "To the glory of God and in lasting memory of 5268 Australian soldiers who fought on Gallipoli in 1915 and have no known graves and 456 New Zealand soldiers whose names are not recorded in other areas of the Peninsula but who fell in the ANZAC area and have no known graves and also of 960 Australians and 252 New Zealanders who fighting on Gallipoli in 1915 incurred mortal wounds or sickness and found burial at sea."

Perhaps the best words come from my fellow traveler, written in the Day Book we kept of our journey during that three month camping journey through Europe.

> We had a very quiet group once again after our afternoon at Gallipoli, especially amongst the Aussies. Some of the men who died were only 17 years old. There were lots of memorial graves for those soldiers whose graves couldn't be located. Looking at the cliffs it was obvious we didn't have a chance against the Turks. We can be thankful that a few survived Gallipoli.
>
> Never has such a victory been won in such defeat. Victory was not the measure of bravery in this place. Gallipoli is the ANZAC spirit that lives on even today. Even if we question their quest today, there is no denying the respect one feels for the courage they had in fighting for their cause. It made me feel proud to be an Australian. Perhaps one inscription on one of the numerous graves said it all. "A Dinkum Aussie." Someone made an interesting comment that we'd seen more of Gallipoli than many of the soldiers. There were no getting odds here. It sure was one hell of a place to die so far from home. Lest we forget. And the band played Waltzing Matilda.
>   (by Debbie Caldow)

I was lucky enough to win the Day Book at the end of our trip in 1983. Looking back on all the entries, the power of the words still impresses me 23 years later. And the power of the deeds never dies.

When we walked through the graves that day in Gallipoli, I heard snatches about "the man with the donkey." That evening I asked about the story.

Private John Simpson Kirkpatrick was an Englishman who joined the merchant marine at age 17, ending up in Australia. He enlisted and ended up in the 3rd Field Ambulance as a stretcher bearer. He landed at Gallipoli on Aug. 25, 1914.

Simpson decided he could better accomplish his task by using a donkey. Three weeks after landing, he was killed one morning by a Turkish bullet, while on his way to retrieve wounded. While there are differing opinions about his fame, which may have been used as spin to promote the war at home, Simpson's bravery has never been questioned.

Windy would be proud. I felt a special bond with John Simpson that evening on that far away shore, hearing about a man and his donkey.

We spent that night at a campground close to Gallipoli. Most of us gathered our sleeping bags and went down on the beach to sleep. With the waves rushing in and the gorgeous sunset, I felt a sense of peace but also a presence of being watched over. Maybe those soldiers who died so far from home were watching over their great-great grandchildren, nieces and nephews and a couple crazy Yanks. Wouldn't surprise me a bit.

I remember telling the Gallipoli story to Rich Clark, former Salem Vet Center Team Leader.

"You know, I've always wondered what happened to this Australian Major I worked with over in Nam," he said. "We had Aussies with us there. Wonder what happened to him."

I will travel to Australia and New Zealand and maybe I can find Rich's Major. There are Aussie bikers who were on *Run For The Wall* too. And, how about meeting that prolific author of the books, *The Blue Day Book*, *Looking For Mr. Right*, and *The Book For People Who Do Too Much*?

His name is Bradley Trevor Greive, a graduate of Australia's Royal Military College. He "served as a paratroop platoon commander before leaving military service to seek creative misadventure." My kind of Aussie! He also has a pet rabbit named Biff, so he's good to go in my book.

Get me an airplane ticket. There are stories downunder. Have you got Aussie or Kiwi stories? G'Day mate!

Author's Note: A special thank you to Joseph Kaposi of Perth, Australia. He made me a great bunch of drawings entitled, "Wabbits at War," while I was on that Autotours EX57 European camping trip in 1983. Though he referred to my quest for a rabbit figurine in every country as "Bunny Hell," I still have all his wabbits.

Resources:
Gallipoli by Alan Moorehead
Ashes of Vietnam: Australian Voices by Stuart Rintoul
"Down Under in Vietnam" by James Warren, *MHQ: The Quarterly Journal of Military*
    History, Summer 1994, Vol. 6, No. 4

Web Sites:
Australian War Memorial
www.awm.gov.au

http://grunt.space.swri.edu/aussimen.htm/austwall.htm

PART THREE

USING WRITING TO HEAL

Chapter 27

Harnessing Anger and Humor

Operation Iraqi Freedom or Embed Me Please!
I know why veterans get fat. The United States keeps going to war and reporters keep asking stupid questions.

During Operation Iraqi Freedom I had to ration my television viewing. Either that or fly to Qatar and kick some serious news media butt. I can say that. I'm a woman veteran and a former newspaper reporter. I believe in freedom of speech. I've defended it. But I do not believe in freedom of stupidity.

My personal preference would have been close captioned thoughts of what the military brass were actually thinking in the CNN scrollbar during the press briefings.

These are my answers to my all time favorite stupid reporter questions.

Actual Question: "Do you know where the POWs are?"

Closed Caption Scroll: If I do, you're the last idiot I'm going to tell. Every man and woman we've got is hunting for them. If we could get the mine clearing dolphins to walk on sand, we'd use them too. Do you have any brains or are you just here for show?

I must have gained three pounds of chocolate weight after that question.

Actual Question: "How could they make a wrong turn in the desert?"

Closed Caption: Have you looked at the desert? Not a lot of traffic signals.

When I was with the Fourth Infantry Division at Fort Carson, Colorado, in the 4th Supply and Transport Battalion, we trained for war by getting lost. Not on purpose. It just happened. I repeat, have you looked at a desert? At Fort Irwin, California, for desert training, the Brigade Headquarters we were supporting managed to set up our operations behind enemy lines. I was not happy about this state of affairs. It's not easy navigating in the desert, in the dark, in a sandstorm, without a GPS. Until you've breathed, eaten, and shit sand, you just don't understand the challenge.

But the all time classic question?

Actual Question: "This advance is bogging down isn't it?"

Closed Caption: It's been five days, you idiot, want to give us a week or two? Does anybody study history? We were in Vietnam for NINE YEARS. That's like 365 times 9. Do the math.

Do Bar Fights Count?

That one question put at least five pounds of chocolate weight on me, probably six. "This is not a microwave war," I told co-workers. You try to gather 30,000 of your closest friends, put them on the Oregon/California border and tell them to capture Los Angeles. THEN start shooting at them, throw in a wild fire and an earthquake for giggles. See if any of them make it to the first Texaco station. Actually, we Oregonians would love to send something back to California besides electricity for a change.

Yes, I'm a native born Oregonian. Home of Tonya Harding, bankrupt schools in Doonesbury, the Bhagwan Shree Rajneesh, assisted suicide and a terrorist cell. Consider yourself warned. Abnormal behavior is normal here, so I was born to fit in.

What does this all have to do with writing war stories? Reporters will never truly understand the military unless they have served in it. **The only writers who can truly tell the stories are military veterans.**

Think of writing your stories down as civilian education. People are curious about the military. I remember September 11, 2001 and the questions I got about the military.

People Think Rumsfield Calls Me Every Day, or 9-11-01

My clock radio clicked on and I heard the disk jockey stumbling over his words.

"Two airplanes have crashed into the World Trade Center towers."

"What the?" I waited for more. It was 6:45 a.m. Oregon time. September 11, 2001. Dead air followed the announcement. The last time I'd heard this long a pause from KISN FM, the dejays had headed for the doorjamb during a 5.6 earthquake. I must have heard him wrong.

"This is so hard to say," he croaked.

I jumped out of bed and ran downstairs, turned on CNN and watched in horror as black smoke billowed from the twin towers. The words "terrorist" and "aircraft" barely registered when the phone rang.

"Are you watching this on tv?" asked my sister.

"I can't believe it."

"What do you think?" she asked.

"Whoever did this is toast," I replied.

I watched the news while I got dressed and ate, then I went to work. As a county government office, we stayed open for business. I could only imagine the pressure the Sheriff's Office was under. Clackamas County is a bedroom community to Portland, Oregon, a West coast city large enough to be a possible target.

I thought about my former co-workers at the Bonneville Power Administration, a federal power agency. Controllers of the western power grid, they were an automatic target. The radio announced their offices were closed.

The World War II photo in the hallway outside my old BPA office came to mind. It showed Army troops with weapons defending the large transmission towers on Oregon and Washington soil. Here we go, I thought.

All my co-workers and boss had their radios on when I got to work. Managers had turned on television sets in two of our conference rooms. We went about our business in slow motion and horror. The phones hardly rang. Everyone was in shock.

Co-worker Dan Nenow, an Army reservist, and I exchanged looks. We knew what this meant and were aware of the men and women in the military, reserve, and guard putting their lives on the line at that moment protecting the country.

We also knew our domestic warriors; police, firefighters, and emergency medical workers were giving it their all in New York and at the Pentagon. When the news of the plane crash in Pennsylvania came, Dan and I agreed; that plane went down after a fight onboard.

The magnitude of the next few days rocked me as it did my co-workers and the nation. I wondered if my friend Ann, an Air Force lawyer who did Reserve work at the Pentagon, was safe. I wondered if the halls I had roamed in the Pentagon while working there for two months in 1990 were part of the damage site. I knew the drink I had in the Windows on the World Bar at the World Trade Center in 1990 was now a once in a lifetime event. I worried over the frustration and pain of emergency workers and citizens who had nothing to do but mourn the crash site in Pennsylvania, where there was no one to save.

By Friday I saw in my co-workers' eyes, the looks of pain and innocence lost I had only seen in fellow vets eyes. Veterans have always known this country was not safe. Freedom is paid for with the price of men and women's blood, pain, tears, and lives, now and since the birth of our nation.

A surprise to me was the sudden interest in the military from friends and neighbors. Somehow they thought I knew what was going on. I had left the military eight years before, but I wondered if they thought Defense Secretary Donald Rumsfield was calling me every day.

"My sister's husband is a submariner, do you think he's been called to sea?" my hairdresser asked me the following week.

"Yes," I replied. It was hard not to tell her; "Well, every fucking asset we own in the military is on alert and was within minutes. The penguins in Antarctica are probably armed by now."

People outside of the service do not understand the military. I knew my old aerovac squadron was on alert immediately. I knew the National Disaster Medical System of the Department of Veterans Affairs Hospitals was on alert. I knew Special Operations and Special Forces personnel would be in Afghanistan as soon as they could get the go order. The military is full of professionals who train for these very events and then hope they never happen.

"Do you think they will have success in Afghanistan?" a co-worker asked a few weeks later.

"Yes," I replied. "People seem to forget there are New Yorkers on those Navy ships in the Gulf, relatives of the people who died. Besides, the idiots hit the Pentagon. We will get them. As long as it takes. We could just unleash what's left of the New York Fire Department and it wouldn't be a fair fight."

I also knew we would have more veterans and more men and women who would die in the fight to preserve freedom. And the emotional toll would be inhumane for those who worked at the World Trade Center, the Pentagon and Pennsylvania crash sites. Some survivors, spouses and rescuers would commit suicide, and children would grow up without parents. Since the War of Independence in 1776, this country's freedom has come at the ultimate sacrifice of the men and women dedicated to protect and preserve it.

I also know the emotional cost of 9-11 and the days to follow will take years to deal with, each on an individual basis. Some will relive it every day, some will compartmentalize it until a time years from now. For those who want to write about it now, I hope this book will be a guide for you. For those who may write about it 20 or 30 years from now, I hope there will be many more books about the power of writing to heal. Writing this book has been therapy for me.

September 8, 2002, on the eve of the first year anniversary of 9-11-01, I know writing helps me deal with the unimaginable horror.

Some truths I have learned for myself in this process:

1. We will never be the same again. We cannot go back to what we were before 9-11. Those people do not exist. While we mourn family, friends and co-workers who were lost, we must also mourn the loss of ourselves, the people we once were.

2. We will not get over it. We will not get closure. We will get through it. With help from each other, counselors, our faith and our love of freedom, we will get through it.

3. Time can help, but it never goes completely away. Little events, sounds or smells will trigger memories. The talk about going to war with Iraq brought a few bad nights to me. I relive the pre-Desert Storm chemical warfare briefings about how the different chemical agents could kill me, including blisters of water from my own body bursting in my lungs so I could drown on dry land. Then how to inject myself with an Atropine syringe to try to save my life if it did happen.

I also remember handing out live ammunition with weapons, real narcotics and full Atropine syringes to my friends on the medical crews to use with their air and land chemical warfare kits.

Then the critter briefing. I listened to some 52 type of snakes in Saudi Arabia, all poisonous, including the bugger who burrows into the sand in the shade to bite me in the butt.

The other day I was cleaning out my jewelry drawer. A small container rocked me back in time. A pretty white box of matches with gold lettering, it read "Windows on the World, 107th Floor, New York World Trade Center." Posttraumatic Stress comes and goes.

4. I am kind to myself. I have learned to ask for help. Hug puppies. Buy a teddy bear. Give of yourself when you can. Giving to others is a wonderful way to take action. I responded to the President's call those first few weeks and shopped like the commando buyer I am.

I really wanted to get in a tank and do something, but I worked on this book instead. So I could give something that might make one veteran smile, make one veteran know I feel they are important, and to thank every active duty, reserve and guard member out there doing his and her job as we contemplate going to Iraq – again.

Humor is a stress reliever, coping mechanism and form of defense for me. A triple threat. Those are some reasons why there are hysterical military situations. Another reason could be Tom Clancy's remark about the military, "They have the best toys."

Think about it. Who else lets teenagers drive nuclear submarines? And fly planes and park ships? Okay, moor ships as one Navy Commander corrected my sister. We marshal planes, moor ships and what do we do to tanks? Nothing! Tanks get to do whatever they want. Flanking, pinching, whatever.

When I started writing this book it grew from both love and anger. Then the anger seemed to take over. I started the book the first year of teaching the

Writing War Stories class. It got put aside for four years. When I couldn't ignore it any longer, I picked it up and read it.

Depressing!

One of the things I lost after Desert Storm was my sense of humor. (I know, hard to believe.) The funny part is I didn't know it was gone until it returned. My parents assured me they were watching me in case I did something odd.

Given my personal history, odd can be hard to detect. My Army buddy, Jan, gave me the physical version. "The twinkle in your eyes was gone," she said.

"But, I'm back now."

"I know," she replied. "The twinkle is back."

Heaven help the planet.

Looking at the first draft of this manuscript, I knew it needed a big twinkle. Humor is how I cope. I do not ever mean it to dishonor. Well, unless I have a beef with Congress and the Executive Branch. They can take it. Have you checked your sense of humor lately?

I was watching a movie the other day, *The Next Karate Kid.* Some closing lines in the film hit home. Actor Pat Morita is trying to get across the point about choosing when to fight to his new pupil, played by Hillary Swank.

"Fighting not good," he said. "But if you must fight, win."

We will win this fight against terrorism. As long as it takes. Freedom is not free.

A special note for the men and women out there on active duty and on active duty in the reserve and guard. There are more than 24 million veterans in this country. We're old, cranky, and some of us are starting into menopause, but, we've got your back. At home or abroad. Call if you need us.

Author's Note: Memo to the President and Congress: We did go to war in Iraq, again, so increase the funding for the Department of Veterans Affairs. We are not taking adequate care of the veterans we have today, and the war on terrorism is making new veterans every hour. Current and future veterans will need support long after the next war/conflict/police action/humanitarian mission is over. If you want the military to be world police, you need to give them world class support for bearing the burden.

And quit making it look good for the cameras by bumping Afghanistan and Iraq veterans ahead of other veterans for VA care and benefits. A veteran whose leg was blown off in Vietnam needs the same quality and priority of care as an Iraq and Afghanistan veteran injured today. If Congress is going to base benefits and care on who has the most recent blown off body part, I'd like to see recruiters try to put a spin on that slogan.

Don't think you can leverage veterans to fight veterans either. (The Swift Boat Veterans aside.) We vets outside the beltway all know the "real" buddy system, having served in the military. You're only fooling yourselves. Shame on you all.

And while I am at it: It is way past time for the Department of Veterans Affairs to change their slogan. I know Abe Lincoln was a great guy, but to keep using, "For him who has borne the battle and his widow and children" is a direct slap in the face to all women veterans. Also to male widowers whose wives have died. Either copy edit the damn thing or get a new one. It stuck in my craw while I worked at the VA, but now it just pisses me off.

My favorite editorial cartoon of all time ran in the December 13, 1984, issue of *The Oregonian* newspaper. By MacNelly of the Chicago Tribune, it shows the White House surrounded by a group of tanks. The bubble in the White House reads, "The good news is they're ours, Mr. President....The bad news is they're here to talk about these cuts in veteran's benefits."

The more things change, the more they stay the same.

Reach out to a returning troop or a new veteran. Let's take care of each other.

Standing down from my soap box. For now. At ease.

Resources:
Iraq and Afghanistan Veterans of America – www.iava.org
Navy Systematic Stress Management Program –
www-nehc.med.navy.mil/hp/stress/index.htm
Heart of a Soldier by James B. Stewart
The Last True Story I'll Ever Tell: An Accidental Soldier's Account of the War in Iraq by John Crawford
Not A Good Day To Die: The Untold Story of Operation Anaconda by Sean Naylor

Chapter 28

Suicide Sucks and Death is Permanent

"I don't know how to tell you this," Jody said over the phone, her voice breaking. "I wish I was there to hold you."

Before I could even figure out why my former Squadron buddy had called, she blurted out the news.

"Scott committed suicide."

My stomach dropped and I felt immediately ill. Sinking into the chair in my living room on a perfect Mother's Day evening in 1995, my mind could not grasp the shock.

I heard a click on the line. "Just a minute," Jody said. "That might be the Squadron."

While on terminal hold, I started to cry. Scott had been down to visit me just two months ago. He had stayed for the weekend and we had great fun talking and catching up on things. A fellow Medical Service Corps Officer, Scott had been my trainer and mentor when I entered the unit.

He came from a military family, was a fellow writer and alternated between big brother and pesky kid next door. But I never questioned his commitment to the members of the Squadron. Scott was always there for everybody else. Why didn't he know we were there for him?

Jody came back on the line. "Sorry, that was Jan, apologizing for me getting the phone call." Jody had left the Squadron awhile ago after being Executive Officer. Seems they never updated the roster at base operations. When they called about a suicide, Jody asked who it was. They told her Scott and she threw the phone at her husband and burst into tears.

Seems Scott had been over to her house for dinner three weeks earlier. She said she would call me about arrangements and be in touch. "I'm so sorry," she said. All I could do was nod, then cry my eyes out the rest of the night.

Scott and I were buddies. We shared a lot of training missions and goat rope exercises. When Desert Shield turned to Desert Storm I shipped him and Jody out with our first wave of medical crews overseas, and he still kept his sense of humor. He was known for his dry wit and authority flaunting ways.

When I got a chance to talk on the secure line some weeks later to him, he was happy to be working the graveyard shift. "Lot less brass around," he said with a chuckle. "I volunteered."

He volunteered later to work with the Kurds in the North of Iraq after the Gulf War. Or the first Gulf War as we refer to it now. Scott was what was considered a Reserve bum. He was able to make enough to get by working almost full-time for the Reserve. We had so many missions, operations officers were always needed for flights and man days in the unit.

I had become a reserve bum myself after leaving the VA Medical Center in July of 1989. Scott was the only one at the airport when our first group of volunteers left for Saudi Arabia in the fall of 1990. And he was there to welcome Jody home with a group of well-wishers when she came back last from overseas.

Scott had issues, but he never let the Squadron down, except by leaving us too soon. His family had a private funeral. We had a memorial service for him at the Squadron. It was my first time back to the unit in three and a half years.

Everyone was there from the Squadron, our wing and all the other units at McChord Air Force Base that had known Scott. He touched many lives. When you work as a team to get patient aeromedical evacuation flights off the ground, personnel from Fort Lewis and Bremerton knew Scott. All the flight crews and pilots knew Scott. Base operations folks, maintenance crews, the firefighters and the supply and canteen folks all knew Scott.

The Chaplain who presided at the memorial service knew Scott quite well too and had trouble making it through the service. We made it through Desert Shield and Desert Storm without losing one service member. But we lost Scott four years later.

The night after teaching my first *Writing War Stories* class, I had a comforting thought. Scott would have loved this class. The next month as I traveled to Tacoma, Washington, for a romance writer's conference, we made a special stop. I found Scott's grave and shed tears. It took me almost two and a half years to come to some closure with Scott's death, but I learned some things along the way:

1. It was Scott's choice to end his life. I have to respect his choice.
2. He left me with some wonderful memories.
3. He left me some of his words.

Scott had an article published in the Wing Newsletter detailing his adventures in Northern Iraq. It was pure Scott. He also left me his critique of our operations right after Desert Storm. I found it while cleaning out papers several years later. And I have letters he wrote me from overseas.

Scott was a frustrated writer like the rest of us. So, on his behalf, I want to do the one thing for Scott I can do now. Besides trying to teach veterans to write their own stories, maybe one veteran will read this and think twice before committing suicide.

Scott's death blew an emotional hole through our Squadron and through the lives of his family and close friends. The emotional toll from any war only truly begins after everyone comes home and tries to put the pieces back together. For some, the pieces never fit and the pain is too great.

One night in writing class Doug apologized to me for not feeling like doing the in class assignments. "I don't feel much like writing," he said. "A vet friend of mine shot himself in the head today."

"He make it?" I asked.

He shook his head no.

"I'm so sorry, Doug," I said. "I'm amazed you're even here."

"Felt like the place to be," he said.

And I understood. I wrote my first screenplay in part as a catharsis to deal with Scott's death and I dedicated it to him. My words from *Reserve Wars* are as true today as ever.

"Suicide rips a part of your heart out and the damn muscle just keeps on beating."

The one thing I can do for Scott besides try to let all veterans know someone in their life cares? Publish his writing.

Aeromed Reflections

Published in the *446th Associate Press*, September 1991
By 1Lt. Scott U. Hall

December

I called the squadron the Friday before Christmas and was engaged in the usual chitchat when suddenly the conversation turned official – "Report to the Squadron at 0700, Jan.2." This is a joke, right? Christmas would have a bit more meaning than in the past.

January

There is much shock and disbelief at being activated. People joked in the processing line, while getting shots, as they were issued bag after bag. Then the frantic sizing, packing, unpacking, repacking, rumors, saying goodbyes everyday. We finally get word we'll leave for Ramstein AB, Germany, in two days. Everything I do holds significance as I repeat it one final time – a drink from my coffee cup, starting my car, the creak of the door as it closes and clicks shut....

After tearful goodbyes and a long flight, we arrived at Ramstein at 0730 local on Sunday, Jan. 13. Four hours later we get our first inbound load of patients from Saudi Arabia.

The next few months are a blur of vague memories: Missions arriving at all hours, many unannounced; small glitches having a major impact, driving on the flightline at night in the fog, working with other units and nationalities, CNN, patients shivering and smiling as they arrive in snow from the desert; crews displayed a fatigue beyond what a mission causes.

February-March

We were overwhelmed with a taste of mortality as we heard the news of a scud hit in Dhahran; later that Israel has kept out of the battle, then the shooting stops and our collectively-held breath is slowly released to a cheer.

Patients continued to arrive from Saudi Arabia. I helped off-load a burn patient on a litter. He asked if we could let him see a tree before we put him in the ambulance. Yeah, I thought we could handle that request. People begin to go home.

April

I catch a mission downrange. We stopped at King Khalid and King Fahd airports to pick up patients – it was my first view of the sandbox. The Saudi tourist bureau has its work cut out for it. The plane is packed, but no one complains.

On April 24, I arrived at Incirlik, Turkey, to help with Operation Provide Comfort. The next morning a C-130 took us to eastern Turkey. Took me three days to spell Diyarbakir! Our tents were 50 feet from the ramp, 100 yards from the Turkish Air Force's practice bomb range. We had no communications. Whenever we heard a chopper, we merely lifted the tent side to see if the chopper had a red cross on it. If so, we scrambled to it. Only when it rained did our tent have running water.

I caught a chopper to Silopi, on the Iraqi border. Made contact with the hospital, dust-off crews and medical management team.

May

One of the guys, Tom, found a big, ugly bug in our tent. Tom named it Achmed and put it in a water bottle. Achmed died a few days later – must have been the water...

My replacement arrived from Saudi. We found a snake under a wooden pallet we used as a porch. Tom said it was a garter snake, named it Omar, and put it in a box. We later learned all seven types of snakes in the area are poisonous – and Tom said Omar escaped. Nobody went after anything that fell under the floor in the tent.

A few days later I caught a C-130 to Sirsenk, Iraq, to set up airevac operations. The Iraquis are tracking allied aircraft with radar, so we flew low – good for sightseeing. Saddam's summer palace was only a few kilometers away. A Marine gave me a ride up to the British hospital and said everyone walked around the place in someone else's footsteps. Good idea considering the mine signs that lined the road. The Brits used a building that survived our B-52s, but the damage showed.

We had breakfast on truck hoods that served as tables. That afternoon the explosive ordinance guys blew up some stuff they found. I accomplished my duties in Sirsenk and caught an Italian bird back to Incirlik and a real shower.

June

Two badly burned guys arrived from Sirsenk. They were in their early 20s, but you couldn't tell looking at them. We got them on a C-9 to Germany, but one guy died enroute.

Rumors ran rampant that we'd stay till Thanksgiving. Turkey in Turkey, oh boy. More missions, days indistinguishable. Coalition Forces started moving out of northern Iraq. U.S. was being urged to stay till October, along with our allied troops. CINCMAC message said all reservists would be home by July 1.

We waited for a plane to Germany on June 27, and wondered if we'd get pulled off it at the last minute.

On June 30 I landed at Sea Tac in the rain. A gorgeous sight!

When I was going through my letters from Scott and his global travels with Aerovac, I came upon some closing words from him. Written on March 1, 1993, while he was in Egypt playing Aerovac.

I received your letter today, it was real nice to hear from you, and yes; you may use my Omar story, but I want acknowledgement.

And later, on September 4, 1994, from Bahrain, while he was getting ready to go to Mogadishu, Somalia.

You take care and remember, I want honorable mention in your book and nothing too tacky or sappy.

I know Scott was referring to the romance novel I was working on at the time, not the screenplay I later wrote to help me deal with his death. But finally, here he is in a book and I can give him credit and keep it on the up side.

Because I know he is sitting in his tent alongside the runway in military heaven, doing his aerovac operations duties, lifting the canvas tent side when he hears a chopper. And when he sees a red cross, he's making sure another military patient crosses over to be with his and her band of brothers and sisters holding the high ground.

I can hear him say, "Just another day in paradise!"

So what do I hope Scott's tale does for all of us? Writing about Scott helps me deal with his death. I get to honor his deeds as I always planned.

Maybe, just maybe, Scott and I can work as a team once more to save another veteran from committing suicide.

If you are thinking of suicide, please reach out to your fellow veterans, the VA Vet Centers, any medical professional, chaplain, spiritual leader, or crisis hotline.

You may not believe it, but we do care for you and want to help. You are not alone. For those of us left behind, suicide sucks and death is permanent.

Eleven years later I still carry Scott's suicide shrapnel in my heart.

And believe me, I am going to kick his butt good when I see him on the other side. The buddy system is forever. Won't he be surprised!

Resources:

After Suicide – A Ray of Hope, by Eleanora Ross. Contact Ray of Hope to order.

A Special Scar: The Experiences of People Bereaved by Suicide, by Allison Wertheimer

Waking Up, Alive: The Descent, the Suicide Attempt, and the Return to Life, by Richard A. Heckler

Suicide Wall, by Alexander Paul

The American Suicide Foundation, 1045 Park Ave., New York, NY 10028, (800) 531-4477.

Ray of Hope, P.O. Box 2323, Iowa City, IA, 52244, (319) 337-9890.

Chapter 29

Space Shuttle Columbia STS-107

I watched the tiny bright light skim across the heavens. I waved. The astronauts on the Space Station didn't wave back that I could see, but I wanted God to know I had them in my prayers. Tonight it is one week since we lost Columbia and her crew on Feb. 1, 2003.

Somehow I felt reassured watching the trail of the Space Station fly across the northwest skies. With the rain and clouds we get in Oregon, being able to see the Space Station at all is a rare treat. I saw the Space Station four nights straight, marveling at how quickly it moved.

I wondered how the three astronauts on the Space Station were dealing with the death of their fellow space explorers. My thoughts went out to Astronaut David Pettit's family in Houston, while I watched not far from his hometown of Silverton, Oregon.

My prayers also reached out to a girl I knew in high school. She played the flute in the band, sometimes sat with us at lunch and was smart and nice. A year younger than I, I wondered how astronaut Susan Helms was holding up with this personal loss.

But somehow, each night when the space lab appeared in orbit, I celebrated the remarkable resiliency of the human spirit once again. The recent editorial cartoon I saw illustrating the Columbia flying through the pearly gates said it all for me. The Columbia crew were up there sharing secrets with the Challenger Crew and the men of Apollo 11, plus the astronauts who have also passed on.

Must be one hell of a gab fest going on up there. I imagine the astronauts have run into the firefighters, police officers and private citizens from 9-11 too. It makes we wonder why God recruited so many angels in the past two years. Perhaps the current winds of war require replacements in the high choir to keep things stable here on earth.

We all grieve with the families. There is no way to even imagine their sacrifice. They can be comforted knowing their loved ones were doing important work. I would wish each and every one of us could say that when it is our time to leave this earth. Perhaps that is the greatest legacy they leave us in this time of economic strife, war and terrorism.

I remember sitting in a traffic jam on the freeway when I heard the news about the explosion of the Challenger. My stomach rolled and I looked at my fellow commuters. There were expressions of shock and disbelief all around me.

Years later, at Arlington National Cemetery, I saw the tombstone dedicated to the Challenger crew. Now the Columbia's crew would be put close by. My heart also grieved for the men and women who would search tirelessly to recover the crew's remains.

What ever you do in life, do it with love, with gusto, and take risks. We celebrate the crews of Columbia and Challenger by how they lived, full speed ahead with love. I wish we all could leave such an epitaph for our lives.

As I watch the Space Station orbit across my neighborhood again this night, I am reminded how much there is yet to learn about this amazing universe. And I thank the veterans, men, women, and employees of NASA who keep reaching past the stars.

Resources:
NASA – Space Shuttle Columbia and Her Crew
www.nasa.gov/Columbia/home/

Rocketman: Astronaut Pete Conrad's Incredible Ride to the Moon and Beyond **by Nancy Conrad and Howard Klausner**

Chapter 30

Using Writing To Heal A Soldier's Heart

Writing is a process and a journey. As writers we pick words out of the air to try and describe our feelings, emotions, hopes and dreams. We create whole new worlds, explore the depths of human suffering and try to record the overwhelming joys we experience as humans on this little planet called Earth.

Writing can help us to process and heal from the life adventures we have experienced. It also provides a paper therapy concrete way to deal with uncontained feelings of rage, anger, joy and love. It is not a magic bullet to ease pain or a way to avoid the past. Rather, writing is an obstacle course, just like the ones many of us navigated in basic training.

Mike DeMaio, a veteran student and retired VA Vet Center Counselor, found the act of writing his story about the first person he killed in Vietnam helped him to heal. "After writing about it," he said, "It helped to lift some of the pain. I took my bayonet out of the bottom drawer where it was hidden and I brought it out into the open. It gave me some peace."

Even with the awareness of Post Traumatic Stress and Post Traumatic Stress Disorder in today's military, many service members returning from Afghanistan, Iraq and the humanitarian missions in Indonesia and Hurricanes Katrina and Rita will need to deal with the events they have witnessed. Writing is one way to process those experiences.

While it is a nice expectation that returning troops will have all the access to health care and counseling they need, we know this is not true. Most VA Vet Centers today are already at capacity seeing veterans from past conflicts. There is also the added stigma still in many areas of the active duty world that to seek counseling is "wimpy."

Bullshit. I see post traumatic stress as an emotional cancer. Left untreated it will permanently damage and may even kill our soldiers. This has already happened with suicides among active duty troops.

I don't want to lose one more soldier, sailor, airman, Marine or Coast Guardsmen because we couldn't find a way to help our homecoming troops to process what they have been through. I offer writing as one method to help in the journey back from combat to home, reserve and guard duty to civilian status.

There are many other outlets which can be used from the arts. Art therapy includes painting, photography, sculpture, metal work and any other medium veterans can think of to illustrate their journeys. Pet therapy is also a valuable contact to give a veteran unconditional love from a four-footed, finned or furred companion.

How about film? I wrote my first screenplay as a catharsis about being a reservist and losing my good friend, Scott, to suicide after Desert Storm. It helped me to heal and move on with my life. Writing this book has helped me to heal holes I thought were long fixed. It has also been a psyche saving way to deal with 9-11, Afghanistan and the Iraq war for me – to channel my anger and feelings of helplessness.

I think the idea of starting writing groups for returning troops is also an excellent way for them to meet on a regular basis to check in with others who have had the same experience and see how everyone is dealing with the transition. The buddy system doesn't stop when you get home, it really needs to get stronger and take on a whole new commitment.

This is especially true for Reserve and Guard folks who do not have the support or community connections of active duty personnel. Maybe it will be easier for troops to say "I'm going to writing class," instead of saying "I'm going to counseling." I really don't care what anybody calls it, as long as each troop feels they have a way to connect and process what they are going through with others.

Also, I hope to encourage stateside troops to write as well. The medical staffs caring for recent amputees at Walter Reed Army Medical Center are not having an easy time of it either. The Med Evac crews who are transporting more severely injured troops are not having a fun time. The almost forgotten troops in Afghanistan are doing their jobs day in and day out, as well as those folks in Korea, Germany and the Aleutians.

Will it be easy? Nope. Does it take practice to get what you want down on paper? You bet. Is every effort valuable? Absolutely. Does it help give you perspective? I hope so. It can also help you grieve. Even though they tried to give soldiers time to pay respects to their fallen comrades in Iraq and Afghanistan, they still had to get right back into the fray. No time to process the loss. Perhaps writing a letter to your fallen buddy will help you continue the grieving process. Maybe that letter turns into a letter to his or her family. And maybe it turns into a book. Who knows? It's worth a try if you are interested.

Can you put in the fun times? Of course. Weird and stupid things happen in the military and war. Record those happy and off-beat moments.

Do Bar Fights Count?

Years later, when you take a look at what you recorded, you will be amazed at the things you forgot about and can then remember with fondness from the distance of time.

For those of you trying to explore the past with World War II, Korea, Vietnam, Gulf war or peacetime memories, it is never too late to start. If you are interested in writing or exploring those areas of your life now, there must be a reason. Either you want to record these adventures for family, friends or history, or you want to discover what you really learned about yourself during those times.

Bob Morris began writing his stories, which have now turned into a book.

Soon a movie will be coming out based upon a book written by his comrade in arms, *They Marched into Sunlight* by David Moranis.

"When I was at the last reunion, Retired Colonel Len Tavernetti, Captain and commanding officer of Charlie Company, 1/26th in 1967 approached me," said Bob.

"See what you've done by writing a story about the ambush on the 7th of November," Len said.

Bob looked at me. "You helped me get started."

Bob's story, *Ambush Srok Rung*, was passed around his unit association. Now another Blue Spader is researching the ambush to write a book.

I am happy to take the blame. I am also thrilled to be speaking at the 28th Infantry Division's Reunion here in Portland, June 2006. I will get to meet the men I have read so much about through Bob's stories.

Dave Hammond also asked me to speak at the Americal Division Reunion being held here in Portland the same month. I am tickled pink. Think of all those stories waiting out there to be written from these men and women?

Dave has been published in *Military* and *Vietnam* magazines. He is coordinating the National Americal Reunion. The ties we make in the military last for life. If you have lost touch with folks, think about going to a reunion. Remember the buddy system is still in place.

Ann Patchett wrote a wonderful article about the death of her long time friend which appeared in the June 2004 issue of *Vogue*. She started out writing an article which later turned into a book about her friend, *Truth & Beauty*. One sentence of hers in the article struck me quite hard.

"My mom used to say that grief is a debt, and you could pay it now or you could pay it later, but you would pay."

How incredibly true. Ann goes on to talk about what the process of writing gave her in dealing with her friend's death.

"I had started to write this book from such a place of grief and confusion that I really didn't know what I was doing, but the more I wrote, the more I understood. I was allowing myself to stay with her for a while longer. I was also painting a portrait I could keep with me for the future."

Part of my journey in writing this book is much the same. It has been a way for me to honor and deal with Scott's death, to honor all veterans past and present, and to try to give something back. It is also a way to set me free to help other veterans write their stories.

When I finally came upon the notion that if one veteran was helped by this book, then I had accomplished my mission, the book began to move and flow.

Will stories be easy to write? No. But you can tell it like it is. How about this wonderful quote I discovered in a recent used bookstore treasure hunt.

"War is insanity. Men who devote their lives and energies toward the preparation for death and destruction cannot be totally sane. At best, they function under illusions. Like fighting for peace. At worst, they are mad. Fighting for peace is a lot like fucking for virginity," says Charles W. Sasser in his book, *Always A Warrior; The Memoir of a Six-War Soldier*. And that is just the first paragraph of the Foreword! Can't wait to read the rest of his story.

Writing this book has helped me realize my journey was to deal with the sacrifice of veterans and to try to educate others about the true meaning and cost of "Freedom isn't Free."

It never has been. "During World War II approximately 1.3 million members of the American armed forces suffered neuropsychiatric disorders serious enough to debilitate them for some period of time. From American army ground forces alone, 504,000 soldiers were discharged for psychiatric reasons," states Paul Wanke in his article "American Military Psychiatry and Its Role among Ground Forces in World War II," in the January 1999 issue of *The Journal of Military History*.

Writing our stories is one way to process the experience. Veterans are veterans every day, for the rest of their lives. It is time to stop leaving invisible stories along the way.

But how do you decide which stories to write or tell to which people?

Perhaps one of the best examples of this I have seen is by Al Siebert, Ph.D., director of The Resiliency Center and author of *The Resiliency Advantage* and *The Survivor Personality*.

His article "Telling Your Survivor Story" is reprinted here with his permission.

Anyone who survives a high distressing experience will never be the same again. Some survivors remain emotionally wounded for life. They relive and re-experience distressing moments over and over. They often dwell on fears about what could happen to them again or to others.

Many survivors recover fairly well with the help of their family and friends. A few go beyond recovery, however. In their struggle to heal and put their past behind them, they grow and become even better than they were before. They become transformed in ways they value.

Every transformational journey is unique, but heroic survivors have two things in common. First, they integrate the traumatic experience into their public identity and make the experience a defining part of their life story. Second, they talk or write about it in a way that has an inspiring effect on others.

The transformational process of recovery from deeply distressing, traumatic experiences takes many months or years and usually proceeds in three phases:

Into the Fire: Reliving the Fears and Memories

- Your effort to suppress the painful memories and feelings is not working. You have not been able to make the feelings and memories go away. You tried to keep your feelings secret, you didn't tell anyone. You avoided situations that might stir up feelings and memories. You may have attempted to deaden the pain with medications, drugs, and alcohol. Are easily upset by certain statements made by others. You have flashbacks. You wonder "Why me?" You have tried to fake being "normal." You feel isolated, lonely, and have very few close relationships.

- You take the courageous step to relive your traumatic experiences with a friend, a counselor, or a support group of people who have been through similar experiences. Painful memories and feelings get uncorked. You have nightmares. You feel like you are falling into a bottomless well. You find yourself reliving the experience during conversations, at movies, in the store, almost any place. You wish you never started this.

Taking Control Phase: Wrestling for Control of your Spirit

- You repeat, relive, and talk about the experience again and again with good listeners. You write about your feelings in a journal. You discover after awhile that you can tell a shorter version, a summary of what happened with less emotional pain. You feel moments of relief. You sleep and feel better. You notice that there is something freeing from knowing that other people know what you went through and care for you.

- You begin to observe yourself more than ever before. You face your fears. You question your erroneous beliefs and assumptions. You discover that you are not as responsible for what happened as you always believed. You struggle to break free from old emotional habits. You defiantly build positive self-regard. You experience breakthrough insights into yourself and others. You give up old scripts, "games" and ways of manipulating people. You feel embarrassed about what you used to do, but also feel happy about what you are learning about yourself. You see some positive aspects, some benefits from going through all this.

- You dismiss suggestions that you forgive the offender/perpetrator (if any). You still feel angry. You do not want to forgive. You may want revenge, punishment, justice. You may need to take some action to confront, report, publicize or resolve what happened.

Transition Phase: Awkward Efforts in Unfamiliar Territory

- You regress, slide back, or repeat an old pattern you thought you'd left behind. You find that old mental and emotional habits are hard to break. You accept that you are human, forgive yourself, and start over again.

- You decide that for your own well being you will try to forgive, but are very clear this does not mean condoning, approving, or excusing what happened. You don't try to forgive because others say you should. You will forgive only when you feel ready, if you ever do.

- You experiment telling your story to others outside your support group and circle of closest friends. You discover that many people either cannot handle listening for more than a short time or become overly sympathetic and distraught about what you went through. Both kinds of listeners have to be coped with, are dissatisfying to talk with. You face a new challenge, that of learning to develop conscious choices about who you tell about your past, when, and how much you say.

- You struggle with assimilating your traumatic experience into your identity. How do you deal with people who label you by your experience?

- You ask yourself "Is there a gift in this? A blessing?"

Reemerging Phase: Publicly Declare and Validate your Transformation

- You now control your memory of your experience, it no longer controls you. You can stop thinking about it when you want to. You gradually develop the ability to *choose* to:
    a. not talk about your experience when asked.
    b. give a short, *Reader's Digest* summary and then change the subject.
    c. talk in detail with the rare person who is sincerely interested, is a good listener, and will take time to listen.

- You find that you can have two sets of feelings about what you went through. You can have both negative feelings and positive feelings.

- You notice that you have more self-confidence and better judgment than before. Your relationships improve. You have an ability to see through people who are suppressing deep emotional pain, who are trying to fake being "normal" – and you let them do that.

- You make yourself available to others who are just starting to deal with similar traumatic experiences. You are able to listen to them without falling back into your old pain. You encourage and coach them without trying to rescue them. You can talk about what you did and what you learned in a way useful to them.

- You talk with various people about your healing process and your learnings in a way that does not subject listeners to the pain and distress you went through. You can talk about your experiences as an observer and learner. You confess mistakes, bad judgment, weaknesses, and laugh at yourself. Now when you tell your story, you do so without re-experiencing strong distress. When you tell your story you do so for the benefit of others to inspire and encourage them.

- You discover that you have valuable messages for a wider audience, that you have acquired important learnings in the school of life that you want to share with people facing many kinds of difficulties. You realize that without the traumatic experiences you would never have accomplished so much beneficial personal growth. You appreciate that you have managed to convert misfortune into good luck.

- You find your voice. You talk to groups about your experience and what you learned. You may write an article. You may think of writing a book about how the worst thing that ever happened in your life was also the best thing that ever happened. You want others to know that something very good can come out of something very bad.

- You work at making your story of your experience and your healing journey a small part of your larger identity. You avoid letting your experience become your primary identity in your own mind, even though it may be how others often refer to you.

- You find that you are immune from opinions, comments, and statements that used to upset you. You connect with other survivors who have been through their own transformative journey. You appreciate and validate each other's spirit.

- You discover at times that you've gone many days without thinking of the traumatic experience or your long healing journey. You appreciate that your emotional wounds have healed, that you are free from what happened, and that your recovery struggle changed you into a better person than you were before.

Role Model for Others

- You offer your strength and insights to others who are struggling with their pain, anguish, traumas, and crises. You can stay calm and keep your attention on others in distress without having your painful memories stirred up. Your presence is helpful to others who see you as a role model and as proof that a person can heal and be happy again.

- You have the courage and strength to relive all your experiences to write a book that inspires others to cope with their challenges.

When I asked Al Siebert for permission to reprint his excellent articles, he graciously included a message for his fellow veterans. I include it here:

A personal message from one veteran to another ...

    The condition called Post Traumatic Stress Disorder (PTSD) is not a mental illness. It is a normal person's conditioned, neuro-chemical reaction to extreme danger and to gruesome, horrifying experiences. PTSD does not go away by itself, but it does not have to be a permanent, life-long condition either. Thousands of veterans have made the journey out of their lonely swamp of pain and isolation to return home to their families and friends. It takes courage to overcome PTSD, more courage than it took to go into combat, but Kim Cook's book provides you with a map to follow for making the heroic journey back home to a happy life.

    Keep in mind that your goal is not to make memories go away. You have a pair of connected goals. One is to achieve conscious control over your memories so that you control them, they don't control you. With conscious control you don't have to avoid people and situations that might trigger an uncontrolled flood of feelings and memories. With conscious control you can choose to talk or not talk about your experiences when people inquire. The other goal is that you don't go to the other extreme and allow your war experience to become your primary identity. Both goals together lead to your war experience becoming one chapter in the multi-chaptered book about your unique life.

    Whether or not you have some PTSD to deal with is not the main motivation for writing your military stories, however. Your children, their children, and generations that follow will want to know about your experiences. Write your stories for them following the well-tested guidelines provided by Kim Cook. Do it for them.

Al Siebert, PhD
Ex-paratrooper and author of *The Survivor Personality*
Vietnam Veterans Rap Group Leader, Advisor
World Trade Center 9/11 Survivors Network
www.resilencycenter.com

With Al's wonderful words, I would like to think I am on the road to being a role model to others, but I know I slip back sometimes. On the other hand, writing this book has helped me to make personal changes. I've lost weight, took up swing, jitterbug and belly dancing, and I laugh a lot more.

And my sense of humor is back with a vengeance. Carol Burnett said, "Comedy is tragedy plus time." How true.

I am also struck by how the survivor's journey so closely parallels the hero's journey. Amazing coincidence? I think not.

Where are you along the survivor's journey? Are you surprised to learn there is a journey and many others have walked the path too? You are not alone. We are all on this little planet earth together. We are all so much more alike than we care to admit.

Perhaps your journey starts with a single written word. What have you got to lose? I think any process which can lead from grief to joy needs to be given a try. After all, it is guaranteed in the Declaration of Independence. Think not?

"We hold these truths to be self-evident that all men are created equal, that they are endowed by their Creator with certain unalienable Rights, that among these are Life, Liberty, and the pursuit of Happiness."

Think about it. Written words which gave birth to a nation.

Happiness is capitalized. Get it?

Thank you for defending Liberty. Let's all get on with pursuing Happiness.

Resources:
www.legion.org – *The American Legion Magazine*, Feb. 2006, article, "War Head – VA Braces for a Looming Spike in Post-Traumatic Stress Disorder Patients from Iraq and Afghanistan," by James V. Carroll
Courage After Fire: Coping Strategies for Troops Returning from Iraq and Afghanistan and Their Families by Keith Armstrong, Suzanne Best, and Paula Domenici
www.patiencepress.com
www.ResiliencyCenter.com
www.pbs.org/wgbh/pages/frontline/shows/heart/etc/resources.html

Writing To Heal by Dr. James Pennebaker
Article at www.utexas.edu/features/archive/2005/writing.html

"Combat Duty in Iraq and Afghanistan, Mental Health Problems, and Barriers to Care" by Hoge, Castro, Messer, McGurk, Cotting, and Koffman in the July 1, 2004 issue of *The New England Journal of Medicine*
www.combatstress.org.uk/home/default.esp
Soldier's Heart: Survivor's Views of Combat Trauma by Hansel, Steidle, Zaczek and Zaczek
Spare Parts: From Campus to Combat: A Marine Reservist's Journey from Campus to Combat in 38 Days by Buzz Williams
Achilles in Vietnam: Combat Trauma and the Undoing of Character by Jonathan Shay
Odysseus in America: Combat Trauma and the Trials of Homecoming by Jonathan Shay
I Can't Get Over It: A Handbook for Trauma Survivors by Aphrodite Matsakis, Ph.D.
Achilles in Vietnam: Combat Trauma and The Undoing of Character by Jonathan Shay, M.S., Ph.D.
Recovering from War: A Woman's Guide to Helping Your Vietnam Vet, Your Family, and Yourself by Patience Mason
Strong Hearts, Wounded Souls: Native American Veterans of the Vietnam War by Tom Holm
A Piece of My Heart: The Stories of Twenty-Six American Women Who Served In Vietnam by Keith Walker
On Killing: The Psychological Cost of Learning to Kill in War and Society by Lt. Col. Dave Grossman
Civil War Poetry and Prose by Walt Whitman

TV Programs:
The Soldier's Heart, Frontline, March 1, 2005, PBS, www.pbs.org/wgbh/pages/frontline

PART FOUR

TRANSITIONS AND

SHOVING OFF

Chapter 31

Transitions and Parting Shots

When I got out of the Army in 1978, I drove through a snowstorm in Wyoming and barely made it home for Christmas. Less than two weeks later I found myself sitting in a college classroom working on a business degree.

I didn't talk to anyone in my classes for three months. I had no idea what civilians talked about.

That may sound dumb, but it's true. The military is a different world with rituals, rules, and a language all its own. Moving from active duty to civilian life or from activated Guard or Reservist back to civilian life is not an easy transition.

When I look at how the Vietnam veterans were pulled out of combat one day and flown home the next, it's amazing any of them were able to adjust. We learned some lessons after Vietnam, but we forgot others.

With the number of reserve and guard troops, plus active duty troops returning and cycling through Iraq and Afghanistan right now, I feel writing about the changes and transitions is a valuable way to process the rage, anger, joy, triumphs, and pain, whether felt now or thirty years from now.

It takes time. Writing can help process the details, bring back memories, process grief, and record thoughts and actions of what it is like to come back to Kansas, without Toto.

Writing this book was a much longer and larger journey than I expected it to be. Pretty much sums up my military time too. So where do we all go now?

I will keep writing. While this book has been a labor of love, it has also been a forced march at times. But as in a long march, I feel both elated and a little sad it is coming to an end. But then, there is the next hill to climb.

I'm thinking the world needs a military humor fiction writer. I'm trained as a journalist, but I find my mind likes to play with fiction, the ability to weave dreams and worlds of my own making.

My military romance novels were not published. "Too military," I was told. My screenplay *Reserve Wars* won a second place award and a $1,000 prize, but knocked into agent sneers when Demi Moore's *G.I. Jane* came into the theaters at the same time. And still I write.

Do Bar Fights Count?

So as I move back and forth between being a non-fiction writer and a fiction story teller, what parting shots do I have for you?

- Take your DD214 or whatever form number of discharge papers you have down to your courthouse or county/city offices and have it recorded. Then put the original in a fire safe or safe deposit box. Do not carry it around in your wallet. This same advice goes for condoms. Nothing works right if carried in a wallet too long.
- Apply for every Veterans Affairs benefit you can think of, even if you don't think it applies now. Get it on record. It was ten years after Desert Storm when my flight nurse-attorney friend asked me if I ever applied for service connection for my emergency eye surgery. Hadn't even crossed my mind. So, I am now service connected in case my eye decides to pop out again. (I figure the VA knows something is wrong with my head, they're just not quite sure what it is.) It is not possible to know the true cost of war unless the human toll after service is documented. Besides, you earned it!
- Reach out to other veterans and say thank you. All ages, all generations, peacetime and war time. You may be the first person to thank them. What an honor.
- Snoop around. A VA program for low-income veterans and widows is missing paying benefits to about 2 million eligible war veterans and widows because these people don't know they qualify. The pension is for veterans who served during wartime but have fallen into poverty and for widows of veterans who have fallen on hard times. The program has a weird name, "disability pension," but the person doesn't have to be disabled to receive it. Go figure. Veterans can even qualify based on their age. Give the VA a call at 1-800-827-1000 or check out www.vba.va.gov/bin/21/milsvc/benfacts.htm
- If you think you might like to go to your unit's reunion, GO! Now! When Mikel died, one of the things Cindy was so grateful for was they had gone to his reunion and he got to bond again with his brothers. Don't dawdle! I live with an active volcano in my backyard, Mt. St. Helens, so you never know what's coming next in this life.
- Get a tape recorder, digital recorder, IPOD, CD burner, camcorder, computer voice recognition software or Vulcan mind meld and record other veterans' stories as oral and/or video histories for those who can no longer write or prefer not to write. I am planning on writing the *How To*

Write Your Military Stories Workbook so others can interview veterans and fill out the book for them or veterans can do it themselves, like a military diary.

- **Note to current activated and active troops** – the Department of Veterans Affairs is **NOT** associated in any way with the military or Department of Defense. In fact, I have it on pretty good authority they don't cooperate with each other very well either. Seek counseling at the VA or Vet Centers and it will remain completely private. No one will inform the military. If you are having adjustment or mental health concerns, please get thee to a counselor! You're normal!
- Speaking of invisible wounds, Traumatic Brain Injury (TBI) is the "signature wound" of the Iraq War say doctors. "According to the Brain Injury Association of America, 14 percent to 20 percent of combat casualties in past conflicts were diagnosed with traumatic brain injuries. But in Iraq, brain trauma accounts for up to 50 percent of injuries, the group said," according to the article in *The Oregonian* newspaper on Oct. 1, 2005. This condition causes "subtle personality changes, memory loss and difficulties with reasoning," the article explains. This injury is life long and will affect the soldier and their entire family. Get to the VA, Vet Centers or any veteran service organization to get help and learn about the massive impact this injury will have on veterans, their families and veteran healthcare for decades to come.
- Big kudos to the Vietnam Veterans of America for starting The National Gulf War Resource Center at www.ngwrc.org Remember Agent Orange of Vietnam fame? Depleted uranium is just one new nightmare for Gulf War veterans. Check it out and get informed. Writing can include letters to politicians too. Snail or email.
- I would like to see Bar Fights Writing Groups start up at all Vet Centers, Disabled American Veterans, American Legion, and VFW Posts, Veteran Motorcycle groups and anywhere else vets will get together. Every operation needs to have a nifty title, so I am dubbing this **Operation Warrior Scribe**. Then let's do it all over again in Australia, Britain, Canada and Norway. (I have a Norway connection, that's why.)
- Because I hope to become a fiction writer, I also need to launch another mission. Call it **Operation Warrior Read**. A recent article in the March 2005 *American Legion* magazine quoted the Librarian of Congress James H. Billington. His greatest concern?

"If you look at a study the National Endowment of the Arts did this past

Do Bar Fights Count?

year about the decline of reading, the rate is sharpest with the 18-to-22 age group. This is really an alarming statistic. People are concerned that jobs are being exported abroad, but if nobody does the reading, it's very elementary. You're not going to be able to perform well in a high-tech information-based society unless you can read."

Let's start book groups and mug young troops with books. Okay, maybe that is a little much, but feel free to donate books to the troops. By the way, Billington is an Army veteran, so he knows military scholars study, and read, read, read. General Patton sure did.

(If you get a chance to visit the Library of Congress, go. It is the mother ship for writers. On my first visit I was so giddy I almost forgot to breathe.)

- Write. Write. Write.
- Edit. Edit. Edit.
- Write some more.
- Have fun. Play hard, life is short.
- Thank you for your service to your country.
- Thank you for reading this book.
- What's next for you? Need suggestions?
- Someone figure out how to get the Army to let me fire a light antitank weapon (LAW).
- Somebody else figure out how to get me on an aircraft carrier to watch flight operations.
- Everybody try and figure out how I can meet the Navy dolphins. (Yes, the ones with fins – the real Flippers!)
- Someone figure out how to get me inside an M1A1 tank running the obstacle course. (Please provide pillows, a scuba suit, and a snorkel mask too)
- Somebody else figure out how to get me a ride on a C-17.
- Come up with a way to get me a tour of a Seawolf Class Submarine. Not while it's underwater. I was in the Army for a reason.
- Everybody try and figure out how to get me rides in Apache and Blackhawk helicopters. (I think my hips will fit in an Apache. Maybe.)
- How about a ride on an Air Force firetruck with lights and sirens. Maybe I can fire the water cannon too?
- What about that cool new toy, er, berm busting machine the Marines are getting? How about a ride in that? It looks like a Sci Fi vehicle.

- Think I could ever get the chance to touch a Stealth bomber? After I grounded myself first. While it is ON THE GROUND, I might add.
- Someone figure out how to get me a sleepover on the U.S.S. *Missouri*.
- I have a big new project too. I've adopted an aircraft carrier. Not just any carrier, but the U.S.S. *Ranger,* CV61. The U.S.S. *Ranger* Museum Foundation put me on the board before really getting to know me. Poor sailors. We are working to bring her to Portland to be an attraction, museum, memorial and education center. Check out our progress at www.ussrangercv61.com. Can you imagine the classroom space for a military writing conference on her? She is a very big girl and she's gorgeous. I got to crawl around on her in Bremerton. Carriers have a lot of stairs, I discovered.
- And what about all those bar fights? Where are those stories? Chuck wrote about Santa (Gunny) getting busted by the MPs in Saigon, and Bob M. and Bob H. and Dave had quite a few Army bar fight stories. Both during and after military service, I might add. I've thought long and hard and searched my memory. I've never been in a bar fight. Been in biker bars, gay bars, overseas bars, and spent my last night in the Army in a strip bar. I've got to find me a bar fight!
- Get busy out there. There are stories to write and fantasies to fulfill. Mine and yours.
Love Kim
Write On!

Appendix A

Guidelines for Teachers and Counselors

I must be out of my mind. The six men sitting in front of me comprised the first group of *Writing War Stories* students. Who the hell did I think I was to be teaching this class?

Teachers get jitters. I had a grand case. The only thing I could do was press on and see what happened. If nothing else, I had brought a rather odd selection of military books which stood like soldiers at the chalkboard. Students could amuse themselves with the books at the break.

My outline, lesson plans and research to teach the first class had been in progress for more than six months. In 1997, there was not much literature on using writing to heal. I spent time talking with my friends who were VA Vet Center counselors to make sure I was not going to inflict trauma on my fellow veterans.

They assured me it would be fine. I had a structured environment, a class syllabus with assignments and I was there to teach writing. Since I was going to hand out the Vet Center information brochure at the beginning of class, I was doing all I could.

After the first class, I dropped by my friend Rich's house. I told him how the class went and wondered if any of my students would be back next week.

He looked at me and laughed. "They'll be back," he said. A door-gunner in Vietnam and former Vet Center Counselor, I trusted Rich's opinion, but I was still nervous. But, they did come back. A couple of them for three years straight.

In my second year of teaching the class I found an article titled "The Use of Writing in the Treatment of Post-Traumatic Stress Disorders" by Susan C. Feldman, David Read Johnson and Marilyn Ollayos. Part of the *Handbook of Post-Traumatic Therapy*, the book was out of print back then, but I tracked it down at a local college library.

The section titled "Process of Writing" outlined how they recommend care providers use the writing process.

1. Requirement to write, usually with structured guides, and beginning in group sessions, then on their own.

2. Requirement to read their writings and share with fellow veterans and staff; this may evoke catharsis of emotion or demonstration of vulnerability.
3. Receiving feedback from the group, including verbal reassurance and physical comforting.
4. Identification of similarities and differences in experiences among member groups.
5. Sharing written work with significant others.

I was greatly relieved and excited to realize the class I had created a year ago followed all these guidelines. Writing is and will always be therapy for me. The article talked about the process of writing as creation, a defense against death anxiety, a dialogue with self and as testimony to others.

> "Writing is a fundamental act of commitment to the world; through writing, the person is thrown into the world. In contrast, the act of the trauma separates the person from the world. Writing is thus a public act that represents the return of the victim to the world; confronting the sufferer with the reality that bad things can happen for which responsibility must be taken. Writing gives this testimonial solidity and validation, which provide a foundation for transcending shame and achieving forgiveness.
>
> Presenting one's writing to an audience gives distance to the original shameful event. The audience is transformed into both the witness and – through identification with the writer – the victim. Victim and audience are brought closer together. Writing therefore serves to link the victim to the world. The result is the empowering of the victim. Writing reasserts the sense of personal control over the trauma, elevating the victim to the role of teacher/expert/helper."

Since most veterans experience post-traumatic stress and many experience post-traumatic stress disorder, I felt I was on the right road if this is how clinicians were using writing to treat PTSD. War is traumatic, there is no getting around that. So is peacetime. So is terrorism.

> "If the moment of trauma is fundamentally an act of destruction, then writing serves, symbolically, as a restitutive act of creation. To victims of trauma, the act of writing calls forth the realization, 'I

exist; I am not gone.' Once written, the piece acquires its own autonomy: it is no longer in the victim. Writing is a birth."

So, not only does the act of writing memorialize those we served with, it also allows veterans to heal from their trauma and experience a rebirth. Pretty powerful stuff, this writing.

Now there is more information available about using writing to heal. The whole science of bibliotherapy which started in the 1940s is embraced by many practitioners today. And veterans thought we were writing for fun!

During the three years of the class, I saw writing levels change and deepen among all my students. I could tell when they peeled another layer of the pain onion and went deeper to their dark places, when their emotions were allowed to creep out a bit at a time or come rushing in a powerful force when they exposed an ugly monster.

It reminds me of lancing a boil or popping a zit, for a really gross image. Once the infection, poison or pus is out, the wound/trauma can heal.

Writing *War Stories* alum, Jeff Manthos, has gone on to teach a military writing group. He came up with a homework assignment I think is brilliant. He gave his writers the following task: Write the story no one wants to hear. How is that for opening some doors into the soul?

Has every veteran been traumatized? There is no way I can answer that. I do know that every veteran has changed from their military experience. I still fold my underwear in the basic training way, in my case. Some things linger on from our military past.

What have I learned about teaching writing to veterans? A lot more about myself than I knew at the time. Writing this book has been quite a journey too, as I revisit what was a very special time in my life. Do I have recommendations for others? But of course.

Starting A War Stories Writing Group

If you want to start your own "Writing War Stories" group – which I would love every Vet Center on earth to do – here are some guidelines:

1. **Everyone should be a military veteran, Reserve, Guard, Coast Guard or Merchant Marine member.** The bonding that occurs recreates the camaraderie writers experienced in the service. It not only helps recall like memories and events, but allows a closeness which those writers who have

not been in the military don't understand. **It is part of creating the trust bond, which every writing group must have.**

2. The same is true for significant other writing groups. Keep the participants on the same personal experience level to ensure like events and challenges.

3. Choose your leader wisely. Get a professional writing teacher to help with the group or run it. I don't mean an English teacher per se, I mean a working writer – journalist, novel teacher, creative writer or memoir instructor. This is a different type of writing, between sterile non-fiction and academic themes. I use fiction, non-fiction, journalism and screenwriting techniques to bring a student's writing alive. Not all teachers are good for you – refer back to Brenda Ueland's paragraphs in Chapter One.

4. Tolerance for others. Respect for each other is paramount. I made a very big mistake with one veteran during my first class. We were discussing World War II atrocities. I made a sweeping statement that there have been atrocities committed by both sides. I broke a cardinal rule of not honoring his experience.

Another rule is not to compare veterans' experiences. My vet center counselor friends tell me this is a common occurrence among veterans. A vet will say someone who was shot twice is worse off than he is, because he was only shot once. There is no priority of pain. Just as bullets kill during war and peace, all veterans are to be honored and respected.

5. I used a simple form from my novel writing class teacher for constructive criticism. The half sheet of 8 ½ by 11 piece of paper listed the reviewers name, date, title or chapter, name of the writer and then two areas with lines for comments: strengths and suggestions. I made a conscious effort to have the strengths last, so writers would always have some positive feedback about their piece of writing at the end of each critique. (This form is at the end of the Chapter.)

6. Class length was three hours with a break in the middle. We tried for three readings
each night, with a limit of 12 pages of double-spaced writing per person. Class size was best at 13 – 15 students, given the round circle we sat in and handling the size of the group. Stories were always turned in to me to edit before the writer read in class. Not only did this give me a chance to provide personal feedback and editing for each student, it also let me schedule the material for order to be read in class. I always tried to put a difficult reading at the beginning or middle of the class and make sure I kept a story with a more

positive tone as the last reading of the night to provide an uplifting "take away" memory for all of us.

7. At the end of each year we published a class anthology book of stories from everyone
throughout the year. For our last class at the end of the year, we would have a party at a local pub, eat, and autograph each other's books. The book provided a concrete product of what the entire class had accomplished throughout the year. Each story brought back memories for all of us when looking back over the stories.

8. The class goals as stated on my syllabus were:
   a. Complete a 10 to 12 page, double-spaced story or several short two-page stories.
   b. Help veterans discover what they want to write.
   c. Encourage veterans to write their stories.
   d. Develop writer skills.
   e. Discover which writing format – fiction, non-fiction, personal history – best meets each students goals.
   f. Develop acceptance of class critiques.

9. At the start of each term I also had all students fill out the Student Information Sheet. That consisted of:
   - Name, address, zip code, telephone, and email address, if available.
   - List your writing interests (fiction, non-fiction, personal history, articles, etc.)
   - List your writing background (high school, college, etc.) and military unit.
   - What would you like to get out of this class?
     a. Short term goal (1-3 terms)
     b. Long term goal (3 years from now, for instance)
   - What are your reading habits? What do you read? Do you read the kind of material that you would like to write? Do you read for information or pleasure, or both?
   - Do you have established writing habits? (Circle one)
     a. A place of your own in which to write?
     b. A specified, regular time in which to write?
     c. A regular reading and research program?
     d. I've thought about it.

- Do you understand how to study the publishing market?
- Please use the bottom of this paper to write a paragraph or two on why you want to write. (And anything else you would like to add)

10. I made beginning students wait until the third week of class to turn in any outside writing they were working on and they had the same limit as the advanced students–12 pages a week. Sometimes this doesn't work, given story lengths, but most of the time a page or two extra was fine.

And here is the Syllabus so a teacher can see how I structured the course.

Organization of Course:
1. The focus is on in-class writing, class readings and homework.
2. Some lecture.
3. Lessons on writing technique.
4. All assignments should be typed and double-spaced. If students don't have access to a typewriter or computer, please print and double-space your writing.

10 Week Course Outline:
Week One – See Chapter One and Appendix B
Lesson: Introductions. Class organization. The Dynamics of Writing. Vet Center Resources.
Handout: Class syllabus and student information sheet.
Homework Assignment: List five events or scenes you want to write about. Pick one of the five and write the first three paragraphs.
Week Two – See Chapter Two
Lesson: Different types of writing. Where to start.
Handout: Beginnings and Grenada newspaper story.
Homework Assignment: Write two typed pages of the scene you picked. Bring to next class.
Week Three – See Chapter Three
Lesson: Characters, point of view and motivation.
Handout: Tim O'Brien article, "The Reimagined Life"
Homework Assignment: What motivates your character? Write one typewritten page about your main character's background, likes, dislikes. Keep a copy of this, you will turn a copy in to the instructor. Continue to work on your story.

**Beginning students may now turn in private writing they are working on outside of the class to be edited by the instructor. Limit twelve pages a week per student.

Week Four – See Chapter Four
Lesson: Conflict and obstacles.
Handout: "The Hero's Journey" and "The Hunt For Red October"
Homework Assignment: Eavesdrop on conversation – write down two or three interesting sentences you've overheard. Bring the sentences to class. Continue to work on your story.

Week Five – See Chapters Five, Six and Seven
Lesson: Dialogue and the five senses.
Handout: Screenwriting dialogue.
Homework Assignment: Write one page completely of dialogue only. Start each character's speech in a new paragraph. Make two copies. Hand in one copy. Continue to work on your story.

Week Six – See Chapter Eight
Lesson: Setting, active verbs and clichés.
Handout: Clichés defined.
Homework Assignment: Find a picture from your military days. Write three paragraphs about what is happening in the picture. Bring both the photo and the writing to class. Continue to work on your story.

Week Seven – See Chapters Nine, Ten and Eleven
Lesson: Middles and ends, pacing and hooks.
Handout: Top Ten Books List. See my web site at www.warriortales.com It changes.
Homework Assignment: Interview another veteran, perhaps a friend or relative. Bring a two-page, double-spaced typed story about this veteran to class.

Week Eight – See Chapter Twelve
Lesson: The business of writing and publishing. Query letters. Setting writing goals.
Handouts: Query letter examples.
Homework Assignment: Write a query letter for a publication of your choice. Turn in your twelve-page story to the instructor, whether it is 3 to 12 pages.

Week Nine
Lesson: Guest Speaker, usually a military writer.
Handout: Guest speaker biography.

Homework Assignment: Write three paragraphs about another story or anecdote you want to write about. Visit a local bookstore's military section and find out what kind of books are NOT on the shelves.

Week Ten – See Chapter Thirteen
Lesson: Student's stories, course summary, student progress, future writing goals and questions.
Handout: Course evaluation.
Homework Assignment: Write!

And so we would go on. After the first term, I had students return term after term. Once past writer's basic training, I ended up with a group of advanced students and always one or two FNGs per term.

This worked out well since I would give the new student a quick overview at the break or after the class. They would do their assignments and report back to the class the next week. The advanced students would turn in their new stories and we would critique three stories each night.

Each critique sheet had the following items listed based on the format my fiction writing teacher Dee Lopez used.
Writing Critique Sheet (Size 8 ½ x 5 ½)
Your Name:
Date:
Author:
Title:
Chapter:
Strengths:
Suggestions:

One of the many great things about this half-page critique sheet is each author gets 13 to 15 critiques to take home and look at about the work they read aloud in class. I still have many from my fiction writing class.

And that is how I taught the class. Simple as pie, right? Is my way the only way? Nope. Is it the right way? Well, it's my way, so it worked for me. Might not work for others, but at least it gives you a starting point if you want to give this a go. Be my guest!

Resources:
Handbook of Post-Traumatic Therapy by Mary Beth Williams, John F. Sommer, editors
The Courage To Write: How Writers Transcend Fear by Ralph Keyes
Writing From The Inside Out by Dennis Palumbo

Writing As A Way of Healing: How Telling Our Stories Transforms Our Lives by Louise DeSalvo
The Healing Power of Stories by Daniel Taylor, Ph.D.
With Pen In Hand: the healing power of stories by Henriette Anne Klauser, Ph.D.
How To Write The Story of Your Life by Frank P. Thomas
Art and Fear; Observations on the Perils (and Rewards) of Artmaking by David Bayles and Ted Orland
The War of Art: Break Through the Blocks and Win Your Inner Creative Battles by Steven Pressfield
Telling Lies for Fun and Profit: A Manual for Fiction Writers by Lawrence Block
Military Veterans PTSD Reference Manual by I.S. Parrish
I Can't Get Over It; A Handbook for Trauma Survivors by Aphrodite Matsakis, Ph.D.

Appendix B

Veteran Outreach Centers

United States and Australia

The following information is excerpted from The Portland Vet Center brochure:

Officially titled "Readjustment Counseling Services," the Vet Centers are a community-based arm of the Department of Veterans Affairs (DVA).

- Our Mission is to provide a wide range of counseling, outreach, and referral services to veterans and their families.
- Our Focus is to help the veteran work through issues with Post-Traumatic Stress Disorder (PTSD) and/or sexual trauma directly related to active duty service.
- Our Goal is to see that every eligible veteran receives the highest quality service. Our veterans have served their country, now it is our job to serve them.
- Our Hope is to see every one of our veteran clients able to lead more fulfilled, productive lives.

History and Eligibility:
Vet Centers opened in late 1979, providing g free services to Vietnam era veterans. Congress and the president later made Vet Centers available to veterans of Lebanon, Grenada, Panama, the Persian Gulf, and Somaila.

In 1992, Vet Centers were permitted to provide counseling services for all veterans who suffered sexual trauma or sexual harassment while on active duty.

In 1996, President Clinton signed Public Law 104-262, making combat veterans of WW II and Korea eligible for Vet Center Services. He also signed Public Law 104-275, which expanded the dates of Vietnam service back to February 28, 1961.

Currently, Vet Center services are available, absolutely free of charge, to the following two categories of veterans:

- Combat veterans (those who served in the combat theater) from the list below.
- Veterans who experienced sexual trauma (i.e. assault, rape, or harassment, etc.) while serving on active duty at any time, whether during peace or war.

Following is a list of periods of hostility; service during which, makes a combat veteran eligible.**

- Vietnam Era*   05 AUG 64 – 07 MAY 75
- Vietnam combat   28 FEB 61 – 07 MAY 75
- WWII   07 DEC 42 – 31 DEC 46
- Korea   27 JUN 50 – 31 JAN 55
- Lebanon   25 AUG 82 – 26 FEB 84
- Grenada   23 OCT 83 – 21 NOV 83
- Panama   20 DEC 89 – 31 JAN 90
- Persian Gulf   02 AUG 90 – Ongoing
- Somalia   17 DEP 92 – Ongoing
- Yugoslavia**   24 MAR 99 – Ongoing
- Global War/Terror   11 SEP 01 – Ongoing
- Bereavement

*Congress has decided that, as of 01 JAN 04, Vietnam Era NON-combat veterans who have not previously visited a Vet Center will lose eligibility for Vet Center services. Those who have visited before the deadline will retain eligibility, whether they are currently receiving services or not.

**These eligibility criteria apply only to Vet Center services. Eligibility or ineligibility here is not necessarily an indication of eligibility elsewhere through the DVA.

**Call or visit the Vet Center for more information and details.

Confidentiality:
All Vet Centers hold all client information in the strictest confidence in compliance with the Privacy Act of 1975. No information will ever be communicated or made available to any outside agency or person without express written, signed consent from the veteran whose information is concerned.

What is PTSD?

While many veterans readjust well into civilian life in spite of their wartime experiences, many others have found it difficult. Post-Traumatic Stress Disorder (PTSD) is the technical name for what is commonly referred to as "Delayed Stress" or "Shell Shock:" a delayed, often chronic, reaction experienced by normal people exposed to abnormally intense amounts of stress. This type of stress can be encountered in war zones, natural disasters, sexual or repetitive abuse or trauma, and other catastrophic situations. The symptoms can be serious, and usually do not go away on their own.

They include:

- Intense anger, irritability, rage
- Anxiety and chronic depression
- Difficulty trusting people
- Emotional numbness or disassociation
- Guilt over acts done or seen & not prevented
- Survivor's guilt
- Hyper-vigilance (alertness) or being easily startled
- Excessive grief or sadness
- Intrusive memories
- Social isolation and feelings of alienation
- Loss of interest in pleasurable activities
- Low tolerance to stress
- Problems with authority
- Low self esteem
- Difficulty sleeping and/or nightmares
- Substance abuse

No single symptom defines PTSD, but the more symptoms a person has, the greater the likelihood (s)he suffers from it.

Services:

The Vet Center provides the following services to eligible veterans and their families.

- Individual counseling
- Group counseling
- Marital and family counseling

- Sexual trauma counseling
- Information and referrals to community and local DVA resources
- Point of contact for Veteran Service organizations
- Discharge upgrade and military record acquisition assistance
- Veterans' loan library
- Employment assistance*
- Benefits counseling**
- Bereavement counseling

Making a Counseling Appointment:
Anyone wishing to see a counselor must make an appointment. To do this, simply call or stop in. A member of the office staff will fill out a Veterans Information Form and pass that on to a counselor. You will then be called within 24 to 48 hours to inform you of the time and date of an appointment which has been scheduled for you.

If you come in, it is helpful if you are able to bring in a copy of your DD214.

***

When I talked to our county veterans employment representative, he said from what he is seeing the troops returning from Iraq and Afghanistan seem to start having trouble at six to eight months after coming home. I've also had World War II veterans in class who had nightmares crop up fifty years later.

I urge all veterans and their family members who have concerns about any veteran to contact a Vet Center. The last suicide count I saw for Iraq and Afghanistan numbered 18 service members, but there are family members who have also committed suicide after the loss of a soldier.

It's time to fight for our veterans personal happy endings. If you want to help out, please call a Vet Center and offer to volunteer any way you can. They are understaffed and overworked, but they care.

United States Web Resources:

Department of Veterans Affairs Readjustment Counseling Services
www.va.gov/rcs/

Vet Center Voice newsletter
http://voice.i29.net

National Center for PTSD
www.ncptsd.va.gov/facts/general/fs_what_is_ptsd.html

Vet Center 2005 Telephone Directory
www.va.gov/rcs/

Alaska
Anchorage (907) 563-6966
Fairbanks (907) 456-4238
Soldotna (907) 260-7640
Wasilla (907) 376-4318

Alabama
Birmingham (205) 731-0550
Mobile (251) 478-5906

California
Anaheim (562) 596-3101
Capitola (831) 464-4575
Chico (530) 899-8549
Commerce (323) 728-9966
Concord (925) 680-4526
Corona (951) 734-0525
Culver City (310) 641-0326
Eureka (707) 444-8271
Fresno (559) 487-5660
Gardena (310) 767-1221
Oakland (510) 763-3904
Redwood City (650) 299-0672
Rohnert Park (707) 596-3295
Sacramento (916) 566-7430
San Bernadino (909) 890-0797
San Diego (619) 294-2040
San Francisco (415) 441-5051
San Jose (408) 993-0729
Sepulveda (818) 892-9227
Ventura (805) 585-1860
Vista (760) 643-2070

Arkansas
North Little Rock (501) 324-6395

Arizona
Chinle (928) 674-3682
Keams Canyon (928) 738-5166
Phoenix (602) 640-2981
Prescott (928) 778-3469
Tucson (520) 882-0333

Florida
Fort Lauderdale (302) 994-1660
Jacksonville (904) 232-3621
Lake Worth (561) 585-0441
Miami (305) 859-8387
Orlando (407) 857-2800
Pensacola (850) 456-5886
Sarasota (941) 927-8285
St. Petersburg (727) 893-3791
Tallahassee (850) 942-8810
Tampa (813) 228-2621

Georgia
Atlanta (404) 347-7264
Savannah (912) 652-4097

Guam
Agana (671) 472-7161

Hawaii
Hilo (808) 969-3833
Honolulu (808) 973-8387
Kailua-Kona (808) 329-0574

Colorado
Boulder (303) 440-7306
Colorado Springs (719) 471-9992
Denver (303) 326-0645
Fort Collins (970) 221-5176

Connecticut
Norwich (860) 887-1755
West Haven (203) 932-9899
Wethersfield (860) 563-2320

District of Columbia
Washington (202) 726-5212

Delaware
Wilmington (302) 994-1660

Indiana
Evansville (812) 473-5993
Fort Wayne (260) 460-1456
Indianapolis (317) 927-6440
Merrillville (219) 736-5633

Kansas
Wichita (316) 265-3260

Kentucky
Lexington (859) 253-0717
Louisville (502) 634-1916

Louisiana
New Orleans (504) 464-4743
Shreveport (318) 861-1776

Lihue (808) 246-1163
Wailuku (808) 242-8557

Iowa
Cedar Rapids (319) 378-0016
Des Moines (515) 284-4929
Sioux City (712) 255-3808

Idaho
Boise (208) 342-3612
Pocatello (208) 232-0316

Illinois
Chicago (773) 881-9900
Chicago Heights (708) 754-0340
East St. Louis (618) 397-6602
Evanston (847) 332-1019
Moline (309) 762-6954
Oak Park (708) 383-3225
Peoria (309) 688-2170
Rockford (815) 395-1276
Springfield (217) 492-4955

Minnesota
Duluth (218) 722-8654
St. Paul (651) 644-4022

Missouri
Kansas City (816) 722-8654
St. Louis (314) 231-1260

Mississippi
Biloxi (228) 388-9938
Jackson (601) 965-5727

Montana
Billings (406) 657-6071
Missoula (406) 721-4918

Massachusetts
Boston (617) 424-0665
Brockton (508) 580-2730
Lowell (978) 453-1151
New Bedford (508) 999-6920
Springfield (413) 737-5167
Worcester (508) 856-7428

Maryland
Baltimore (410) 764-9400
Elkton (410) 392-4485
Silver Spring (301) 589-1073

Maine
Bangor (207) 947-3391
Caribou (207) 496-3900
Lewiston (207) 783-0068
Portland (207) 780-3584
Springvale (207) 490-1513

Michigan
Dearborn (313) 277-1428
Detroit (313) 831-6509
Escanaba (906) 789-9732, ext. 211
Grand Rapids (616) 243-0385

Nevada
Las Vegas (702) 251-7873
Reno (775) 323-1294

New York
Albany (518) 438-2505
Babylon (631) 661-3930
Bronx (718) 367-3500

North Carolina
Charlotte (704) 333-6107
Fayetteville (910) 488-6252
Greensboro (336) 333-5366
Greenville (252) 355-7920
Raleigh (919) 856-4616

North Dakota
Bismarck (701) 224-9751
Fargo (701) 237-0942
Minot (701) 852-0177

Nebraska
Lincoln (402) 476-9736
Omaha (402) 346-6735

New Hampshire
Manchester (603) 668-7060

New Jersey
Jersey City (201) 748-4467
Newark (973) 645-5954
Trenton (609) 989-2260
Ventnor (609) 487-8387

New Mexico
Albuquerque (505) 346-6562
Farmington (505) 327-9684
Santa Fe (505) 988-6562

Puerto Rico
Arecibo (787) 879-4510
Ponce (787) 841-3260
Rio Piedras (787) 749-4409

Rhode Island
Warwick (401) 739-0167

Brooklyn (718) 624-2765
Buffalo (716) 882-0505
Harlem (212) 426-2200
New York (212) 742-9591
Rochester (585) 232-5040
Staten Island (718) 816-4499
Syracuse (315) 478-7127
White Plains (914) 682-6250
Woodhaven (718) 296-2871

Ohio
Cincinnati (513) 763-3500
Cleveland Heights (216) 932-8471
Columbus (614) 257-5550
Dayton (937) 461-9150
Parma (440) 845-5023

Oklahoma
Oklahoma City (405) 270-5184
Tulsa (918) 748-5105

Oregon
Eugene (541) 465-6918
Grants Pass (541) 479-6912
Portland (503) 273-5370
Salem (503) 362-9911

Pennsylvania
Erie (814) 453-7955
Harrisburg (717) 782-3954
McKeesport (412) 678-7704
Philadelphia, Arch St.
  (215) 627-0238
Philadelphia, Olney Ave.
  (215) 924-4670
Scranton (570) 344-2676
Williamsport (570) 327-5281

South Carolina
Columbia (803) 765-9944
Greenville (864) 271-2711
North Charleston (843) 747-8387

South Dakota
Martin (605) 685-1300
Rapid City (605) 348-0077
Sioux Falls (605) 330-4552

Tennessee
Chattanooga (423) 855-6570
Johnson City (423) 928-8387
Knoxville (865) 545-4680
Memphis (901) 544-0173

Texas
Amarillo (806) 354-9779
Austin (512) 416-1314
Corpus Christi (361) 854-9961
Dallas (214) 361-5896
El Paso (915) 772-0013
Fort Worth (817) 921-9095
Houston Westheimer Rd.
  (713) 523-0884
Houston N. Post Oak Rd.
  (713) 682-2288
Laredo (956) 723-4680
Lubbock (806) 792-9782
McAllen (956) 631-2147
Midland (915) 697-8222
San Antonio (210) 472-4025

Utah
Provo (801) 377-1117
Salt Lake City (801) 584-1294

Virginia
Alexandria (703) 360-8633
Norfolk (757) 623-7584
Richmond (804) 353-8958
Roanoke (540) 342-9726

U.S. Virgin Islands
St. Croix (340) 778-5553
St. Thomas (340) 774-6674

Vermont
South Burlington (802) 862-1806
White River Junction
    (802) 295-2908

Washington
Bellingham (360) 733-9226
Seattle (206) 553-2706
Spokane (509) 444-8387
Tacoma (253) 565-7038
Yakima (509) 457-2736

Wisconsin
Madison (608) 264-5342
Milwaukee (414) 536-1301

West Virginia
Beckley (304) 252-8220
Charleston (304) 343-3825
Huntington (304) 523-8387
Martinsburg (304) 263-6776
Morgantown (304) 291-4303
Princeton (304) 425-5653
Wheeling (304) 232-0587

Wyoming
Casper (307) 261-5355
Cheyenne (307) 778-7370

Australian Veteran Resources: (From the VVCS web site)

Vietnam Veterans Counseling Service www.dva.gov.au/health/vvcs/vvcs.htm
  Veterans' line 1-800-011-046 Nationally

The Vietnam Veterans Counseling Service (VVCS) is a specialized, free, confidential Australia wide service for Australian veterans and their families.
  VVCS staff are professionally qualified with skills in working with life problems faced by veterans and their families. They can also provide a wide range of programs and treatment for war or service-related mental health conditions.

Who can use the VVCS?
- Australian veterans of all conflicts and peacekeeping operations.
- Partners, ex-partners and dependent children of veterans with issues arising from the veteran's overseas service.
- Sons and daughters of Vietnam veterans with issues relating to their parent's service.
- Certain current and ex members of the Australian Defence force.

  DVA entitlement is not required to access services.

What services VVCS provides:
- Individual, couple and family counseling
- VVCS Outreach Program
- Group Programs
- Referrals
- Veterans Line
- Information, Education and Community Support

Referrals to VVCS Services

- Veterans and/or members of their families can refer themselves.

- Medical Practitioners, other service providers, community agencies and ex service organizations can provide written or verbal referrals to VVCS services.
-

DVA Fact Sheets on the web: www.dva.gov.au/factsheets/default.htm

Australian Veteran Organizations:

Regular Defence Force Welfare Association – www.rdfwa.org.au
Links to veteran organizations – www.rdfwa.org.au/links.htm
Australian Government Department of Veterans' Affairs – www.dva.gov.au

They also have writing and art competitions, like the 2005 DVA-RSL (Qld) Writing Competition through the DVA Queensland State office of Commemorations. Not to be outdone, Victorian veterans can enter the Victorian Story Writing and Art Competition. See the Vetaffairs June 2005 issue on the web at www.dva.gov.au/vetaffairs/index.htm
On page 2.

Australian War Memorial – http://awm.gov.au
The Australian Centre for Posttraumatic Mental Health – www.acpmh.unimelb.edu.au

How is this for a great link? Callsign Vampire, the 1st Australian Field Hospital Association – www.callsignvampire.org.au The only Australian Field Hospital with Australian nurses in Vietnam.

United Kingdom Veteran Resources:

Veterans Agency – Ministry of Defence – www.veteransagency.mod.uk

Combat Stress-Ex-Services Mental Welfare Society
www.combatstress.org.uk/home/default.asp

Canada Veteran Resources:

National Defence – www.forces.gc.ca

Canadian Persian Gulf Cohort Study Report: Summary

Do Bar Fights Count?

www.forces.gc.ca/health/information/engraph/ShortGWV_e.asp

Veterans Affairs Canada – www.vac-acc.gc.ca

Royal Canadian Legion – www.legion.ca

Appendix C

Online Resources

Online resources are listed at the end of each chapter. Here are some additional sites. These are information sources and no endorsement is implied.

Online Veteran Resources (Subject to change)

www.va.gov

Fact sheets: America's Wars – www1.va.gov/opa/fact/amwars.html
    Women Veterans Population – www1.va.gov/opa/fact/women-vets.html

Veteran Data :
www.va.gov/vetdata/Demographics/Vetpop2004/vp2004v1.htm

Veteran Service Organizations :
www1.va.gov/vso/index.cfm?template=view&SortCategory=4

Other Government Sites:
www.defenselink.mil

www.army.mil

www.navy.mil

www.af.mil

www.marines.mil

www.vetbiz.gov

Veteran Organizations & Supporters
www.uso.org

www.military.com

www.militarycity.com/valor/honor.html

www.armytimes.com, www.airforcetimes.com, www.navytimes.com, www.marinetimes.com

www.iava.org – Iraq and Afghanistan Veterans of America

www.booksforsoldiers.com

www.vetbizjournal.com

www.treatsfortroops.com

www.woundedwarriorproject.org

www.unmetneeds.com

Permissions

Grateful acknowledgment is made to the following for permission to reprint previously published material:

GrayWolf Press: Excerpts from *If You Want To Write* by Brenda Ueland, copyright © 1938 by Brenda Ueland, copyright © 1987 by the Estate of Brenda Ueland

Christopher Vogler: Excerpt from *The Writer's Journey; Mythic Structure For Storytellers & Screenwriters* by Christopher Vogler (Michael Wiese Productions Book, 1992). copyright © 1992 by Christopher Vogler.

Steven Tice: Excerpt from "From Trauma to Enlightenment: The Survivor's Journey" copyright © 1991 by Steven N. Tice, M.A. in The Post-Traumatic Gazette, Volume 1, No. 5, January-February 1996

Al Siebert: "Guidelines for Listening to War Veterans," and "Telling Your Survivor Story," copyright © 2002 by Al Siebert.

Major Jessie Massey: "Sons Return Father's Remains Home From Vietnam after 34 Years," copyright © 2002 by Joint POW/MIA Accounting Command (JPAC), Public Affairs

Casualties of War: This Piece originally aired on KATU-TV and KATU's web-site beginning on December 24, 2005 Copyright © 2005 KATU-TV – All Rights Reserved

Kim Cook: Excerpt from "Fire in The Caboose!" copyright © 1984 by the Newport News-Times, Newport, Oregon

1Lt. Scott Hall, 40th AES: "Aeromed reflections," copyright © 1991 by Air Force Reserve Command

Handbook of Post-Traumatic Therapy, edited by Mary Beth Williams and John F. Sommer, Jr., Copyright © 1994 by Greenwood Press. Reproduced with permission of Greenwood Publishing Group, Inc., Westport, CT.

Exercise Nine Shopping List

Smell – Use ground cloves, vanilla, or a spice which evokes childhood memories.

Touch – Marshmallow, peanuts in the shell, stress ball.

Taste – Mints, chocolate anything, (be aware of diabetics or allergies) pretzels.

Hearing – Didgeridoo from Australia, belly dance music, classical music, thunderstorms.

Vision - Pictures of exotic lands, a photograph, an old calendar picture.

About The Author

Kim Cook developed and taught the *Writing War Stories* class at Mt. Hood Community College in Gresham, Oregon, from 1997 to 2000.

She served as an enlisted woman in the U.S. Army from 1975 to 1978 with the 4th Supply and Transport Battalion, Fourth Infantry Division, Fort Carson, Colorado. She participated in Reforger to Germany and desert training on Bulldog Safari I at Fort Irwin, California, both in 1978. Kim was commissioned as an Aeromedical Evacuation Operations Officer in the Air Force Reserve 40th AES at McChord Air Force Base, Washington, from 1988 – 1993. She mobilized her Squadron for Desert Shield and was a state-side activated reservist during Desert Storm.

Kim's writing has appeared in *Army*, *The Officer*, *The Writer* and *Romance Writers Report* magazines, *Spear Tips*, the 9th Air Expeditionary Group base newspaper at Ali Al Salem Air Base, Kuwait, and numerous newspapers.

Kim's writing awards include the $1,000 prize in the 1997 Oregon Film and Video Foundation Screenplay Contest for her script *Reserve Wars*. She earned three first place finishes in interview, feature, and photography categories from the National Federation of Press Women in 1983.

Kim is a former newspaper journalist and photographer, VA Medical Center public affairs officer, video production coordinator and print buyer. She holds a bachelor's degree in business administration and an associate degree in journalism arts technology.

She is a member of the American Legion Oregon Post 1, National 4th Infantry (Ivy) Division Association, AeroMed Evac Association, Romance Writers of America, Willamette Writers, and Oregon Press Women. Kim is on the Board of Directors of the U.S.S. *Ranger* Museum Foundation.

She lives in the Portland, Oregon, metropolitan area and tries to not buy more books than her house can hold.

Get Started Writing!

To contact Warrior Tales, LLC

Visit www.warriortales.com

To order books contact:

www.booklocker.com

For more information:

Warrior Tales, LLC
P.O. Box 1628
Clackamas, OR 97015

Tel: (503) 740-1850
Email: wartales@warriortales.com

Warrior Tales, LLC, is a Service-Disabled Woman Veteran-Owned Small Business listed in the Central Contractor Register at www.ccr.gov

Printed in the United States
46829LVS00007B/121-306